*For the executive or the entry-level employee
*For assistants, secretaries, temps, and support staff
*For students, job hunters, and career changers

THE ENCYCLOPEDIC DICTIONARY OF BUSINESS TERMS

This A-to-Z handbook contains information you need at your fingertips for day-to-day usage, quick reference, and an increased understanding of today's business world. From the ancient language of the legal profession to up-to-date computer terminology, it's the one book no one in business should be without.

Most Berkley Books are available at special quantity discounts for bulk purchases for sales promotions, premiums, fund-raising or educational use. Special books, or book excerpts, can also be created to fit specific needs.

For details, write to Special Markets, The Berkley Publishing Group, 200 Madison Avenue, New York, New York 10016.

THE ENCYCLOPEDIC DICTIONARY OF BUSINESS TERMS

Mary A. De Vries

BERKLEY BOOKS, NEW YORK

If you purchased this book without a cover, you should be aware that this book is stolen property. It was reported as "unsold and destroyed" to the publisher, and neither the author nor the publisher has received any payment for this "stripped book."

THE ENCYCLOPEDIC DICTIONARY OF BUSINESS TERMS

A Berkley Book / published by arrangement with
the author

PRINTING HISTORY
Berkley edition / March 1997

All rights reserved.
Copyright © 1997 by Mary A. De Vries.
This book may not be reproduced in whole
or in part, by mimeograph or any other means,
without permission. For information address:
The Berkley Publishing Group, 200 Madison Avenue,
New York, New York 10016.

The Putnam Berkley World Wide Web site address is
http://www.berkley.com/berkley

ISBN: 0-425-15612-5

BERKLEY®
Berkley Books are published by The Berkley Publishing Group,
200 Madison Avenue, New York, New York 10016.
BERKLEY and the "B" design are trademarks
belonging to Berkley Publishing Corporation.

PRINTED IN THE UNITED STATES OF AMERICA

10 9 8 7 6 5 4 3 2 1

CONTENTS

Preface	vii
Guide to the Dictionary	ix
Standard Business Terms	1
Jargon	265
Foreign Expressions	283
Unusual Words	299
Cliches	317
Abbreviations	333
General Business Abbreviations	335
Technical Business Abbreviations	364
Business Organization Abbreviations	395
Prefixes and Suffixes	405
Prefixes	407
Suffixes	414
Appendix	421
Fraction and Decimal Equivalents	423
Large Numbers (American System)	424
Roman Numerals	425
Cardinal and Ordinal Numbers in Five Languages	426
Mathematical Signs and Symbols	431
Greek Letter Symbols	435
Foreign Currency	436
Principal National Holidays of Other Countries	446
Area Codes: United States and Canada	457
Time-Period Designations	460
Dates and Times in Five Languages	462
Easily Misspelled Words	467
Index	476

PREFACE

In the twenty-first century, businesspeople will be challenged as never before with a complex and wide-ranging language that defines their work. Gone are the days when it sufficed to have a limited basic vocabulary, consisting largely of common accounting and financial terms. Businesspeople now speak and write about subjects as diverse as fiber optics and human engineering.

With more than 3,500 definitions, *The Encyclopedic Dictionary of Business Terms* presents a comprehensive collection of important terms in dozens of key areas of business activity. A list of these areas and a detailed description of the way the dictionary is arranged are presented in the "Guide to the Dictionary."

Because of its broad coverage, encyclopedic descriptions, extensive cross-referencing, and numerous examples, the dictionary will be useful to all businesspeople in virtually any position or level of employment, from secretarial and other support staff to supervisors, administrators, and managers to corporate officers. In addition, the dictionary represents an affordable guide to the language of the business world for students and instructors in business courses and for anyone else who wants to understand the language of business.

Information used to prepare the entries was drawn from many authorities and businesses across the United States, including a number of specialists who spent many hours collecting and contributing information, reviewing entries, answering questions, and making valuable suggestions about what to include and how best to present it.

My sincere thanks go to James R. Spear, CPA, and Dennis Evans, independent exclusive insurance agent, Sedona, Arizona; Carolyn W. Baldwin, attorney-at-law, Baldwin & de Séve, Concord, New Hampshire; Tina Hrevus, communications coordinator, Edward D. Jones & Co., Maryland Heights, Missouri; Jean McCormack, broker, TNT Property Management, Prescott, Arizona; Judith Grisham, administrator, Harvard University, Cambridge, Massachusetts; and Alice Hubbard, manager, Word Processing Services, Vacaville, California. Their contributions not only helped to ensure the accuracy and completeness of the entries but also made the project much more enjoyable and satisfying.

GUIDE TO THE DICTIONARY

Subjects covered. More than 3,500 definitions are presented in entries that cover the key areas of business activity, including the following:

management, business communication, domestic commerce, international trade, economics, statistics, mathematics, retailing, wholesaling, sales, marketing, purchasing, advertising, mail order, personnel management, insurance, real estate, investments, finance, credit, banking, accounting, taxes, business law, information processing, records management, word processing, telecommunications, electronic messaging, computer technology, travel, and meetings.

Description of the entries. Each entry consists of an entry head in bold type, followed by either a brief definition or a detailed definition and description, depending on the requirements of the term. The entry **real property,** for example, is adequately defined with a brief entry; the entry **bond,** however, requires not only a definition of the general term *bond* but also descriptions of the many different kinds of bonds. When additional terms are thus defined within a single entry, those terms are printed in an italic face.

Organization of the entries. Entries are separated into seven key sections according to type of language: "Standard Business Terms," "Jargon," "Foreign Expressions," "Unusual Words," "Cliches," "Abbreviations," and "Prefixes and Suffixes."

1. **Standard Business Terms:** This is the main, encyclopedic part of the dictionary, with detailed definitions and descriptions of important business terms. Here you will find a well-rounded collection of more than 1,000 definitions, with some entries consisting of several subentries or including numerous definitions of additional terms. The entries represent a contemporary basic business vocabulary, such as *assets, breach of contract, corporation, trademark,* and *word processing.*

2. **Jargon:** Although all business terms are a form of specialized language (*jargon*), this part contains those terms that most authorities have classified outside of standard terminology. Here you will find nearly 200 terms, such as *across the board, bait and switch pricing, log on, niche market,* and *outsourcing.* However, in case you expect to find some of these terms in the "standard" collection, cross-references are given there, and the index will also direct you to any term in question.

3. **Foreign Expressions:** Many businesspeople enjoy sprinkling their speeches and letters with foreign expressions, and many Latin as well as some French terms have always been prominent in business law and other areas. In today's global economy, foreign expressions are even more important; and a literate, successful busi-

nessperson should be familiar with a working variety, including the nearly 300 common foreign terms listed here, such as *ad hoc, de facto, ex officio, quo warranto,* and *sine die.*

4. **Unusual Words:** Some business speakers and writers like to flex their linguistic muscles with unusual and difficult words. You may read them in a letter, report, magazine, or newspaper or hear someone use them while addressing a conference or conversing at a social-business event. Regardless, you will be embarrassed if you don't know their meanings. More than 200 unusual terms used in business are defined here, including *adumbrate, circumforaneous, feracious, malversation,* and *objurgate.* Because the words in this part are often unfamiliar and difficult, the entry heads include syllabication to help you with word division and pronunciation.

5. **Cliches:** Certain cliches are widely used in business—against the advice of language instructors and to the dismay of international readers who tend to translate everything literally. This group of entries, therefore, might be considered a list of terms you should *not* use in business. The more than 200 definitions given here can also serve as a guide to rephrasing such expressions in ordinary English. Included is a variety of trite expressions, such as *acid test, hive of industry, pay through the nose, track record,* and *wave of the future.*

6. **Abbreviations:** Informal memos, purchase orders, contract bids, and numerous other business documents are replete with abbreviations. The 700 general abbreviations listed here, such as *acv (actual cash value), cwo (cash with order), i/l (import license), o/s (out of service), w/o (without),* are used in nontechnical material. The nearly 800 technical abbreviations, such as *ade (automatic data entry), fde (field decelerator), lna (low-*

noise amplifier), pfr (peak flow rate), and *s/w (standard weight),* come from the technologies in the scientific and technical side of business. Also provided here are more than 150 abbreviations of organizations that serve the business community, including *BEMA (Business Equipment Manufacturers Association), FASB (Financial Accounting Standards Board), NSA (National Standards Association), NTSB (National Transportation Safety Board),* and *PIMA (Paper Industry Management Association).*

7. **Prefixes and Suffixes:** It is difficult to build a strong business vocabulary without knowing the principal prefixes and suffixes that can be combined with bases, stems, and roots to change their meanings. The first list has more than 100 prefixes, such as *bi- (biweekly), con- (concurrent), de- (deactivate), intra- (intrastate),* and *retro- (retroactive),* and the second list has more than 100 suffixes, such as *-cy (bankruptcy), -fold (twofold), -ician (technician), -ment (advancement),* and *-worthy (trustworthy).*

Cross-references. Each cross-reference entry head is printed in bold type, and the other term to which you are referred is also given in bold. All cross-references appearing within a regular entry are printed in bold as well. Most of the nearly 700 cross-reference entries refer you to additional terms that are defined within the entries, such as "**capital asset** See **asset.**" Cross-references are also included when terms are known by more than one name, such as "**hard disk** See **disk.**" In other cases, cross-references are given to terms in another part of the book, such as "**bottom line** See **JARGON: bottom line.**"

Tables, models, lists, examples. A principal advantage of an encyclopedic-style dictionary is that detailed supplementary material can be included, and the entries in "Standard Business Terms" have an abundance of such supporting information. In the entry **debit and credit,** for example, you will find a table that shows at a glance whether a debit or credit will increase or decrease a particular type of account, and in the entry **income statement,** you will find an actual model of this type of financial statement. Also, whenever practical, definitions and other information are presented in a list format to allow for quick scanning and easy comprehension. Many entries, however, consist of definitions that are best explained or clarified by creating a ficticious example. The entry **coinsurance** therefore has a paragraph explaining how to do certain calculations in an imaginary situation. All such models or explanatory paragraphs are set apart from the rest of the entry discussion and are always preceded by the word *Example* in italics.

Appendix. The dictionary has a number of other useful tables and lists that are not related to any entry, including several that will be particularly helpful to those who have contacts with people and companies in other countries. This type of information is collected in the appendix. No entry pertains to fractions and decimals, for example, so the table "Fractions and Decimal Equivalents" appears in the appendix. Also provided here is a variety of other reference material that is useful to businesspeople, such as lists of foreign currencies and easily misspelled words.

Index. The various terms from all parts of the book are combined in a single alphabetical list in the index. Therefore, if you are uncertain whether to look up the term *pro rata* in the "Foreign Expressions" or the "Standard Business Terms" collection, simply check the index.

STANDARD BUSINESS TERMS

A

abandon To clear **computer** work from **memory** without saving it on **disk**. Users who don't want to retain their work can choose the option of closing a **file** or exiting the program without saving the work or edits just completed. If this option is chosen, any editing that was performed will be lost. If a new document is started and then abandoned without saving it on disk, the entire new document will be lost.

See also **JARGON: abort.**

abandonment Voluntarily relinquishing or surrendering tangible or intangible property or a claim or right to it, with no intention of regaining **title** or possession and without naming a successor. An example of *tangible property* is a house; an example of *intangible property* is a **patent.**

Intent is an important part of legal abandonment. If there is no intention to abandon property, it is not *legally* abandoned.

Example: A person might have a heart attack and, as a result, involuntarily have to leave his or her car unattended on a city street. Although it may appear to have been abandoned, it was not intentionally (legally) left on the property, and no one else may claim it.

Voluntary abandonment does not release someone from all obligations associated with his or her property.

Example: If a person has a **lease** or **mortgage** on property that requires monthly payments, that obligation cannot be cancelled simply by leaving the property. The requirements of the lease or mortgage remain in force.

What happens to abandoned property depends on the situation. It may, for example, revert to someone who had a previous interest in it, or it may revert to the state.

abbreviations A shortened form of a word or phrase. Broadly, the term includes three types of words and phrases:

1. *General abbreviations* are words that have letters omitted in the middle (*nat'l: national*) or the end (*admin.: administration*). When the missing letters occur in the middle of a word, an apostrophe is used in the position of the missing letters, and the final period is omitted. When the missing letters occur at the end of a word, no apostrophe is required, and the final period is included.
2. *Initialisms* usually consist of the first letter of each important word in a phrase (*fyi: for your information*). In speech, each letter in an initialism is pronounced: *f-y-i*.
3. Acronyms also usually consist of the first letter of each important word in a phrase (*PIN: personal identification number*). In speech, however, the initials are pronounced like an actual word: *PIN*.

Although the style of writing abbreviations differs among industries and professions, the lists of general and technical abbreviations given later in this book are written in a widely accepted business style. Also included later is a list of abbreviations of business organizations, most of which are written in capital letters.

The trend with initialisms and some acronyms is toward lowercase letters and no punctuation. An exception to this occurs with abbreviations that look the same as an actual word. For example, the word *cap* (no punctuation) refers to something that is worn on the head; the abbreviation *cap.* (with punctuation), which is spelled the same, refers to "**computer-aided p**roduction."

Authorities recommend that writers put a period after abbreviation letters spelled the same as an actual word to signal that the letters represent the abbreviation, not the word. The period is omitted, however, when an abbreviation is written in all capital letters (*CAP*), because that in itself usually signals that it is an abbreviation, not an actual word.

abort See **JARGON: abort.**

abrogate To abolish, annul, repeal, revoke, or cancel, especially by authority; to set aside; to make a law void through legislative action. The act of abrogation voids or puts an end to a rule, law, or other authoritative directive.

absentee owner Someone who does not personally reside on or manage the property he or she owns. The owner of an apartment complex, for example, may live in another city and retain a local property manager to manage the complex.

abstract A summary of a larger statement or document; a condensed history of a court case (*abstract of record*) or of **title (2)** to property (*abstract of title*).

Formal **reports** commonly have a brief summary of the document in the **front matter** positioned immediately following the table of contents and list of illustrations. This summary may consist of text-style paragraphs, or it may be written as an itemized list of key points.

abstract of record See **abstract.**

abstract of title See **abstract.**

acceleration clause A clause in a loan **contract,** installment **agreement,** or other document that gives a lender the right to declare that an entire debt or the remaining balance is due immediately if the borrower **defaults** or violates a provision of the document. A credit card agreement, for example, might state that if the cardholder fails to make payments on time, the issuer has the right to demand immediate payment of the entire indebtedness.

access See **JARGON: access.**

accommodation endorsement See **endorsement.**

account 1. In general, a customer or client; a record pertaining to a business association or relationship established with a customer or client, often to allow future payment of current purchases, as in an *open account* or *charge account*.

2. In finance, a record maintained for a bank or brokerage customer, under the customer's name, that shows customer deposits and withdrawals.

3. In **accounting,** a bookkeeping record of business transactions reported by making **debit and credit** entries. An account is set up for each of the **assets,** each of the **liabilities,** the stockholders' **equity,** and each item of revenue or expense.

A company's **chart of accounts** lists the individual general **ledger** accounts, such as "office equipment." A *control* (or *controlling*) *account* is a general ledger account that shows the totals of debit and credit entries in a subsidiary ledger, such as an accounts payable ledger. It thus provides a summary of the detailed entries of the subsidiary ledger.

accounting A system for providing and maintaining information about a person or organization; a system of record keeping and reporting that enables businesses to monitor their financial positions and determine profits (see **gross profit; net income**), taxable income (see **gross income**), and other information essential to management.

An accounting system includes the following three aspects:

1. The records used to enter transactions
2. The process of making entries in the books of account
3. The preparation of **income statements, balance sheets,** and other necessary financial reports

Standard Business Terms

As indicated in the following list, various federal and state organizations determine the system of accounting used by a business.

1. The advisory statements of the Financial Accounting Standards Board (FASB) have been adopted by all types of businesses as basic accounting principles.
2. The rules and regulations of the Internal Revenue Service affect how the accounting records are maintained and what information must be reported.
3. The rules and regulations of the **Securities and Exchange Commission (SEC)** govern the accumulation and reporting of securities information.
4. In addition to the influence of organizations at the federal level, the requirements of state and local authorities affect overall procedures in business accounting.

An accounting system has two general types of *records:* original entry and final entry.

1. *Records* (traditionally called "books") *of original entry* refer to the **journals** in which transactions are first recorded.
2. *Records* (books) *of final entry* refer to the **ledgers** into which amounts are transferred from the journals.

An accounting system uses one of two general *methods* of accounting: a cash basis or an accrual basis.

1. In *cash accounting,* income is reported when received, regardless of the periods to which it applies; expenses are reported when paid, regardless of the periods to which they apply.
2. In *accrual accounting,* income is allocated to the periods to which it applies, regardless of when it is received;

expenses are allocated to the periods to which they apply, regardless of when they are paid.

An important part of the accounting process is *cost accounting*, which refers to the systematic recording, analysis, and reporting of the costs of labor, materials, and **overhead** used in manufacturing products and providing services. Through cost accounting, management can determine the unit cost of production and set prices accordingly.

Certified public accountants (CPAs), who have passed national examinations and have met the requirements of the states in which they practice, are qualified to develop and manage accounting systems, prepare and interpret financial statements, prepare tax returns, and perform an **audit.** Public accountants may have many of the same skills of a CPA but have not completed the necessary examination or have not met all state requirements for certification.

accoutrement See **UNUSUAL WORDS: accoutrement.**

accrual accounting See **accounting.**

accrued asset See **assets.**

accrued dividend See **dividend.**

accumulated dividend See **dividend.**

acknowledgment A formal declaration made before a duly authorized person, such as a **notary public,** that ensures a document's legal validity (see example). The one who signs an acknowledgment declares that the signing is a voluntary act before an authorized person. This act entitles the legal document to which it is appended to be recorded and filed.

Unlike an **affidavit,** which can stand alone as a document, an acknowledgment is always appended to another document. Also, whereas an affidavit is sworn to, an acknowledgment is not. In addition, only the officer taking an acknowledgment signs it, not the person making it, as in the case of an affidavit.

Example: Acknowledgment

STATE OF
COUNTY OF

On this _____ day of _____, 19___, before me, _____, the undersigned officer, personally appeared _____, known to me or sufficiently proven to be the person whose name is subscribed to the within instrument and acknowledged that he executed the same for the purpose therein contained.

IN WITNESS WHEREOF, I have hereunto set my hand and official seal.

_____
Notary Public

My commission expires _____

acronym See **abbreviations**.

actual cash value In insurance, the cost of replacing property that has been damaged or destroyed. The actual cash value is generally calculated as the cost of comparable new property less **depreciation** or obsolescence.

Example: If a desk that initially cost $500 had depreciated by $275, its actual cash value would be $500 − $275 = $225.

actuary A mathematician who calculates insurance or **annuity** premiums, **dividends,** and reserves for policies; conducts statistical studies and prepares mortality and other tables; and prepares **annual reports.** To become an actuary, a candidate must pass pertinent business and mathematical examinations.

addendum Something that is added, such as an **attachment** to a **contract** or a supplement to a book. An addendum to a **lease,** for example, might describe penalties for late rental payments.

add-on See **JARGON: add-on**.

address 1. In **computer** use, the location where information is stored in **memory.** Each specific location is identified by a name, number, or code label. Users who want to find a particular item can use that identification to tell the computer which item of information to locate.

2. In **telecommunications**, the label that represents either the terminal where **data** originate or the destination of the data.

ad hoc See **FOREIGN EXPRESSIONS: ad hoc**.

adjourned meeting A continuation of a previous regular or special **meeting** that had to adjourn until a later date and time but *before* the next regular session. (In formal meeting conduct, a *session* is a series of meetings where business is continued from one meeting to another until the session ends.)

When a quorum is not present, for example, a meeting may be adjourned to another date when the required number of people will be in attendance.

If an adjourned meeting is desired, the motion (see **parliamentary procedure**) to adjourn must make this clear; that is, it must specify an adjournment to a future designated date and time. Otherwise, a simple adjournment is final, and any future meeting will be treated as an entirely new meeting, not a continuation of the previous meeting.

adjournment See **adjourned meeting.**

adjustable-rate mortgage (ARM) See **mortgage.**

adjustment bond See **bond.**

ad valorem See **FOREIGN EXPRESSIONS: ad valorem.**

advance An amount paid before expenses are incurred or before income is earned.

Example 1: A businessperson might receive a travel advance before incurring any travel expenses. The person receiving this type of advance would then request reimbursement only for additional expenses not paid out of the advance.

Example 2: A writer might receive an advance against future royalties before a book is written and money is actually earned. The person receiving this type of advance would begin receiving royalty payments only after the publisher had recovered (deducted) the amount of the advance from initial sales.

affidavit A written statement made or taken under oath before a duly authorized person, such as a **notary public** or officer of the court, affirming that the statements made are true (see example). Although an affidavit may be attached to a court document to support the facts stated in the document, it is a

Example: Affidavit

STATE OF

COUNTY OF

                      AFFIDAVIT

_____, being duly sworn, deposes and says:

    She is the President of_____ Corporation and that _____

_____

_____.

                              _____

                                      President

Sworn to [or affirmed] before me this _____ day of _____, 19__.

_____

     Notary Public

document in itself and need not be attached to something else. In this respect, it differs from an **acknowledgment,** which is always attached to another document. Also, an affidavit, unlike an acknowledgment, is sworn to and is signed by both the person making the declaration and the officer receiving it.

Although the sworn-to clauses may differ depending on where they are used, they generally follow a similar style and wording.

aftermarket See **JARGON: aftermarket.**

agency A relationship in which an agent is authorized to act on behalf of the person doing the authorizing (**principal**). The acts of an agent or agency are then binding on the principal. The third party in such a relationship is the individual or company with whom the agent or agency conducts business on behalf of the principal.

An agency may have one of two levels of power.

1. It may have broad *general power* to represent the principal in all or most situations.
2. It may have *limited* or *special power* to represent the principal only for a specific purpose or only in a limited number of areas.

An agent may be a person or an organization, such as a bank. In either case, the agent or agency observes three basic rules.

1. It is subject to the wishes and control of the principal.
2. It owes allegiance to the principal, not to a third party it may deal with, in all matters pertaining to the principal's business.
3. **Title** to any of the principal's property that is involved in business activity handled by the agent or agency remains with the principal.

See also **fiduciary.**

agent See **agency**.

agiotage See UNUSUAL WORDS: **agiotage**.

agreement An arrangement or mutual assent between legally competent parties that often precedes a formal **contract.** Some authorities use the terms *agreement* and *contract* interchangeably. Others prefer to use the term *agreement* only in reference to an act, promise, or informal arrangement that does not carry the legal obligation of a formal contract.

Algol Acronym for **Alg**orithmic **L**anguage; see **language**.

algorism See UNUSUAL WORDS: **algorism**.

algorithm A procedure or sequence of instructions that tells how to solve a problem. Broadly, any established sequence of steps for accomplishing a task, such as the steps for changing the image drum in a copier, is an algorithm. Unlike a **heuristic** method of problem solving, an algorithmic method has to consist of a finite number of steps and clear, precise instructions that are guaranteed to provide the correct solution.

alien corporation See **corporation**.

aliquot See UNUSUAL WORDS: **aliquot**.

alphanumeric A combination of alphabetical and numerical representation; also known as *alphameric*. Alphanumeric **data** items may include any of the 26 letters, 10 numerical digits, or other special symbols, such as the asterisk (*), that are machine readable. Filenames (see **file**), for example, may be alphabetic only, numeric only, or alphanumeric: *c:\SLI\T$-a.doc*.

alpha storage See JARGON: **alpha storage**.

alternative dispute resolution See **arbitration**.

amalgamation The act of consolidating or merging two or more companies to form a new company.

amendment A correction or other change in a law or legal document, such as a **contract;** the formal process of amending something. After corrections or other changes have occurred, the law or document that was amended continues in force in its changed form.

In **meetings** that are conducted under the rules of **parliamentary procedure,** amendments are made by making a motion "to amend" (to change or revise something) and then by approving the motion with a majority vote.

Example: "I move that we amend the motion to _____ by striking out the words _____ and inserting the words_____."

A motion to amend must be seconded, after which it can be debated before the vote on it is taken.

An amendment to a document can be changed in the same way that an original document can be changed, by making a motion "to amend the amendment." This motion also must be seconded and approved by majority vote. However, a motion to amend an amendment cannot itself be amended.

American Stock Exchange (AMEX) See **stock exchange.**

American Stock Exchange (AMEX) Market Value Index See **stock index.**

amicus curiae See **FOREIGN EXPRESSIONS: amicus curiae.**

amortization An **accounting** procedure for reducing gradually the cost value of an amount or **asset** over a designated time. The value of a fixed asset, such as a building, or an intangible asset, such as a **franchise,** is reduced by allocating the original cost over the life of the asset (see **depreciation**).

Borrowers can amortize a debt by making a series of periodic payments, as with a **mortgage,** to the lender or creditor. Often, the procedure for paying down a debt calls for equal periodic payments made at designated equal periods. With this method, each payment consists of **interest** on the outstanding debt and part of the **principal.**

amotion See **UNUSUAL WORDS: amotion.**

analog A type of mechanism in which the data are represented in a continuous manner or along a continuous scale. Therefore, a value can occur anywhere within a specified range as, for example, a temperature point on a mercury thermometer. Most **computers,** by contrast, are **digital** devices.

annual report The annual record of a **corporation**'s financial position and operating results sent to shareholders (see **stockholder**) and other interested persons at the end of its fiscal year (see **fiscal period**). The report may include a description of the company's operations, audited (see **audit**) financial statements, and a letter from or introduction by the president or chairman of the board (see **board of directors**) commenting on the year's activities, the company's current status, and plans for the future. Since annual reports are used for public relations purposes, they may be attractive, well-designed publications that rival slick magazines.

The size of an annual report and the amount and type of information presented depends on the organization. Public corporations, for example, are required under the rules of the **Securities and Exchange Commission** (see **stock exchange**) to provide an audited **income statement** and **balance sheet** as well as certain other information for stockholders. Other types of organizations may design and write annual reports primarily to stimulate the interest of customers and prospective customers, to create better employee relations, or for other informational purposes.

annuity A form of insurance **contract** specifying that a fixed or variable sum of money be paid to a designated person (*annuitant*) at designated intervals for life or for a certain number of years. Annuities may be fixed or variable, depending on the type of payments made.

1. With a *fixed annuity,* the amount is paid out in regular installments.
2. With a *variable annuity,* the payments are made based on a guaranteed number of units and are made in variable amounts for specified periods.

Usually, a main purpose of an annuity is to provide monthly, quarterly, semiannual, or annual income to an annuitant during his or her lifetime. Since an annuity usually provides regular payments to the purchaser throughout his or her life, it differs from life insurance, which is payable to a **beneficiary** only upon the holder's death.

Three common forms are the ordinary annuity, annuity due, and deferred annuity.

1. An *ordinary annuity* provides for payments to the annuitant at the end of the period.
2. An *annuity due* provides for payments at the beginning of the period.
3. A *deferred annuity* provides for payments beginning after two or more periods have elapsed.

Capital in an annuity grows on a tax-deferred basis. In all annuities, however, the annuitant has an interest in the payments only, not in the principal fund from which the payments are made.

answer In legal matters, the defense's formal pleading (statement) in response to the plaintiff's formal **complaint.** This written statement offers an opportunity for the defense to deny all or some of the allegations made by the plaintiff. The answer may include affirmative statements provided to support the position of the defendant and may even include counterclaims against the plaintiff.

antitrust laws Statutes (see **statutory law**) that regulate trade to encourage free competition and to prevent the restraint of trade, monopolies, and unfair practices in **interstate commerce.** As a result of these statutes, any cooperative intent or effort by two or more parties to restrain trade is illegal.

Both the states and the federal government have adopted legislation to prevent associations or combinations that hinder competition. On the federal level, two antitrust laws and their successors have had a major impact for nearly a century.

1. The *Sherman Act* (1890), the first major act, made illegal any **contract,** combination, or conspiracy aimed at restraining trade or commerce; any monopoly; and any conspiracy or combination designed to monopolize. In 1937, the *Miller-Tydings Act* amended and updated the 1890 Sherman Act.
2. The *Clayton Act* was adopted in 1914 in response to weaknesses in the Sherman Act. It sought to stop anti-competitive practices, such as price discrimination, and to regulate practices in **stock** acquisitions and other areas where unfair practices might arise. In 1936, the *Robinson-Patman Act* was passed to reinforce the 1914 Clayton Act.

APL Abbreviation for **A P**rogramming **L**anguage; see **language.**

appendix See **back matter.**

applications software See **software.**

appreciation The increase in an **asset**'s value over time; in taxes, the difference between the fair market value of property and a taxpayer's cost or **basis.**

arbitration The process of an impartial third party hearing and determining a case involving a controversy, without the use of litigation. The arbitrator or panel of arbitrators that makes a determination is selected by the parties in a dispute. The decision in settling a dispute is binding on all parties, provided they agreed to this provision beforehand.

Arbitration is common in labor-management disputes and may be used to settle a variety of problems, from deciding the interpretation of **contract** clauses to breaking a deadlock in contract negotiations. Although arbitration is usually voluntary among commercial organizations, it is compulsory for public utility **corporations** and municipal services in cases involving public safety or convenience.

Those who want to avoid the judicial process may use a form of *alternative dispute resolution (ADR)*, which might involve binding or nonbinding arbitration or mediation. In *mediation*, a neutral mediator helps the parties arrive at a mutually acceptable resolution.

archetype See **prototype; UNUSUAL WORDS: archetype.**

arithmetic mean See **mean.**

array A collection of **data** consisting of a group of single elements (numbers or character strings) of the same type, all connected and arranged in a logical and meaningful pattern. Because this type of data structure has a single label (name), instructions can be applied to the entire array or to any of the array elements (parts). Users can select and retrieve certain data from an array by specifying the name of the array and the particular element's location within the array.

Arrays may be classified as one- or two-dimensional data structures.

1. A *one-dimensional array*, called a *vector*, has values arranged in either a single horizontal row or a single vertical column.
2. A *two-dimensional array*, called a *matrix*, has values listed across and down in both rows and columns.

arrearage See **arrears.**

arrears The state of being behind or late (being "in arrears") in making required payments or fulfilling other obligations. The amount of a past-due obligation is known as the *arrearage*.

arrogate See **UNUSUAL WORDS: arrogate**.

articles of incorporation Also called *certificate of incorporation* or *charter;* a document filed with the designated state official to create a private **corporation**. The statement must meet the general corporation laws and filing requirements of the state in which the instrument is filed.

The articles state pertinent information about the creation of the entity, including the following five items:

1. Name of the corporation
2. Principal place of business
3. Purpose of the corporation
4. Names and addresses of the incorporators
5. Amount of **capitalization** of the corporation

artificial intelligence The branch of **computer** science that deals with the simulation of intelligent behavior in computers; the capability of a machine to imitate human behavior. An example of artificial intelligence is the capability of a computer to solve an algebraic equation. However, artificial intelligence extends beyond the processing of **alphanumeric** data into areas such as human-voice recognition and game playing.

1. With human-voice recognition, the computer must be given a dictionary and the rules of the language being used. Difficulty occurs when the same words are used in a different context, such as when using the expression "How nice" sarcastically. The computer, therefore, must be able to follow a recognizable set of instructions in all applications.

2. With games that have limited options, a computer may be programmed to calculate possible moves from a given position and then to determine the consequences of each possibility so that it can eliminate paths that would be incorrect.

artificial language See **language**.

ASCII Acronym for American Standard Code for Information Interchange, pronounced as "ASK-EY"; a worldwide standard for information storage and interchange in **data processing** and communications systems and equipment. Using the ASCII code (see table), it is possible to store virtually any kind of **data** by translating each character into the code.

Standard ASCII uses seven **bits** for each character code plus one bit used for error checking, providing 128 symbols (0–127), 96 of which are displayable characters (see table). Extended ASCII character sets use all eight bits for character codes, providing 128 additional codes (up to 256 total). Since the basic, or standard, ASCII code does not include **graphics** characters, **computers** generally use an extended character set for work involving graphics.

When an extended character set is available, you can produce additional characters on screen by pressing the *Alt* key and simultaneously typing the correct code on the numeric keypad. For example, you can create the character *è* by pressing *Alt* and typing *138*. **Software** manuals commonly include a list of codes and the characters they will produce. However, not all printers will print out higher-order characters even though they may appear correctly on the computer screen.

The following table lists the basic ASCII symbols and compares decimal and **binary** values.

Symbol	Decimal Number System	Binary Value
NUL (Null character)	00	0000 0000
SOH (Start of heading)	01	0000 0001
PST (Start of text)	02	0000 0010
ETX (End of text)	03	0000 0011
EOT (End of transmission)	04	0000 0100
ENQ (Enquiry)	05	0000 0101
ACK (Acknowledge)	06	0000 0110
BEL (Bell)	07	0000 0111
BS (Backspace)	08	0000 1000
HT (Horizontal tabulation)	09	0000 1001
LF (Line feed)	10	0000 1010
VT (Vertical tabulation)	11	0000 1011
FF (Form feed)	12	0000 1100
CR (Carriage)	13	0000 1101
SO (Shift out)	14	0000 1110
SI (Shift in)	15	0000 1111
DLE (Data link escape)	16	0000 0000
DCI (Device control 1)	17	0001 0001
DC2 (Device control 2)	18	0001 0010
DC3 (Device control 3)	19	0001 0011
DC4 (Device control 4)	20	0001 0100

Standard Business Terms

Symbol	Decimal Number System	Binary Value
NAK (Negative acknowledge)	21	0001 0101
SYN (Synchronous idle)	22	0001 0110
ETB (End of transmission block)	23	0001 0111
CAN (Cancel)	24	0001 1000
EM (End of medium)	25	0001 1001
SUB (Substitute)	26	0001 1010
ESC (Escape)	27	0001 1011
FS (File separator)	28	0001 1100
GS (Group separator)	29	0001 1101
RS (Record separator)	30	0001 1110
US (Unit separator)	31	0001 1111
SP (Space)	32	0010 0000
! (Exclamation mark)	33	0010 0001
" (Quotation)	34	0010 0010
# (Number sign)	35	0010 0011
$ (Dollar sign)	36	0010 0100
% (Percent)	37	0010 0101
& (Ampersand)	38	0010 0110
' (Apostrophe)	39	0010 0111
((Opening parenthesis)	40	0010 1000
) (Closing parenthesis)	41	0010 1001
* (Asterisk)	42	0010 1010
+ (Plus sign)	43	0010 1011

24 THE ENCYCLOPEDIC DICTIONARY OF BUSINESS TERMS

Symbol	Decimal Number System	Binary Value
, (Comma)	44	0010 1100
- (Hyphen or minus sign)	45	0010 1101
. (Period or decimal point)	46	0010 1110
/ (Slant)	47	0010 1111
0	48	0011 0000
1	49	0011 0001
2	50	0011 0010
3	51	0011 0011
4	52	0011 0100
5	53	0011 0101
6	54	0011 0110
7	55	0011 0111
8	56	0011 1000
9	57	0011 1001
: (Colon)	58	0011 1010
; (Semicolon)	59	0011 1011
< (Less than sign)	60	0011 1100
= (Equal sign)	61	0011 1101
> (Greater than sign)	62	0011 1110
? (Question mark)	63	0011 1111
@ (At sign)	64	0011 0000
A	65	0100 0001
B	66	0100 0010
C	67	0100 0011
D	68	0100 0100
E	69	0100 0101
F	70	0100 0110
G	71	0100 0111
H	72	0100 1000

Symbol	Decimal Number System	Binary Value
I	73	0100 1001
J	74	0100 1010
K	75	0100 1011
L	76	0100 1100
M	77	0100 1101
N	78	0100 1110
O	79	0100 1111
P	80	0101 0000
Q	81	0101 0001
R	82	0101 0010
S	83	0101 0011
T	84	0101 0100
U	85	0101 0101
V	86	0101 0110
W	87	0101 0111
X	88	0101 1000
Y	89	0101 1001
Z	90	0101 1010
[(Opening bracket)	91	0101 1011
\ (Reverse slant)	92	0101 1100
] (Closing bracket)	93	0101 1101
^ (Circumflex)	94	0101 1110
_ (Underscore)	95	0101 1111
` (Grave accent)	96	0110 0000
a	97	0110 0001
b	98	0110 0010
c	99	0110 0011
d	100	0110 0100
e	101	0110 0101
f	102	0110 0110
g	103	0110 0111
h	104	0110 1000

Symbol	Decimal Number System	Binary Value
i	105	0110 1001
j	106	0110 1010
k	107	0110 1011
l	108	0110 1100
m	109	0110 1101
n	110	0110 1110
o	111	0110 1111
p	112	0110 0000
q	113	0110 0001
r	114	0111 0010
s	115	0111 0011
t	116	0111 0100
u	117	0111 0101
v	118	0111 0110
w	119	0111 0111
x	120	0111 1000
y	121	0111 1001
z	122	0111 1010
{ (Opening brace)	123	0111 1011
	(Vertical line)	124	0111 1100
} (Closing brace)	125	0111 1101
~ (Tilde)	126	0111 1110
DEL (Delete)	127	0111 1111

asked price See **quotation**.

assembler A program that converts instructions written in a low-level **programming** language (*assembly language*) into machine **language**. The commands and functions in an assembly language are expressed in words rather than numbers. To be read by a **computer**, instructions have to be converted to machine language, which is written in **binary** code.

An assembler can also handle other tasks, such as detecting and flagging errors resulting from misuse of the language, such as an invalid number.

assembly language See **assembler; language.**

assets Things of value owned by an individual or a business. Assets are considered in different ways, such as fixed, intangible, current, noncurrent, capital, accrued, frozen, hidden, and liquid.

1. *Fixed assets* are physical resources, such as plants, machinery, land, and mineral resources, used to produce goods and services. They are not intended for resale to customers, and except for land, they are subject to **depreciation.**

2. *Intangible assets* are privileges and acquired or developed rights, such as a **franchise, trademark, patent,** leasehold (see **lease**), and **goodwill.** Although a right granted by the government, such as a patent, may be represented on paper, intangible assets generally lack the physical substance that a fixed asset, such as a building, has.

3. *Current assets* are short-term assets in that they pertain to a normal business operating cycle, such as one year. Examples of such assets are cash, accounts receivable, **inventory,** marketable securities, and other assets that may be converted into cash or sold within the normal course of business.

4. *Noncurrent assets* are fixed assets, such as **real property** and equipment, that will *not* be converted into cash or sold within a normal business operating cycle.

5. *Capital assets* are used in production, rather than used for resale, and are held for a long period. They may include tangible fixed assets, such as land and equipment, or intangible assets, such as patents and goodwill.

6. *Accrued assets* (also called *accrued revenue*) refers to money that has been earned or has been accumulated over time but has not been received at the end of a specific **accounting** period. An example is rent that is due but has not yet been received.
7. *Frozen assets* are any assets or resources that cannot be sold or otherwise disposed of without the company suffering a loss. In some cases, assets such as property may be frozen by a court pending settlement of a dispute. See also **attachment.**
8. *Hidden assets* are any assets or resources that have a higher value than stated or are not readily identified in an organization's financial statements.
9. *Liquid assets* are any assets in the form of cash, such as a checking account, or any other assets that can be quickly converted into cash, such as a marketable security.

The total assets of a business at any time are stated on its **balance sheet** (see example in that entry). Current assets, including accrued assets, are usually listed first, followed by investments and other assets; fixed assets; and, finally, goodwill, leaseholds, and so on.

assigned-risk plan A form of insurance coverage for undesirable or high-**risk (2)** applications. Businesses and individuals may need insurance in situations that create more liability than insurers like to assume.

Example: A company may have filed an above-average number of claims for worker injury, or an individual may have had more automobile accidents than conventional coverage is designed to accommodate.

In high-risk cases, state governments require insurers to provide coverage, which is usually offered at higher rates, so that all parties will have protection regardless of the exceptional situation.

assignment Generally, the transfer of an interest in a right or property from one party (*assignor*) to another party (*assignee*). An assignment may be oral or written, and it may be a formal document or an **endorsement** on another document.

> *Example 1:* A **stockholder** may assign legally held **stock** to someone else by filling in the reverse side of the certificate or by having a separate assignment prepared (printed forms are usually available).
>
> *Example 2:* A person who sells property may assign the insurance policy on the property to the buyer, or the holder of a life insurance policy may assign it as **collateral** when taking out a loan.
>
> *Example 3:* An assignor may use his or her accounts receivable as collateral in a promissory **note.** If the assignor fails to honor the terms of the note, the assignee may use the assigned receivables as payment.

Assignments may be made by operation of law as well as by an act of the **principals** (assignor and assignee). For example, an assignment may be made by the courts in cases of death or **bankruptcy.**

assumable mortgage See **mortgage.**

attachment 1. In general, a supplement, **endorsement,** or rider, such as an addition to an insurance policy.

2. A legal proceeding by which property is officially taken into custody; the writ that orders such seizure. For example, a debtor's property may be seized to use as security for a debt in a claim made by a creditor.

attestation The act of authenticating a legal document by signing it as a witness to the signature of the party making the instrument. The witness, who signs at the request of the party making the instrument, is referred to as a *subscribing witness*.

The statement that describes the circumstances regarding the signing of an instrument is the *attestation clause*. The wording of this clause varies depending on the document. A **will,** for example, may have a very long clause placed to the left of the signature, whereas a simple business **contract** may have only a few words placed before the signature line.

```
              Example 1:


In the presence of:


_____


              Example 2:


Signed and delivered in the presence of:


_____
```

attestation clause See **attestation.**
audioconference See **teleconference.**
audit **1.** In general, an evaluation or investigation to determine whether a firm's procedures and operations are efficient and in compliance with company rules, regulations, and policy. Companies commonly use internal personnel to conduct

the audits that are designed to test and monitor internal matters. These audits have various names, such as *internal audit, compliance audit,* and *management audit.*

2. In **accounting,** an audit is made to verify the accuracy of the accounting records and financial **accounts** of a company. A formal audit is often done by an independent certified public accountant who, upon completion, provides an audit opinion. This type of audit is known as an *external audit.* When the firm uses its own personnel to do the financial audit, it is known as an *internal audit.* Frequently, both inside and outside accountants are involved.

Auditors verify the company's **assets, liabilities,** and **capital** as of a certain date. They also verify financial transactions that occurred during the period ending on that date.

Audited financial statements are required in various situations, such as when a company is applying for a loan or must issue an audited **annual report** to shareholders.

automation Automatically controlled operation; the technique of making systems, machines, or processes operate automatically with minimal human intervention. Automation in the workplace is a reflection of technological advances that have altered job-skills requirements. Although in some cases such advances have resulted in layoffs, transfers, or termination of employment, often they have created new opportunities. Secretaries, for example, may be able to participate in managing new technologies, such as computerized **databases,** rather than perform traditional tasks, such as sorting and filing manually.

auxiliary storage Secondary storage; an external **computer-**controlled storage device, such as a **disk** or tape, as opposed to internal computer storage (**memory**).

average 1. In general, a description, such as years of education completed, that typifies or generally explains the makeup of all members in a group. An average of a group of numbers is calculated in the same way as an arithmetic **mean,** by adding all numbers in the group and dividing the sum by the number of items.

2. For investments, see **stock index.**

axis One of the reference lines from which distances or angles are measured in a coordinate system. An axis is often referenced by the letters x, y, or z.

1. In Cartesian coordinates, the x-axis is the line $y = 0$; the y-axis is the line $x = 0$.
2. In a business graph, the x-axis, or the "categories" axis, is usually horizontal; the y-axis, or the "values" axis, is usually vertical.
3. In a three-dimensional graphics image, the z-axis is the dimension of depth.

B

baby bond See **bond**.

backlog An accumulation of unfinished work, unprocessed materials, or unfilled orders; the value of a company's unfilled orders.

back matter The concluding parts of a book or a book-length **report** or other document.

Appendix. The appendix (if used) is the first item in the back matter. Although a chapter within a document may have one or more appendixes, such material is often collected at the end of the document in the back matter.

Generally, material is well suited for an appendix if it is not an essential part of the text but is a helpful elaboration or explanation. The body of a survey questionnaire that was mentioned or summarized in the text, for example, might be printed in full as an appendix.

When there are several appendixes, they may be numbered (*Appendix 1, Appendix 2,* and so on) or lettered (*Appendix A, Appendix B,* and so on). Appendixes may also have titles: *Appendix 1: Sales by Region, 1995–1997.*

Notes. When notes are not collected at the ends of chapters, a section, commonly called *endnotes,* may be placed after the appendix in the back matter. Endnotes may be grouped by chapter, with chapter numbers and titles used as subheads above each applicable group of notes.

Even when a document contains endnotes, it may also have bottom-of-page *footnotes*. The footnotes may be strictly expository (containing text-style discussion), whereas the endnotes may consist of only source citations.

The style of notes should follow the employer's preferred style or the discipline of the writer. Writers may use business guides, such as *The Prentice Hall Style Manual;* specialized style guides, such as the *Style Manual* of the American Institute of Physics; or general guides, such as *The Chicago Manual of Style.*

The following style for book and article citations is widely used in general business documents. Notice that a shortened form may be used to cite an earlier source that was previously stated in full.

Examples:

1. Ronald Michaelson, ed., *Bottom-Line Management* (Portland, Oreg.: Business Management Press, 1996), 41, 301–7.
2. Ellen Miles-Kantor, "Desktop Publishing in the Millennium," *Office Technologies Today,* 30 (March 1995): 16–18, 21.
3. Michaelson, *Bottom-Line Management,* 53.

Glossary. If definitions of numerous difficult technical or foreign terms would be helpful, they may be given in alphabetical order in a glossary following the notes section. The style might resemble the short entries in this dictionary.

Bibliography or *reference list.* Like the endnotes section, a bibliography or reference list may be placed at the end of each chapter or in the back matter, after the glossary.

Different types of bibliographies and reference lists may be used, depending on the writer's objectives. The form may be a *bibliographical essay,* with a discussion of useful sources. It may be a single *list* alphabetized by author or alphabetized within various sections under appropriate subheads. When comments are desired, but not as a bibliographical essay, the alphabetical list of entries may be annotated, with a brief comment following the source data in each entry.

When a list contains sources for every work mentioned in the text, it may be titled "Works Cited." When all works consulted while writing the document are mentioned, it may be called "Works Consulted." More commonly, the list contains only certain sources selected by the author for mention; it is then called a "Select Bibliography" or a "Selected Bibliography."

Whether a bibliography or reference list is used often depends on the type of in-text citations desired. If the writer refers readers to a name and title (see Miles-Kantor, "Desktop Publishing," 6), the reader will need an alphabetical bibliography to find the full data on Miles-Kantor's "Desktop Publishing" article. But if the writer refers readers to a name and date (Miles-Kantor 1995, 17), the reader will need an alphabetical name-date reference list to locate the full data for Miles-Kantor's 1995 piece.

In a straight alphabetical bibliography, entries might look like the following examples. Notice that a succeeding entry by the same author would have a long dash instead of the name.

Examples:

Michaelson, Ronald. *Accounting for Nonmanagers*, 2d ed. New York: Halstrom and Kennedy Publishers, 1989.

————, ed. *Bottom-Line Management*. Portland, Oreg.: Business Management Press, 1996.

Miles-Kantor, Ellen. "Desktop Publishing in the Millennium." *Office Technologies Today*. 30 (March 1995): 16–30.

In a name-date reference list, the date is moved from the end of the entry to the beginning in a position immediately after the name.

Examples:

Michaelson, Ronald. 1989. *Accounting for Nonmanagers*, 2d ed. New York: Halstrom and Kennedy Publishers.

_____, ed. 1996. *Bottom-Line Managers*. Portland, Oreg.: Business Management Press.

Miles-Kantor, Ellen. 1995. "Desktop Publishing in the Millennium." *Office Technologies Today*. 30 (March): 16–30.

Index. An index is the last item in the back matter. If both name and subject indexes are used, the name index precedes the subject indexes. A separate name index may be helpful in a book with extensive discussion of and reference to various persons.

The complexity of an index depends on the text. In some works, one or more levels of indented subentries may appear under the main entry line.

Example:

Software, 117
   applications. *See* Applications software
   command-driven, 29
   groupware, 119
   high-level language, 67–68
   integrated, 16, 92–97
   low-level language, 69–71
   menu-driven, 30
   operating system, 11, 101–102
   user friendly, 8, 17–19

backup A copy of a document, **file,** or program. **Computer** users *back up* information when they want to be certain that important information stored on a hard **disk** will not be lost in case of disk failure or other problem that affects **data** storage. Frequently, the information is copied onto a removable diskette and stored in a secure area apart from the operating computer.

bailment The act of delivering **personal property** in **trust** to someone else. Except in the case of a **consignment** sale, it is usually implied that the property will be returned to the owner after the objective of the bailment has been met.

Four common forms of bailment are the actual bailment, involuntary bailment, bailment for hire, and bailment for mutual benefit.

1. An *actual bailment* refers to the actual or constructive (implied) delivery of goods to a *bailee* (the person who keeps the goods for someone else) or an agent (see **agency**) of the bailee.
2. An *involuntary bailment* refers to the unintentional leaving of one person's goods in another person's possession, as in the case of a car left on another's property after an accident.
3. A *bailment for hire* refers to a **contract** whereby the bailor (the one who delivers the goods) agrees to compensate the bailee, as in the case of paying a garage where a car is stored.
4. A *bailment for mutual benefit* is similar, except that an additional benefit is involved, as in the case of also asking the garage to wax the car during the bailment.

bait and switch pricing See **JARGON: bait and switch pricing.**

balance sheet A statement showing the **assets, liabilities,** and **capital** (see **equity**) of an organization on a specific date (see example). A balance sheet differs from an **income statement** in that it provides information about a company on a certain *date* rather than for a selected *period*.

The word *balance* in "balance sheet" points to the basic **accounting** equation that is observed in listing **accounts** in a certain order.

Example: Assets = Liabilities + Equity (A = L + E)

To depict this equation, accounts on the balance sheet are grouped into major categories. The "assets" accounts include current assets, investments, fixed assets, and intangible and other assets. The "liabilities" and "equity" accounts include current liabilities, long-term (noncurrent) liabilities, and owners' equity.

In the *account form* of balance sheet, the assets are listed on the left side of a page and the liabilities and owners' equity on the right side. In the *report form,* the accounts are stacked one above another in a single column, as illustrated in the example. However, the specific accounts that are listed on a balance sheet depend on the type of company and its financial activities. Regardless of the specific accounts that are listed or the particular format that is used, the totals on the statement must be consistent with the equation A = L + E.

balloon mortgage See **mortgage.**

balloon payment See **JARGON: balloon payment.**

bank draft The written order of one bank to another bank where it has funds deposited authorizing the other bank to pay a specified amount to the person or organization named on the draft (*payee*). Bank drafts may be described as sight or time drafts.

1. With a *sight draft,* the bank is directed to pay the amount due to the payee on demand.
2. With a *time draft,* the bank is directed to pay the amount due to the payee at a stated future time.

See also **bill of exchange.**

bankruptcy The legal process under federal law by which a debtor deals with a state of **insolvency.** The Bankruptcy Act provides for both the relief and rehabilitation of debtors by reconstituting the debtors' financial and business operations.

Example: Balance Sheet

J. Brentmire and Co., Inc.
Balance Sheet
December 31, 1997

ASSETS

Current assets
Cash		$ 15,000
Accounts receivable, net		59,000
Inventories		127,000
Prepaid insurance		2,000
Total current assets		203,000

Fixed assets
Land	$ 162,000	
Buildings	675,000	
Furniture and fixtures	59,000	
Equipment	196,000	
	1,092,000	
Less accum. deprec.	612,000	
Total fixed assets		480,000

Other assets
Long-term investments	53,000	
Goodwill, net	56,000	
Other assets	4,000	
Total other assets		113,000

TOTAL ASSETS — **$796,000**

LIABILITIES & OWNERS' EQUITY

Current liabilities
Accounts payable		$ 67,000
Notes payable		158,000
Accrued salaries payable		5,000
Taxes payable		7,000
Total current liabilities		237,000

Long-term liabilities
Bonds payable	202,000	
Total long-term liabilities		202,000
Total liabilities		439,000

Owner's equity
Common stock	253,000	
Retained earnings	104,000	
Total owners' equity		357,000

TOTAL LIABILITIES AND EQUITY — **$796,000**

Bankruptcy may be voluntary or involuntary.

1. Under *voluntary bankruptcy,* a party that is unable to pay its debts files a petition to have its **assets** fairly and equitably distributed among creditors, after which it is considered free of debt.
2. Under *involuntary bankruptcy,* the creditors petition to have a debtor declared insolvent by a court so that they can receive at least part of what is owed them. However, proceedings cannot be brought against a farmer or certain corporations, such as a municipal corporation.

Chapters 7, 11, and 13 are three common codes that provide for relief of debtors.

1. In straight bankruptcy, *Chapter 7* allows for all or most of a company's **assets** to be liquidated to pay off creditors.
2. Under *Chapter 11*, a company is given time to reorganize with the aim of becoming more profitable so that it can pay off its debts.
3. *Chapter 13*, designed for wage earners, allows them to retain possession of their property while paying creditors over a certain period as specified in a court-approved plan.

barcode A type of code imprinted on labels that can be read by a scanner or wand specifically designed for this purpose. A familiar example is the wand that retail checkout clerks use to read product labels and record sales. See **optical character recognition (OCR).**

bargain and sale deed See **deed.**

barter A form of trade in which goods or services, rather than money, are exchanged; the thing that is exchanged.

Example: A painting company might agree to paint the offices of a landscaping service if the landscaping service will agree to landscape the painting company's property. This type of exchange of services occurs without any payment of money by either party.

BASIC Acronym for **B**eginners **A**ll-Purpose **S**ymbolic **I**nstruction **C**ode; see **language.**

basis The amount or value on which something else is based; a base measurement used to calculate **amortization, depreciation,** capital gains or losses, and other amounts. Generally, *basis* is the original cost in acquiring an **asset.** Thereafter, the basis must be adjusted by adding capital expenditures and deducting depreciation (*adjusted basis*).

batch processing A type of **computer** operation in which several items are grouped for processing together. Program instructions are thus executed one after another—in one batch—without the user's intervention.

Although efficiencies can be realized by using batch processing, the disadvantage is that error correction or other adjustments can be dealt with only after the computer has finished with the entire batch. With *interactive processing,* where the user can intervene, the results are seen on screen, and adjustments can be made without having to wait until a batch has been run.

baud A variable unit of **data** transmission speed. This speed is the number of pulses or discrete signal events per second, with one baud equaling one **bit** per second in the case of a **binary** channel. Fax machines, for example, have built-in **modems** that transmit data at a rate expressed in bits per second (bps), such as 9,600 bps or 14,400 bps. The term *baud* derives from Emile Baudot, an inventor who contributed to the development of **telecommunications.**

bear See **JARGON: bear.**

bearer bond See **bond**.

beneficiary The person or thing designated to receive the proceeds of a deceased person's life insurance policy or something from the estate of a deceased person; the one designated to receive the benefits of a **trust**.

The recipient may or may not be a relative and could even be a pet; the recipient may also be a charity or any other organization—anyone or anything designated to receive proceeds or benefits by the person making a **will** or trust or owning a life insurance policy.

bibliography See **back matter**.

bid price See **quotation**.

bid and asked price See **quotation**.

Big Board See **stock exchange**.

bilateral contract See **contract**.

bill of exchange A **bank draft;** a negotiable written order signed by the issuer that requires the receiver or addressee to pay a third party a specified amount of money. A bill of exchange is common in international transactions where the receiver of goods is required to pay a specified amount before **title** to the goods can be transferred.

bill of lading A **contract** between a shipper and the transportation company that carries the shipper's goods; a receipt that lists the goods being shipped. The bill, which states the terms of the contract, can also serve as a document of **title**, with the party in possession of the bill assuming ownership of the goods being shipped.

bill of sale A written document that transfers goods, **title** to the goods, or other interest from a seller to a buyer. The bill states the terms and conditions of the transaction and certifies the transfer of ownership.

binary A type of number system that has a base of 2 (two possible digits—0 or 1), as opposed to the more familiar decimal system that has a base of 10 (10 possible digits—1 through 10). A **computer** can work more easily with a binary system since it need select only from two states: on or off, open or closed, 0 or 1. The following table gives examples of decimal and binary equivalents:

Decimal	Binary
0	000
1	001
2	010
3	011
4	100
5	101
6	110
7	111
8	1000
9	1001
10	1010

binder 1. In real estate, the preliminary **agreement** under which a purchaser makes a deposit (**earnest money**) as evidence of a commitment to purchase **real property;** the payment itself.

2. In insurance, a temporary **contract** provided by an insurance company that gives coverage until a permanent policy can be issued. The binder obligates the insurance company to the same extent as specified in the actual policy that is being prepared.

bit An abbreviation for **b**inary dig**it**; see **binary.**

blank endorsement See **endorsement.**

blanket insurance A broad type of insurance coverage used for group-health and property insurance. A blanket group-health policy covers a group of individuals, such as a team, who are not identified individually but are subject to the same hazards. Blanket coverage for property may apply to one of the following three situations:

1. Two kinds of property, such as a building and its contents, in the same location
2. The same kind of property, such as buildings, in two or more locations
3. Two kinds of property in two or more locations

With a blanket policy, all property may be covered without a specific limit on a particular property and regardless of its location. Coverage, therefore, remains in effect even when merchandise is moved from one building to another at various times.

blanket mortgage See **mortgage**.

blind trust See **trust**.

block 1. In **data processing**, a unit of information that is processed or transferred; a section of text or other material that is highlighted on screen so that a **computer** operation, such as copying or deleting, can be performed on it as a unit.

2. In finance, a large quantity of **stock,** such as 10,000 or more shares, or a large dollar amount of **bonds,** such as $200,000 worth or more, that is held or traded.

blue chip See **JARGON: blue chip**.

blueprint A photographic reproduction, such as an architectural plan, often made with white lines on a blue background or blue lines on a white background; a printer's **proof** of pages in a document showing how they will appear when printed.

In **printing,** this final proof is given to customers for their use in checking for errors, omissions, and other problems. Those who handle the **proofreading** at this stage should check for problems such as the following:

1. Missing or incorrectly placed pages

Standard Business Terms

2. Facing pages that are not equal in length
3. Misplaced illustrations
4. Errors noted earlier when proofreading page proofs that still have not been corrected

blue-sky laws A reference to state statutes (see **statutory law**) that regulate sales and other matters pertaining to the securities of **corporations** sold through investment companies. The purpose of the laws is to prevent the sale of securities of fraudulent companies and to protect the public from this danger.

board of directors A group of individuals elected by **stockholders** to manage a **corporation.** In organizations that have no stockholders, such as a nonprofit professional association, the board is elected by the membership.

A director may be an employee of the organization or someone from the outside who has an interest in the affairs of the organization (*outside director*). The corporation's **bylaws** and certain state statutes (see **statutory law**) affect board composition and service, including the following provisions:

1. Qualifications for service
2. Residency requirements
3. Number of directors allowed
4. Term of office
5. Election rules
6. Resignation procedure
7. Powers while in service
8. Liabilities while in service
9. Compensation requirements or restrictions
10. Location and frequency of meetings

Usually, a board must have at least three directors, often more, who serve a term of one or more years. These directors are not normally compensated for serving on the board but may be compensated for duties beyond the scope of board requirements.

Although directors occupy a **fiduciary** position (see also **trust**), they are not personally liable for losses caused by accident or by errors in judgment. They are, however, subject to any federal or state statutes that pertain to liabilities while they are in service.

Directors usually may conduct ordinary business, such as getting a bulletin printed, for the organization without interference from stockholders or members, except in areas where the bylaws or statutes require consent of the entire body. Binding business activity, however, such as accepting a government contract, must be undertaken as a group, not on an individual basis, at the directors' meetings where the board discusses and votes on relevant matters.

boilerplate See **JARGON: boilerplate.**

bond A promise to pay a specified sum on a specified date; an **interest-**bearing certificate issued by a government or private **corporation** that represents a form of indebtedness and an obligation of the issuer to the purchaser (*bondholder*). The formal **agreement,** or *deed of trust,* between an issuer and a bondholder is known as an *indenture*.

Both public and private organizations issue bonds as a means to raise money, sometimes in large amounts, and individuals buy them to earn money. Bonds may or may not be taxable.

1. A *corporate bond*, issued by a private corporation and traded on major exchanges, provides interest income to holders that is taxable.
2. A *municipal bond*, issued by a state or local government, provides interest income that may or may not be taxable.

A common measure of whether a bond is taxable is who benefits and how much. When a bond benefits private parties to a certain extent, for example, it is generally taxable. Therefore, whereas the income from a *public-purpose bond* is usually tax-exempt, that from a *private-purpose bond* is usually taxable unless specifically exempted.

A bond is a promise to pay the holder a specified amount of both interest and **principal,** and the payments are often scheduled as regular interest payments during the period of the bond, with the principal paid at **maturity.** A corporate bond sometimes may be converted into corporation **stock** rather than cash upon maturity. Bond periods until maturity vary but commonly run for 10 or 20 years.

Bonds may be secured or unsecured.

1. *Mortgage bonds* are secured by a corporation's **pledge** of **real property,** such as a plant and equipment.
2. *Debentures* are unsecured bonds backed only by a corporation's promise to pay or by its general **credit** standing.
3. *General obligation (municipal) bonds* are secured simply by the ability of the governmental body to collect money through taxes if needed.
4. *Revenue bonds*, used to fund public projects such as an airport, are paid from income received through the projects.

Bonds have various features and are known by different names depending on the particular feature.

1. *Redeemable* or *callable bonds* have a "bond redemption" feature that gives corporations the right to **call** in bonds before maturity.
2. *Convertible bonds* allow the holder to exchange them for another form of security, such as stock.

3. *Sinking-fund bonds* require the issuer to set aside a certain amount periodically to reduce the bond indebtedness.
4. *Baby bonds* are any bonds issued in denominations less than the standard $1,000 bond.
5. *Coupon bonds* are a form of *bearer bond*, with interest coupons that are detached and presented for collection of interest payments; that is, interest is paid to the bearer.
6. *Registered bonds* are registered in the name of the owner and must be signed by the owner before transfer can occur.
7. *Income* or *adjustment bonds* allow corporations to pay interest only when they earn it.
8. *Joint bonds,* common in railroad financing, are backed by two or more guarantors.
9. *Savings bonds* are issued by the U.S. government in various small denominations.
10. *Serial bonds,* issued by municipalities on the same date, have various maturity dates scheduled at regular intervals.
11. *Series bonds* are groups of bonds issued under the same indenture on different dates with different maturity dates.

Bonds are sometimes sold before maturity at a lower or higher price than the price at maturity. The difference between the **face value** or maturity value and the current market price is known as the *bond discount* or *bond premium,* depending on whether the market price is more or less than the maturity value.

See **bonding** for a description of *fidelity bonds* and *performance bonds.*

bond discount See **bond.**

bond dividend See **dividend**.

bonding Contracting to assume liability for failure to perform a designated task or for liability in the case of dishonesty involving someone in a position of **trust** (see **fiduciary**). Two examples of bonding are the performance bond and the fidelity bond.

1. A *performance bond* is an **agreement** whereby an insurance company assumes liability when a contractor fails to perform work or services by a certain date.
2. A *fidelity bond* is another form of insurance that provides coverage for an employer against loss caused by employee dishonesty or mishandling of funds.

bond premium See **bond**.

bond redemption See **bond**.

book value The value of individual **assets** as shown in the **accounting** records of the individual or corporate owner. Book value, which may be more or less than current market value, is generally based on an equation that deducts **depreciation** from the cost of the asset.

Example: Actual cost of an asset – allowances for depreciation = book value

The book value of a *fixed asset*, such as a building, is commonly calculated as cost plus additions and improvements less allowances for depreciation. The *net asset value* per **bond** or per share of **stock** is reached by dividing the number of bonds or shares of preferred or common stock into the company's total net asset figure.

bottom line See **JARGON: bottom line**.

breach of contract The intentional or unintentional failure to comply with a duty imposed by law or to perform an act called for in a **contract**. Someone might, for example, fail to deliver goods that were guaranteed in a contract to be delivered by a certain date. However, to receive **damages** in a lawsuit for some failure, an injured party must show that the alleged losses directly resulted from the breach.

breach of warranty The violation of an express or implied **agreement** in which a seller (*warrantor*) gave a promise or assurance concerning the **title,** quality, content, condition, or performance of something; providing a false **warranty** to a buyer (*warrantee*).

When something such as merchandise is deficient in terms of the guarantee or promises of the warranty, the buyer may return the item and ask for a refund, reduced price, or replacement item. In other situations, a buyer may choose to take legal action against the seller for **damages** resulting from the breach.

breakeven point 1. In general, the point at which income equals expenses. For businesses, when sales revenue is more than the breakeven point, there is a profit; when it is below the breakeven point, there is a loss.

2. In investments, the dollar price at which a securities transaction will produce neither a gain nor a loss.

broadcast In **computer** use and **telecommunications,** to send one message simultaneously to more than one receiver. With the appropriate equipment, for example, a user can send a fax (see **facsimile**) or **electronic-mail (E-mail)** message to numerous recipients all at once rather than transmit the message to one receiver at a time.

budgeting See **zero-base budgeting.**

buffer A storage area where information is held temporarily. A printer (see **printing**), for example, usually processes information more slowly than the **computer;** therefore, the **data** from the computer are held in the printer's buffer until it is ready to process the information at its own pace.

bug See **JARGON: bug.**

bull See **JARGON: bull.**

bulletin board system An electronic communication and mailing system in which **computer** users in different locations are connected to the system through the use of a **modem** and the telephone lines, enabling them to leave or retrieve messages, exchange **software,** and perform other tasks. Users who exchange software, however, do so at the risk of infecting their own system with a virus (see **JARGON: virus**).

Various organizations offer an electronic bulletin board system (BBS) for customers and other interested parties. The U.S. Government Printing Office, for example, has a BBS that users can call to browse through a roster of serviceable items.

burden rate See **overhead.**

bus See **central processing unit (CPU).**

bus topology See **local area network (LAN).**

bylaws Rules and regulations adopted by an organization to regulate its activities and to set forth the rights and duties of officers, directors (see **board of directors**), and **stockholders** or members. The bylaws may also include articles on standing rules and parliamentary rules of order (see **parliamentary procedure**), unless these items are published as separate documents.

1. *Standing rules* are rules (resolutions) affecting the organization and its members that are subject to the will (vote) of the majority at any **meeting.** These rules may not be in conflict with the constitution, bylaws, or rules of order but may be adopted or changed at any meeting without prior notice.

2. *Rules of order* are parliamentary rules describing the proper and orderly procedure for transaction of business at a meeting. These rules should include a provision

about the required procedure for making **amendments** to the rules.

The bylaws are considered permanent rules and regulations, although they may be amended by strictly following the prescribed conditions for amendment stated within them. Unlike standing rules, which may be written and adopted at any meeting by the directors or members, the bylaws are usually drafted by legal counsel.

The articles in the bylaws cover a variety of topics pertinent to the organization's management and operation.

1. Duties of officers and directors
2. Elections and nominating procedure for officers and directors
3. Duties of committees
4. Stockholder or membership requirements
5. Type, frequency, and location of meetings
6. Requirements for calling a meeting and notifying members
7. Quorum requirements
8. Designation of the fiscal year (see **fiscal period**)
9. Amendment requirements and procedure
10. Standing rules (if not a separate document)
11. Parliamentary rules of order (if not a separate document)
12. Other rules and regulations (if needed)

byte A group of eight adjacent **bits,** such as 0101 0110. In **computer** storage, each byte can hold the equivalent of one character. Computer **memory** is commonly listed in terms of kilobytes (K or KB) and megabytes (MB or meg).

Example: 1K = 1,024 bytes; 1MB = 1,048,576 bytes

More than 200 combinations exist for the eight bits, or binary digits, that make up a byte. See **ASCII** for examples.

C

cafeteria plan See **JARGON: cafeteria plan.**

call 1. In investments, the right or option of a buyer to purchase a specific number of shares of **stock** at a prearranged price by a fixed date; the right or option of an issuer of callable or redeemable preferred stock to demand that holders surrender the stock for cash; the right or option of an issuer to redeem **bonds** before their **maturity** date. Like **puts,** calls are traded in 100-share units.

The part of an **agreement** between an issuer and a buyer that describes the call is known as the *call feature*. The price at which a bond or preferred stock can be redeemed by the issuer is known as the *call price* or *redemption price*.

2. In banking, the right of a bank to demand that the entire **principal** of a secured loan be repaid immediately. A bank may "call" a loan when a borrower fails to fulfill the requirements of the loan **contract,** such as failing to make timely payments (see **default**).

callable bond See **bond.**

callable preferred stock See **stock.**

call option See **call.**

call price See **call.**

cambistry See **UNUSUAL WORDS: cambistry.**

camera-ready copy Material intended for **printing** that is complete, finished, and ready to be photographed in preparation of making a **plate** used in printing. Camera-ready **copy** should have been previously read and checked for errors and other problems (see **copyedit; proofreading**) and corrected or revised as necessary before final approval was given to proceed to the photographic stage.

cap See **JARGON: cap.**

capital The money, tangible or intangible property, and other accumulated wealth of an individual or **corporation;** a corporation's **assets;** those corporate assets used to create profits (see **gross profit; net income**). Capital may be routinely used for an existing corporation or may represent funding for a new venture.

1. *Working capital,* or *net working capital,* refers to the assets used in everyday operations (current assets less current **liabilities**) that are immediately available. Working capital is a measure of an organization's *liquidity*, that is, its ability to meet current liabilities or convert current assets into cash or cash equivalents.
2. *Venture capital* refers to the financing provided to start new ventures or to expand or improve the condition of existing companies. Since this type of financing often involves some **risk,** it is also known as *risk capital.*

capital asset See **assets.**

capital goods The fixed **capital,** or durable goods, such as equipment and buildings, that are used over a period of years to produce other goods.

capitalization The total amount of a **corporation's** outstanding **stocks** and **bonds;** the total value of **capital stock,** paid-in **capital,** and borrowed capital. The term *capitalization* is sometimes used interchangeably with *capital structure*, although authorities disagree whether long-term debt is part of the capital structure.

The term *capital structure* is often used in reference to components of the financial structure, and *capitalization* is more often used in reference to the structure as a whole.

capital stock The outstanding shares of common and preferred **stock** representing the aggregate ownership interest of a **corporation**. A capital stock **account** is set up in the **accounting** records of a corporation to reflect income from the sale of stock.

capital structure See **capitalization**.

carrier See **common carrier**.

cash accounting See **accounting**.

cash disbursements journal See **journal**.

cash dividend See **dividend**.

cash flow The sources and uses of cash during an **accounting** period (see **fiscal period**); the changes that affect the cash **account;** cash receipts less cash disbursements from a particular **asset** or operation for a specified period.

The management of a company wants to have enough cash to meet its needs at any time. Since one of management's most important functions is to ensure the availability and efficient use of cash, it needs to have a complete picture of the movement of cash, or liquid assets, in and out of the company during each accounting period. This picture, used in analysis and in preparing a cash budget, is best represented by developing a cash flow statement based on the same **data** used in preparing a **balance sheet** and **income statement**.

A cash flow statement lists the sources that have produced cash (*inflow*) and shows where cash has been spent (*outflow*). The difference between the two is the balance in the cash account as of a certain period.

cashier's check A check drawn by a bank against its own funds and signed by a cashier. The check may be sold to a customer, issued to a borrower, or used by the bank to pay its own obligations.

cash receipts journal See **journal.**

cathode ray tube (CRT) An electron tube used in visual displays, such as a **computer** monitor or a television screen. An electron gun sends a beam used to form images by repeatedly sweeping across a display screen and striking phosphors (light-emitting substances) that are then illuminated on the inside of the screen. A color monitor has a separate gun for the colors red, blue, and green and separate phosphors on the inside of the screen.

The terms *CRT, monitor, display,* and *video display* are often used interchangeably in reference to the unit that contains or provides for a computer's on-screen display.

caveat emptor See **FOREIGN EXPRESSIONS: caveat emptor.**

CD-ROM See **disk,** *Optical disk.*

cell See **cellular technology; spreadsheet.**

cellular technology Mobile telephone communication capability based on the transmission of signals through a system of exclusive geographical areas, known as *cells,* that are connected to a series of transmission towers.

The Federal Communications Commission set up the cellular geographic service areas to handle mobile telephone service to and from automobiles and other moving vehicles and to connect users to the worldwide telephone **network.** The system allows for expansion in that if a particular cell becomes overcrowded, it can be subdivided to handle the increasing volume of traffic.

Cellular technology permits calls to be dialed from a moving vehicle in the conventional manner and then picked up by the nearest base station located in one of the established cells. The receiving station transmits the call to a central switching office that handles a group of cells and is itself connected to the worldwide telephone network.

As a user travels in a moving vehicle (called *roaming*), calls are automatically switched from one cell to another. Each new cell continues the task of uninterrupted transmission to the switching office. Therefore, users can continue to use cell phones as long as the areas into which they drive have transmitting cells available.

central bank The Federal Reserve System; a national bank established by federal authorities that sets monetary policy, issues currency, controls the money supply and **interest** rates, and works to protect the public interest. It also holds deposits that represent the reserves of other banks and transacts government business.

The Federal Reserve System has 12 regional banks that provide check clearing, hold commercial bank deposits, and control **credit.** The regional banks, which are privately controlled, are located in Atlanta, Boston, Chicago, Cleveland, Dallas, Kansas City, Minneapolis, New York City, Philadelphia, Richmond, St. Louis, and San Francisco. The governors of the Federal Reserve Board and the presidents of the regional banks handle a variety of responsibilities, from buying and selling foreign currencies (see list in **APPENDIX**) to regulating the functions of commercial banks.

centralization Concentration of authority at the top. With this form of management, decision-making and policy-making functions are reserved for top management, rather than spread out geographically or delegated to lower levels, as in the case of **decentralization.**

central processing unit (CPU) That part of a **computer** consisting of the primary storage (see **memory**), the arithmetic-logic unit (ALU), the clock, and the control unit. The CPU receives information, interprets it, executes instructions, and transfers information to and from other components, such as the keyboard. It does this over the computer's *bus,* which is its **data** highway through which instructions are transmitted.

See also **chip; microprocessor.**

Centrex See **telephone system.**

certificate of incorporation See **articles of incorporation.**

certified check A bank check that is requested by a depositor and that the bank guarantees will be covered by sufficient funds on deposit. When a depositor asks that a certified check be drawn against his or her **account,** the bank immediately charges the depositor's account. Therefore, when the depositor presents the check to the intended recipient (*payee*), the payee can cash it immediately without risk that the depositor might not have sufficient funds to cover it.

Certified checks are commonly used in real estate and securities transactions where cash payment or the equivalent is required. An advantage to this type of check is that the *payee* knows funds are available to cover the check. A disadvantage is that the *payer* cannot stop payment once a payee has received a certified check.

certified public accountant (CPA) See **accounting.**

certiorari See **FOREIGN EXPRESSIONS: certiorari.**

Chapter 7 bankruptcy See **bankruptcy.**

Chapter 11 bankruptcy See **bankruptcy.**

Chapter 13 bankruptcy See **bankruptcy.**

character Any symbol, such as a letter, number, punctuation mark, or **graphics** symbol, used to express information. A character occupies one **byte** of **memory** in a **computer.** The table given in the entry **ASCII** contains the standard ASCII character set.

charitable corporation See **corporation.**

charter See **articles of incorporation.**

chart of accounts A numbered list of **accounts** in a **ledger** that is used to classify, identify, and locate ledger items. A chart of accounts has a range of numbers for each financial category so that new items can be added later to any category. Four-digit numbers are used in the chart of accounts illustrated on page 60.

chattel A legal term for **personal property,** such as a car or boat. Unlike **real property,** such as land or a building, chattel refers to movable goods. A chattel **mortgage,** for example, is a loan **contract** that uses movable personal property, rather than immovable real estate, as security.

chattel mortgage See **chattel; mortgage.**

chip A miniature **integrated circuit** made from semiconductor material, usually silicon, with millions of components existing on a chip smaller than a fingertip. The two common types of chips are **memory** chips and **microprocessors.** A *memory chip* contains blank memory ready to receive information; a *microprocessor* houses an entire **central processing unit (CPU).**

civil law The body of federal or state laws that deals with the rights of a private citizen; the body of law developed from Roman law, used in Louisiana and various countries throughout the world, especially in Western Europe; Roman-based jurisprudence, especially as defined by the Justinian code.

Civil Rights Act of 1964 See **discrimination; equal opportunity.**

class action A reference to a lawsuit brought by one or more representative members of a larger group of people who have a common interest or complaint. A few employees who have a grievance, for example, might initiate a class-action lawsuit on behalf of all employees in the organization who share the grievance.

This type of lawsuit must be certified as a class action by a trial court before it can proceed. If it receives proper certifi-

Example: Chart of Accounts

```
           N. T. WASHINGTON, INC.
                 LISTING OF
               GENERAL LEDGER
          DATE PRINTED: 01\16\97
```

G/L ACCT NUMBER	ACCT NAME
	CURRENT ASSETS
1000	CASH IN BANK
1001	CASH IN BANK - CHECKING
1002	CASH IN BANK - SAVINGS
1300	ACCOUNTS RECEIVABLE - TRADE
	FIXED ASSETS
1500	FURNITURE/FIXTURES
1510	OFFICE EQUIPMENT
	CURRENT LIABILITIES
2000	ACCOUNTS PAYABLE - TRADE
	CAPITAL
3000	CAPITAL STOCK
3010	ADD'L PAID IN CAPITAL
3050	RETAINED EARNINGS
	INCOME
4000	SALES REVENUE
	COST OF SALES
5000	COST OF SALES
	EXPENSES
6000	ADVERTISING
6010	AUTO EXPENSE
	OTHER EXPENSES
9999	INCOME TRANSFER

cation, all members of the class must receive notice of the action and must be given an opportunity to exclude themselves if they so desire.

Clayton Act See **antitrust laws.**

clearinghouse 1. In banking, a voluntary association of banks where checks, **notes,** drafts, and other items held by one member and owed to another are exchanged and where balances between the banks are settled.

2. In securities transactions, a **stock exchange** or **commodities** exchange, which helps to settle the debits and credits among members.

clip art Illustrations that are printed in books or stored on **disk** and may be purchased for use in **word processing, desktop publishing,** and other applications requiring decorative or artistic material. Typically, you may select and use a certain number of pieces in brochures, newsletters, and other documents without permission.

Because the illustrations are simultaneously available to anyone else who wants to use them, they cannot be considered original or exclusive art; nevertheless, many of the pieces represent professional-quality **graphics** and provide a low-cost source of artwork for budget-conscious users.

close corporation See **corporation.**

closed-circuit television A video system limited to a particular location or group, such as a company plant or company employees. Closed-circuit television is used by organizations for various in-house activities, such as security systems, training programs, safety monitoring of work areas, and promotional films.

See also **teleconference.**

closed corporation See **corporation.**

closed end Having defined limits regarding time or money, such as a closed-end investment company that has fixed capitalization. A closed-end **mortgage,** for example, does not allow additional borrowing without the consent of the first mortgagee, and a closed-end **mutual fund** starts with a set number of shares instead of creating additional shares on demand.

Compare with **open end.**

closed-end fund See **mutual fund.**

closely held corporation See **corporation.**

closing 1. In **accounting,** "closing the books" by transferring revenue and expense **accounts** at the end of an accounting period to summary accounts. After closing entries have been made, with revenue accounts debited and expense accounts credited (see **debit and credit**), the account balances will be zero as a new year begins.

2. In real estate, the final steps in a transaction between a seller and a buyer that complete a sale of **real property.** A *closing statement* is presented listing the various costs, such as property taxes and recording fees, that the buyer or seller must pay.

closing entries See **closing.**

closing statement See **closing.**

closing the books See **closing.**

cloud on the title See **encumbrance; title.**

COBOL Acronym for Common Business Oriented Language; see **language.**

codicil A supplement to an existing **will** that legally changes or alters it.

coinsurance The amount of **risk** shared by an insurer and insured.

In property insurance, the *coinsurance clause* defines what percentage the insurer will pay for a loss.

Example: If a building is valued at $500,000, the policy specifies 80 percent coinsurance ($400,000), the building is insured for $350,000, and the loss is $270,000, the insurer would pay $236,250 as follows: $350,000/$400,000 × $270,000 = $236,250.

In health insurance, the coinsurance clause specifies the amount of a loss that the insured will assume. Often, the insurer will pay 75 or 80 percent of the covered medical expenses, after the **deductible,** and the insured must pay the remaining 25 or 20 percent. After a certain limit is reached, such as $5,000, the insurer will usually pay 100 percent.

collateral The property, money, or other item of value that is offered as a **pledge,** or security, when taking out a loan.

Example 1: A company that wants to borrow $75,000 and has $200,000 **equity** in a building might use the building as collateral for the loan.

Example 2: An individual who wants to borrow $10,000 and has a car with a clear **title** (fully paid for) worth $15,000 might use that property as collateral for the loan.

If the borrower **defaults,** the lender is entitled to sell the pledged property as a means of ensuring that the loan is repaid.

collusion A secret **agreement** between two or more parties that intend to do something fraudulent (see **fraud**), illegal, or deceitful.

colophon See **UNUSUAL WORDS: colophon.**

color coding The use of different colored paper, labels, **file** folders, or other material to make identification and location of items on shelves and in cabinets easier and faster and to help prevent and spot misfiles.

comaker Someone who signs a note along with a borrower to provide additional security on the loan. The comaker is jointly liable with the borrower for the borrower's obligation. Thus if the borrower defaults, the comaker must repay the loan.

command A signal that you give to a **computer** to tell it to perform a certain task, such as file a document. In *command-driven programs,* you give a command by pressing the required keys for the desired task. In a *menu-driven* program, you select the command you want from an on-screen **menu** that lists possible tasks, such as file, edit, and format.

command-driven program See **command.**

commercial paper An unsecured and usually discounted short-term promissory **note** with a flexible **maturity** range up to 270 days. This type of obligation is issued by **corporations,** banks, and others who want to borrow money; the notes are purchased by investors, directly or through brokers, who have available cash to buy the paper and in essence lend money to the issuer. Commercial paper is usually backed by the issuer's bank line of **credit.**

commodities Goods that are traded in bulk, such as grains and metals. Commodities are bought and sold on a commodities exchange or a spot market. The different *commodities exchanges* are registered with the *Commodities Futures Trading Commission*, which regulates all commodities traded in organized contract markets.

A *spot market* refers to a commodities market where goods are sold for cash, often by telephone rather than on an exchange floor, with arrangements for immediate delivery. A *futures market* is a commodity exchange set up for trading in *futures contracts* (see **futures**).

commodities exchange See **commodities.**

commodities futures See **commodities.**

Commodities Futures Trading Commission See **commodities.**

common carrier A company that provides transportation of people or goods for hire as well as communications and other related services.

common law A system of jurisprudence, originating in England, that is based on court decisions (*judicial precedent*) rather than legislatively enacted statutes (**statutory law**). Common law, which is the basis of laws in most states, is a written form of law but is called the *unwritten law* to distinguish it from written statutes enacted by legislatures.

common logarithm See **logarithm.**

common stock See **stock.**

communications protocol See **protocol.**

compact disk See **disk.**

comparative negligence See **contributory negligence.**

compatibility The capability of equipment or **peripherals** to be connected and function together without special devices or adaptors; the ability of one company's **computer** to run the **software** of another company's computer and to use the same **commands** and **formats** as another.

Compatibility may be partial or complete. One machine, for example, may be able to run part but not all of another machine's software. When software is fully compatible, a **file** produced by one application, such as **word processing,** can be imported into another application, such as into a **spreadsheet.** If compatible, both can use files created in the same format.

compiler See **language.**

complaint In law, the plaintiff's formal *pleading* (statement) in a lawsuit describing the facts of a preliminary charge against the accused and asking for **damages** or other relief. A complaint is usually the first document filed in a lawsuit.

compound interest See **interest**.

computer An electronic device that can be programmed to carry out instructions and process **data** at high speed. It can receive data (see **JARGON: input**), manipulate it, store it (see **memory; disk**), and display or print out the results (see **cathode ray tube [CRT]; printing; JARGON: output**).

The first computer, the Electronic Numerical Integrator and Calculator (ENIAC), was built for the U.S. Army in 1945. Although the ENIAC was a huge machine, computers used in business today range in size from large, central *mainframe computers* to intermediate-size *minicomputers* to small-size *microcomputers*, such as the personal computer, to even smaller, portable *notebook computers* and other pocket-size devices.

A modern computer can store its own instructions and is capable of rapid processing of text, numbers, **graphics,** symbols, and sound. The equipment (**hardware**) operates and produces results through programs (**software**) that tell it what to do. The hardware includes these components:

1. The primary unit for interpreting and executing instructions, known as the **central processing unit (CPU)**
2. Input devices, such as a keyboard (see **Dvorak keyboard** and **qwerty keyboard**) or **mouse**
3. Memory to store programs, documents, and other data
4. Storage devices, such as a hard **disk**
5. Output devices, such as a printer (see **printing**) or monitor

See also **language; programming**.

computer-aided design (CAD) See **graphics**.

computer-assisted retrieval (CAR) See **micrographics**.

computer conference See **teleconference**.

computer document conference See **teleconference**.

computer graphics See **graphics**.

computer printer See **printing**.

computer-telephony integration See **telephone system**.

conditional endorsement See **endorsement**.

conditional sale A sale in which the buyer receives possession and use of purchased goods while **title** remains with the seller as security, pending fulfillment of some condition, such as receiving the buyer's payment of a final installment.

conference A type of **meeting** between two or more persons for the purpose of discussing matters of common interest and exchanging ideas and opinions. Executives and staff may hold daily conferences in their company offices, or an organization, such as a professional association, may hold annual or other large conferences for its membership. Sometimes small meetings, such as a meeting of the **board of directors,** will be scheduled as part of a large conference.

When large conferences have equipment or other exhibits, they are often called *conventions*. A smaller gathering set up only for information exchange and instruction or training is often called a *seminar* or *workshop*.

Large conferences have formal programs, with a variety of sessions scheduled during one or more days. Experts on the scheduled topics are invited to "present papers" (speak) to members who register for the sessions of their choice. The papers may be collected and published in a book known as the *conference proceedings*.

Tours, lunches and dinners, and other special events are often planned during the conference. Attendees and spouses frequently stay at the hotel or near the facilities where the conference is being held.

A large conference requires extensive planning, and numerous committees may be formed to make arrangements in a variety of areas, including the following:

1. Budgeting
2. Site selection
3. Hotel reservations
4. Equipment rental
5. Program development
6. Exhibits
7. Printing and mailing
8. Transportation
9. Meals
10. Entertainment
11. Advance and door registration
12. Postconference evaluation

Computer programs (see **software**) designed especially for conference planning and scheduling are helpful in making arrangements for large conferences. Also, large organizations may have in-house **desktop publishing** capability or may be offered the assistance of member companies that can provide this service.

For a description of *document* or *computer conferences, videoconferences,* and other methods of remote conferencing, see **teleconference.**

conference proceedings See **conference.**

confidential mailbox See **mailbox.**

configuration The setup of **hardware** and **software** in a **computer** system. The choices that must be made in selecting components and programs may be complex, depending on user needs. A business may have to select an **operating system** and specify various aspects of the system, such as the amount of random-access **memory** (RAM), the size of the hard **disk,** the number and size of floppy drives, and the type and size of the monitor (see **cathode ray tube [CRT]**).

The **parameters** for a particular applications program, such as the **default** (*preselected*) settings for line spacing and margins, are then stored in a *configuration file*. The computer can check this **file** each time it runs a program.

configuration file See **configuration.**

conglomerate See **corporation.**

consideration See **contract; mortgage.**

consignment A **bailment** for sale or care; the delivery and transfer of goods, such as furniture, without transfer of **title,** from a seller (*consignor*) to a dealer (*consignee*) who agrees to sell the goods for the consignor.

According to the terms of the consignment agreed to by the parties, the consignee will remit a percentage of the proceeds to the consignor and will retain a percentage (*commission*) for his or her efforts. However, if the consignee does not sell the goods within an agreed-upon period, the property must be returned to the consignor.

constructive receipt In taxes, the concept that income must be reported according to the date that it is made available to a taxpayer, not the date when a taxpayer physically receives it, deposits it, or cashes a check.

Example: If a check was written and sent to a taxpayer on December 30, 1996, but the taxpayer did not receive or deposit it until January 5, 1997, it was nevertheless constructively received in 1996 and must be reported as income in 1996.

consumer price index (CPI) A statistical measure of changes in the cost of goods and services to wage earners (*consumers*) as determined by a monthly survey of the U.S. Bureau of Labor Statistics. The index, stated as a percentage of the cost in a base period, includes the costs of food, housing, electricity, and transportation. Since it measures changes in consumer prices, it is regularly used as a measure of **inflation.**

continuous inventory See **inventory.**

contract A binding **agreement,** enforceable at law, between two or more parties who mutually agree to do or not to do something. According to the **statute of frauds**, certain contracts to be enforceable must be in writing; in other cases, a contract may be oral or written and formal or informal, as desired by the parties. All contracts concerning the sale of goods are governed by the **Uniform Commercial Code (UCC).**

Four elements must be present for a contract to be enforceable at law.

1. There must be an offer and an acceptance.
2. The contracting parties must be of legal age in their state and be legally competent to contract. **Corporations** may be additionally limited by their **articles of incorporation** or by restrictions in various state statutes.
3. The terms of the contract may not call for acts that are illegal, such as **price fixing.**
4. There must be *consideration,* something of value given to the party that makes a promise (*promisor*) by the other party (*promisee*).

Contracts are known by different names that describe the type of contract, such as the unilateral, bilateral, oral, quasi (or implied), cost-plus, and output contracts.

1. With a *unilateral contract,* consideration is not given to the promisor by the promisee.
2. With a *bilateral contract,* mutual promises are made, and each party becomes both a promisor and a promisee.
3. With an *oral contract,* the terms are presented and agreed to orally, and there is no written instrument or signature involved.
4. With a *quasi* (or *implied*) *contract,* founded in Roman law and English **common law,** an agreement is created

by law for reasons of justice and, therefore, sometimes without the assent of the parties.

5. With a *cost-plus contract,* common in government agreements, a contractor is paid a sum that includes his or her costs plus a specified percentage representing the contractor's profit.
6. With an *output contract,* one party agrees to deliver his or her entire output to another party, who in turn agrees to accept it.

contributory negligence The legal principle that an injured person at least in part caused his or her own injury.

Example: A person shopping in a store may have failed to notice a cautionary sign, such as "WET FLOORS," and as a result was injured in a fall. The person was therefore injured not only because the store had wet floors but also because he or she failed to notice the cautionary sign.

More common now is *comparative negligence* whereby the responsibility for an injury is divided between a plaintiff and a defendant based on "relative" negligence. Under this principle, plaintiffs can receive **damages** only in proportion to their fault.

control account See **account; ledger.**

convention See **conference.**

conventional mortgage See **mortgage.**

convertible bond See **bond.**

convertible preferred stock See **stock.**

copy A manuscript before it is produced in final form; advertising text. Manuscript copy is often copyedited by an editor who marks corrections and improvements on the manuscript pages. The copyediting (see **copyedit**) is done by using **proofreading** marks. These marks are commonly understood by those who produce finished documents by typesetting and **printing** in outside firms or by **word processing** or **desktop publishing** handled in-house.

copyedit To prepare **copy** for typesetting, **desktop publishing, printing,** or some other stage in the production of a document. Copyeditors may do minimal or extensive work, depending on their assigned duties and the needs of a document, from rewriting to styling (determining the style and consistency of capitalization, punctuation, spelling, and so on). Corrections or refinements are made directly on screen with a **computer** or marked directly on the manuscript using **proofreading** marks.

Copyeditors who work for companies that prepare newsletters, house organs, **reports,** books, and other documents often have a preferred style that they must follow. This style is usually detailed in an in-house or outside style guide that covers spelling, punctuation, capitalization, and other matters, such as the preparation of reference citations (see examples in **front matter**).

Various organizations use style books that can be purchased in bookstores or ordered directly from the publisher. Well-known guides include *The Chicago Manual of Style, The Prentice Hall Style Manual, The New York Times Manual of Style and Usage,* and the *United States Government Printing Office Style Manual.* Also available are specialized guides, such as the Harvard Law Review Association's *Uniform System of Citation.*

copying See **xerography.**

copyright Legal protection of documents, **computer** programs (see **software**), recordings, films, and other creative works of authors and artists as provided by statute (see **statutory law**) and **common law.** The Copyright Office in the Library of Congress, Washington, D.C., has forms available to use in registering legal ownership for the period allowed by law.

Those works that are not protected by copyright are said to be "in the **public domain**" and may be freely reproduced without permission. In cases of protected works, however, writers must be careful not to violate restrictions or prohibitions on using another's creation without permission (*copyright infringement*).

Material in legally copyrighted works can be used without permission only for purposes of news reporting, teaching, or critical commentary. Persons who use material in this way should nevertheless credit the source of the information. However, the systematic photocopying or other reproduction and distribution of copyrighted material is strictly prohibited by law. Even spontaneous photocopying and distribution in classrooms must be minor or brief, with the number of copies made not exceeding the number of students in a class.

See also **patent; trademark.**

copyright infringement See **copyright.**

corporate bond See **bond.**

corporate raider See **JARGON: raider.**

corporation A legal entity, separate and distinct from the employees or people who own it (**stockholders**), chartered by a state or the federal government to conduct business. In a corporate form of organization, which provides limited liability, an owner can lose only what he or she has invested and can easily transfer ownership by selling **stock.** (See also **limited liability company.**) Continuity of existence is ensured since new owners purchase the stock of the previous owners who are selling it. **Capital** can be relatively easily obtained by increasing the number of owners.

One or more persons may file an official statement known as the **articles of incorporation** (also *certificate of incorpo-*

ration or *charter*) with the appropriate state official. Once an organization is chartered and begins operations, it must strictly follow the laws of the state under which it is incorporated.

Corporations are known by various names that describe their organizational status and function, such as the domestic, foreign, out-of-state, alien, de facto, de jure, charitable, nonprofit (or not-for-profit), for-profit, closely held (or close), privately held (or closed), parent, subchapter S, professional, public service (or utility), public, and publicly held corporations, as well as the conglomerate and holding company.

1. A *domestic corporation* is organized to do business in the state in which it is incorporated.
2. A *foreign corporation* is either chartered under the laws of a state other than the one in which it does business or is organized under the laws of a foreign country.
3. An *out-of-state corporation* is another term for a foreign corporation that is chartered under the laws of a state other than the one in which it does business.
4. An *alien corporation* is another term for a foreign corporation that is organized under the laws of another country.
5. A *de facto corporation* exists in fact or in good faith but has not met all of a state's legal requirements.
6. A *de jure corporation* exists in law as well as in fact since it has met all incorporating requirements.
7. A *nonprofit* (or *not-for-profit*) *corporation,* such as a religious body, is a tax-exempt organization that has no **capital stock,** pays no **dividends,** and operates for a charitable, humanitarian, or educational purpose.

8. A *charitable corporation,* such as a humane society, is a nonprofit corporation that operates for a charitable purpose.
9. A *for-profit corporation* is a taxable business organization that issues stock, pays dividends, and operates to make a profit.
10. A *closely held* (or *close*) *corporation* has a limited number of stockholders, sometimes from the same family, has some stock available for trading, and conducts business less formally than a regular corporation.
11. A *privately held* (or *closed*) *corporation* also has a limited number of stockholders but does not offer any stock for public trading.
12. A *parent corporation* owns the majority of shares of stock of another corporation (a *subsidiary*) and thus has control over it.
13. A *subchapter S corporation* is a small corporation that elects to be taxed as a **partnership** but whose stockholders enjoy the benefits of limited corporate liability.
14. A *professional corporation* is an association of one or more licensed members of a profession, such as the legal profession, who continue to practice their profession while enjoying tax and other benefits of incorporation.
15. A *public service* (or *utility*) *corporation*, usually franchised (see **franchise**) by a governmental authority, is organized to supply services, such as electricity or water, regarded as a public necessity.
16. A *public corporation* is a government-owned corporation, such as the U.S. Postal Service, or a subdivision of the state, such as a school district.
17. A *publicly held corporation* sells stock to the public under the regulation of the **Securities and Exchange Commission.**

18. A *conglomerate* is a widely diversified corporation composed of subsidiaries united through mergers and acquisitions.
19. A *holding company* is a corporation that has partial or complete interest in other companies and owns enough stock to control their policies and management.

correlation A relationship or association, which may be positive or negative, between two separate things or phenomena.

Example: If it is true that as educational level increases among job applicants the opportunities for employment also increase, there is a *positive* correlation between the two variables "educational level" and "employment opportunity."

A statistical measure known as the *correlation coefficient* is used to determine the degree to which the movements of two such variables are related.

correlation coefficient See **correlation**.

correspondence format See **format**.

cost accounting See **accounting**.

cost-plus contract See **contract**.

coupon bond See **bond**.

coupon yield See **yield**.

covenant A written promise or binding **agreement** between two or more parties to do or not to do something. In real estate, a **deed** may have a covenant that restricts how the property may be used, or the developer of a subdivision may have recorded certain restrictions that apply to owners. For example, an owner may not be allowed to place a storage shed on any landscaped area. This type of covenant is known as a *restrictive covenant*.

credit 1. In business transactions, the amount of indebtedness that a customer may incur. Banks, credit card companies, retail institutions, and other lenders and sellers set up **accounts** for customers with *credit lines* (also called *lines of credit*) up to which a customer may purchase goods and services by charging them and paying later either in full or in installments.

Suppliers commonly offer *open accounts* to customers based on a customer's credit history and financial trustworthiness. An open account enables a customer to purchase goods and services "on account" **interest**-free for a short term, usually 30 days or less.

A business traveler going to another country may purchase a *letter of credit* from a bank that testifies to the holder's creditworthiness. The letter of credit can be drawn against at other banks worldwide until the face amount is exhausted.

2. In **accounting,** an entry on the right side of an **account** in a **ledger.** See **debit and credit.**

credit line See **credit.**

crossover See **JARGON: crossover.**

crosstalk See **JARGON: crosstalk.**

cumulative preferred stock See **stock.**

cumulative trauma disorders See **ergonomics.**

Curb, the See **stock exchange.**

current asset See **assets.**

current yield See **yield.**

Cu See-Me conference See **teleconference.**

cybernetics The study of control processes and communication in biological, mechanical, and electronic systems, particularly in artificial systems and living organisms; the theoretical study of control processes and communication between people and machines to help improve machine efficiency.

Cybernetics has been used to advance technology through better forecasting, systems modeling, and the development of **artificial intelligence.**

cyberspace See **JARGON: cyberspace.**

D

damage control See **JARGON: damage control.**

damages The monetary compensation allowed by law that is awarded to someone who has been injured by the action of another; monetary compensation for a legal wrong, such as **breach of contract,** or for a **tort,** such as negligence; the sum an insurance company pays an insured party for covered losses that have been incurred.

The term *pecuniary damages* is used when losses are defined in monetary terms. The term *punitive damages* refers to the portion of compensation awarded by a court above the amount allowed for actual damages. This type of award is made as punishment for a willful wrongdoer and as reparation for the injured party.

data Factual or numerical information; figures, characters, and words that can be transmitted digitally and stored in machine-readable form (see **computer**; **JARGON: input**). The word *data* is the plural of *datum;* the latter is seldom used, however, since references to factual or numerical information in computer processing usually involve more than a single fact or number.

databank See **database.**

database Also called *databank;* a collection of **data** organized in a systematic manner to allow for rapid search and retrieval of selected items by **computer.** Although a database may be as small as an office telephone list, the term more often refers to a much larger collection, such as a national or international directory.

In-house databases may be accessed using database **software,** or collections may be purchased on CD-ROM (see **disk**). Outside databases may be accessed by **modem** and telephone either through the **Internet** or, by subscription, through one of the commercial on-line (see **JARGON: on line**) service providers, such as CompuServe or America Online.

database management system A **software** package that is designed to set up, maintain, and access a **database.** A database management system (DBMS) enables users to update and sort **data** and to store and retrieve information. For example, a DBMS for a large mailing list would likely allow users to sort and retrieve addresses by geographic region, zip code, or some other designation.

data processing The traditional term for using **computers** in all stages of **data** handling, from collection to entry (see **JARGON: input**) to processing to storage (see **disk; memory**) to output (see **JARGON: output**). The term *information processing* is used more often today to refer to the systematic sequence of operations performed on data.

debenture See **bond.**

debit and credit Entries that are made in a *double-entry bookkeeping system* to record additions or subtractions from an **account.** In this type of system, each account has two possible entries. A *debit entry* is recorded on the left side, and a *credit entry* is recorded on the right side. Whether a debit or credit entry increases or decreases an account depends on the type of account.

The following table lists the main types of accounts and indicates whether you must use a debit or credit to increase or decrease each one.

Type of Account	To Increase	To Decrease
I		
Assets	Debit	Credit
Expenses	Debit	Credit
Cost of Sales	Debit	Credit
II		
Liabilities	Credit	Debit
Equity	Credit	Debit
Income	Credit	Debit

debug See **JARGON: debug.**

decentralization The delegation or spread of decision making and policy making geographically or to lower levels of management, such as to branches or departments. Unlike the objectives in **centralization,** the goal with decentralization is to place responsibility in the hands of those most directly involved with the regular operations of the company.

decibel A unit used to measure relative electrical power or acoustic (sound) level. A decibel (db) represents a ratio that compares a particular level to an arbitrarily established standard. A microphone or stereo speaker, for example, is commonly rated in decibels above or below a certain standard. Regardless of the original intensity or level in matters of sound, the smallest amount of change that the human ear can detect is about 1 db.

decree See **judgment.**

deductible Any amount that can be deducted from a **principal** amount; a common term in insurance policies referring to an amount that the insured must pay before the insurance company begins paying benefits on a claim. A policy's *deductible clause* specifies the amount of the deduction.

A deductible may be very low, such as $50, or very high, such as $10,000. Some persons elect to have a very high deductible, particularly in health policies, to qualify for a lower **premium.**

deed A signed legal document that conveys **real property** from one party to another. The one selling, or conveying, his or her interest is called the *grantor,* and the one receiving it is the *grantee,* who may or may not be the actual purchaser. Someone else, for example, may have purchased the property to give to the grantee.

The text of a deed includes information about the relevant parties; a description of the property being conveyed and any associated **encumbrances,** such as a **lien** or **mortgage;** the selling price of the property or other consideration, such as a gift; any **covenants** (promises) of the parties; and the type of deed.

Examples of deeds are the warranty, bargain and sale, quit-claim, sheriff's, statutory, gift, and trust deeds.

1. A *warranty deed* transfers **title** in *fee simple* (absolute ownership of and unconditional power to dispose of real property) and guarantees that the title is free and clear of encumbrances.
2. A *bargain and sale deed* transfers title to the buyer but does not provide any **warranty** about the validity of the title.
3. A *quit-claim deed* is a form of release wherein the grantor gives up (releases) any interest that he or she has to the grantee but does not warrant the title to be valid.
4. A *sheriff's deed* is given for property purchased at a public sale, such as a sheriff's or court-ordered sale of property.
5. A *statutory deed* is a short form of deed wherein certain covenants and warranties are omitted since they are required by statute (see **statutory law**) and thus are binding whether or not the deed includes them.

6. A *gift deed* conveys real property with something other than money, such as love and affection, for consideration.
7. A *trust deed* (also called *deed of trust*) is used in place of a mortgage to finance the purchase of real property by having the debtor convey bare legal title (title without the right of possession) to a trustee as security for the benefit of the lender (the **beneficiary**) until the buyer has repaid the loan (see **trust**).

deed of trust See **bond; deed; mortgage; trust.**

de facto corporation See **corporation.**

defamation See **libel; slander.**

default 1. In finance, the failure to make timely payments on a loan, to fulfill some other condition of a **contract,** or to meet some other legal obligation. Depending on the specific terms of the contract, different consequences may result.

Example: The entire amount of a loan may become due and payable immediately (**acceleration**) if default occurs, or property used as a **pledge** (security) in a loan may be claimed by the lender to pay off the debt.

2. In **computer** use, a selection that a computer automatically makes when the operator does not choose another option.

Example: If two printers are connected to a computer, the *default printer* is the one that the computer automatically chooses for **printing** unless the operator intervenes and directs the computer to use the other printer.

Default settings, such as margins of 1 inch and paragraph indentions of 1/2 inch, are incorporated into a computer program as automatic settings—those that the computer always uses in the absence of operator intervention. However, if a user nearly always prefers different margins and indentions, the pertinent defaults can be changed accordingly so that the user's preferred settings will automatically be chosen by the computer.

default setting See **default**.

defeasance clause See **mortgage**.

deficit 1. In general, an inadequacy or deficiency.

2. In financial matters, a financial shortage or **net loss** caused by an excess of expenditures over income; the excess of a company's **liabilities** over its **assets** and reserves.

deflation Generally, the reverse of **inflation;** a continuing decrease in the prices of goods and services or a continuing increase in the purchasing power of money caused by a reduction in available currency and **credit.** Unlike deflation, *disinflation* refers to a slowing down in the rate of price increases.

de jure corporation See **corporation**.

demand deposit A checking **account;** money deposited in an account that authorized persons may withdraw (demand) by writing a check, by using an automated teller machine, or by making a transfer of deposited funds to another account.

demography See **UNUSUAL WORDS: demography**.

depositary See **depository**.

deposition A question-and-answer form of statement that is made by a witness under oath in response to an attorney's oral questions (called an *oral deposition*) or in response to written questions that are read to the witness by an officer taking the deposition (called a *deposition on written interrogatories*).

deposition on written interrogatories See **deposition**.

depository A place, such as a library, where something is deposited for safekeeping; a bank where money is deposited and held temporarily until it is transferred to a different branch or bank. The term *depository* is sometimes used interchangeably with *depositary,* although the latter may also refer to a person to whom something is entrusted.

depreciation 1. In taxes, the deduction allowed to taxpayers for a loss in the value of property used in business or held for the production of rent or of royalty income, such as income from oil or gas. The property must have a useful life that can be determined and must be something that wears out over time, becomes obsolete, or loses value for another reason.

2. In economics, the loss of an **asset's** value because of age, wear, or other conditions.

desktop publishing (DTP) The production of printed matter, such as a newsletter, with a desktop **computer** and special **software** designed to combine text and **graphics.** As an advanced form of **word processing,** desktop publishing is used in business to produce a wide range of material, from magazines to business forms to training manuals to product brochures.

DTP has many advantages. The technology, for example, enables operaters to see pages on screen as they will look when printed, and the software offers a variety of **typefaces** and sizes (see **point**), with special graphics features and sophisticated page-layout capability.

Word processing operators can often apply the same skills to in-house DTP that they use in ordinary word processing tasks. However, the operators must also have an understanding of typography, graphics, and scanning procedures. Companies that have the appropriate equipment and software, as well as trained operators, may realize cost savings by using in-house DTP instead of higher-cost outside typesetters and printers.

diagnostic See **diagnostic routine.**

diagnostic program See **diagnostic routine.**

diagnostic routine A set of instructions designed to pinpoint **computer** malfunctions, **programming** errors, mistakes in **data,** and other problems. A *diagnostic program* is a computer utility program devoted exclusively to testing **hardware** or **software** for such problems; the term *routine* is often used to mean part of a program. Frequently, the term *diagnostic* alone is used to refer to any checking procedure.

dialog box See **menu.**

differential cost See **marginal cost.**

digital The representation of information in discrete (separate) form, with digits or numbers, as opposed to representing it in continuously varying form (see **analog**).

Example: A clock that displays a series of changing digits to represent time at discrete intervals, such as seconds, is a *digital* device; one that shows time with continuously moving hands on the clock's face is an *analog* device.

Most **computers** are **binary** digital devices and allow two values, 0 and 1. By contrast, an analog indicator, such as a mercury thermometer, could have values anywhere on its scale. However, digital computers can receive and transmit **data** in analog form by using analog-to-digital and digital-to-analog converters that change information from one form to another.

direct numerical control See **numerical control.**

disclaimer A renunciation, repudiation, denial, or disavowal of one's legal right or claim; a formal refusal to accept an interest or estate; a statement whereby one denies or refuses to accept liability or responsibility for or association with something.

discrimination Unfair and unequal treatment based on a person's nationality, race, age, religion, or sex in matters involving employment, housing, education, voting rights, and access to public facilities. Various fair-employment-practices acts, such as the Equal Employment Opportunity Act of 1972, the Age Discrimination Act of 1967, and the Americans with Disabilities Act of 1990, as well as the Civil Rights Act of 1964 are aimed at preventing discrimination in the workplace.

Sexual harassment is an example of discrimination that has received increasing attention since the 1980s. According to the Equal Employment Opportunity Commission guidelines, *sexual harassment* is any unwelcome behavior or attention, including language, gestures, or physical contact, that focuses on an employee's sex rather than his or her employment status.

The guidelines specify that sexual favors may not be made a condition of employment or advancement and that it is illegal to use sexual references or gestures to create a hostile or intimidating work environment. Companies may, in fact, be held legally responsible for acts of sexual harassment committed by an individual in the firm.

dishonor A refusal, with or without justification, to pay a **negotiable instrument** when it is presented for payment.

Example: A bank might *justifiably* refuse to pay a check if there are insufficient funds in the drawer's **account** to cover the check. An individual, however, might *unjustifiably* refuse to make required payments on a **note** simply because he or she instead chose to spend the money on a vacation.

disinflation See **deflation.**

disk A common medium for permanent **data** storage available in magnetic or optical form.

Magnetic disk. Known primarily as a *hard disk* or *diskette* (*floppy disk*), magnetic disks are writable, which means that information can be recorded on them; rewritable; and erasable. The circular, platelike disk, which has a magnetically encoded surface, rotates to permit the storage and retrieval of data by one or more read/write heads (see **disk drive**).

A hard disk is often permanently fixed in its disk drive, whereas a diskette is always removable. Some hard drives, however, take removable cartridges. Since diskettes are removable, they are frequently used for **backup** copies that can be stored in a clean, secure, remote location.

A hard disk operates at high speeds and has extensive storage capacity. Removable diskettes, which are most often used in 3 1/2- and 5 1/4-inch sizes, are available in single- or double-sided and standard-double or high-density versions. The 3 1/2-inch diskette is rigid and more durable than the flexible 5 1/4-inch diskette. All diskettes have far less storage capacity than a hard disk and work at much slower speeds.

Optical disk. Known primarily as *CD-ROM* (compact disk, read-only memory), *WORM* (write once, read many times), and *erasable optical disk* (erasable and reusable), these small, circular, removable disks, available in the same sizes as a magnetic diskette, have a reflective coating that can be read by a laser. They are more rugged and require less care than a magnetic diskette.

Optical disks are especially well known for their vast storage capacity of hundreds of megabytes (see **byte**) of **data**. A single CD-ROM, for example, may contain numerous large encyclopedias and dictionaries. Sometimes called *laser disks,* they can be used for mixed media, such as data and voice, as well as both still and moving images.

Optical disks, which must run on a special disk drive, are more expensive and slower than a magnetic hard disk. But because of their huge storage capacity, they offer businesses a practical option for exceptionally large in-house **databases.**

disk drive The device that reads or writes (records) **data** on magnetic **disks** (hard disks and diskettes, or floppy disks) and on optical disks (CD-ROM, WORM, and erasable disks). A *disk-drive controller* controls the operations of the disks connected to the **computer.**

Diskettes and optical disks are manually inserted into a drive. Although a hard disk may be attached to a computer as a separate boxlike device, it is usually built into the computer along with the drive heads, which do the reading and writing, all in a sealed mechanism.

A personal computer may have several drives, including a hard-disk drive, at least two floppy-disk drives (to accommodate both 3 1/2- and 5 1/4-inch magnetic diskettes), and, possibly, a CD-ROM drive.

An optical-disk drive can accommodate more data than a hard-disk drive, which in turn can handle more data than a floppy-disk drive. In matters of speed, however, the hard drive operates faster than either the optical or floppy disk drive. In general, the technology for optical-disk drives is slower than that for magnetic-disk drives.

diskette See **disk.**

display screen See **cathode ray tube (CRT).**

disposable income Also called *discretionary income;* the remaining income available to consumers after they have paid for food, clothing, and housing and have made all necessary debt payments.

divestiture The process of selling a business or an **asset,** usually because it is unprofitable or because it no longer fits in a company's overall plan.

dividend The portion of a **corporation's** total earnings and profits (see **gross profit; net income**) that is distributed to **stockholders.** Corporate dividends, which are taxable, are paid quarterly, semiannually, or annually in amounts set by the **board of directors.**

Common types of dividends are the stock, cash, optional, bond, property, accrued, and accumulated dividends.

1. *Stock dividends* are paid in distributions of additional **stock,** rather than in cash.
2. *Cash dividends* are usually paid by check.
3. *Optional dividends* are paid in either cash or stock, as requested by the stockholder.
4. *Bond dividends* may be paid in the form of corporate **bonds,** if not prohibited by statute.
5. *Property dividends,* which are offered as an option in lieu of cash, are paid in surplus property, such as surplus stock that one corporation holds in another.
6. *Accrued dividends* are regular dividends that are accumulated between payment dates.
7. *Accumulated dividends* are regular dividends that are unpaid as of a due date.

documentation A collection of documents or records; the set of user instructions accompanying a **hardware** or **software** package. **Computer** documentation may be supplied on **disk** or in **hard copy.**

document conference See **teleconference.**

domestic corporation See **corporation.**

dot matrix printer See **printing.**

double-entry bookkeeping See **debit and credit.**

Dow Jones Industrial Average See **stock index.**

download See **JARGON: download.**

downsize See **JARGON: downsize.**

downtick See **JARGON: downtick.**

downtime See **JARGON: downtime.**

drop ship A method of delivering merchandise directly from a manufacturer to a **retail** customer, rather than to the retailer who would otherwise have to reship the item to the customer. With the drop-ship method, the retailer promotes and sells the merchandise as usual, but the manufacturer stores it and does the shipping. Since ownership of the merchandise stays with the manufacturer until the retailer's customer buys it, a retailer can avoid **inventory** costs by using the drop-ship method.

dumb terminal See **workstation**.

duplexing See **duplex system**.

duplex system A **telecommunications** system that enables simultaneous and independent transmission of **data** between two terminals (see **workstation**). The two common types are the half-duplex and full-duplex systems.

1. A *half-duplex system* provides for transmission in both directions but not simultaneously.
2. A *full-duplex system* allows both simultaneous and independent transmission.

The term *duplex system* should not be confused with *duplexing,* which is the use of duplicate **hardware** to ensure that there is another component in reserve in case one fails.

Dvorak keyboard A simplified keyboard configuration for typewriters and **computers** designed to increase the speed and ease of typing, named after American educator August Dvorak. With this configuration, the left hand carries slightly less than 50 percent of the load, and the right hand carries slightly more than half of it. The arrangement of characters is designed to reduce the distance that fingers have to move and hence to reduce fatigue from hand movements.

Compare **qwerty keyboard**.

dye-sublimation printer See **printing**.

dye-thermal printer See **printing**.

E

earnest money A deposit; down payment; money that a buyer gives with an offer to purchase **real property.** Earnest money is usually placed in a trust **account** or with an **escrow** company. By law, a real estate broker may not commingle earnest money with the real estate firm's general funds. After the transaction is completed, the earnest money is credited to the buyer's down payment.

easement A legal right to make limited use of someone else's property for a special purpose, such as to lay pipelines across the other person's property to reach your own or to cross someone else's land to reach a highway. If a user has already had this type of use or access for a long period, a court may rule that an *implied easement* exists.

An *express grant of easement*, as opposed to an implied easement, must be in writing, usually as a separate **deed** or a reservation in a deed. Common forms of easement are the right-of-way, right-of-drainage, right to lay pipelines underground, and right to run power lines overhead. Since an easement is an actual "interest" in land, the **statute of frauds** applies.

An easement may arise or be created in various ways, such as by informal agreement, necessity, or prescription.

1. It may consist of an informal **agreement,** rather than a formal **contract,** based on a commonly held opinion about the right.
2. It may be created by *necessity,* as when a larger tract of land has been subdivided into smaller units.

3. It may arise by *prescription,* such as when the use by someone else other than the property owner is adverse to the rights of the owner but has nevertheless been open and continuous with the full acquiescence of the owner.

An easement is sometimes described as a *negative easement.* This is the case when it restricts a property owner from doing certain things with his or her land that would be harmful to another person entitled to use the land. For example, the easement might prevent the owner from placing an object where it would dangerously obstruct the view of someone using the property to enter a highway.

When an easement involves the right of passage of the public over designated land for travel and other special purposes, it is known as a *public easement.*

economy of scale The concept that as production facilities increase their size and capacity, production cost per unit will decrease. Therefore, a large company manufacturing lawnmowers and capable of producing large quantities might have a lower per-unit cost than would be possible in a smaller company.

effective interest rate See **yield.**

elasticity of demand A measure of consumer response to price changes. Demand is elastic when low prices cause the demand to increase and high prices cause it to decrease.

electronic mail (E-mail) A form of communication between **computers** or terminals (see **workstation**) that allows textual messages to be entered, sent, read, stored, and printed electronically. Transmission can occur locally, through machines connected in **local-area networks (LANs),** or over long distances to remote terminals by using a **modem** and the telephone lines. E-mail addresses can be obtained through commercial on-line services (see **JARGON: on line**), such as CompuServe or America Online, or via the **Internet.**

E-mail is appealing to businesses that want to have instant communication and a reduction in paper handling. Using communications **software,** a message can be entered and sent to one person or several people simultaneously. The computer can be programmed to send a message at any time of the day or night. At the destination terminal, it is stored in the receiver's electronic **mailbox** awaiting retrieval. Once retrieved, the recipient can read it on screen or print out a **hard copy.**

In spite of its convenience and speed, E-mail creates special problems not evident with conventional mail. Matters of legality and privacy, for example, are of special concern, especially when security is absent or ineffective and mailboxes can easily be accessed by others.

Many E-mail users also forget that messages may have a different impact on screen and thus should be composed very carefully. When codes and symbols (see **JARGON: emoticon**) or **abbreviations**, such as *BTW* (by the way), are used, it is helpful to include a list of definitions for the recipient.

Compare with **facsimile.**

electronic mailbox See **electronic mail (E-mail); mailbox.**

eleemosynary See **UNUSUAL WORDS: eleemosynary.**

eminent domain The right of a governmental body to take private property and use it for the benefit of the general public, such as in construction of a public highway or park. Under eminent domain, privately owned property may be acquired without the landowner's consent but not without just compensation, as required by the Fifth Amendment to the Constitution.

emoticon See **JARGON: emoticon.**

encumbrance A claim or other liability attached to **real property** that may not prevent a transfer of **title** but may lower the value of the property. Examples are taxes, **mortgages, attachments, leases, liens,** and **easements.**

Example: If an **easement** is granted allowing others to use a portion of property being sold, it may make the entire property less desirable to a buyer and thereby cause its price (value) to decline.

When an invalid encumbrance exists, such as an error in the record of a **title,** that would affect the title if it were valid, it is called a *cloud on the title*. This type of encumbrance may be removed by court action or a quit-claim **deed.**

endnotes See **back matter.**

endorsement 1. In insurance, a written **agreement,** rider, or supplement attached to a policy to add to, subtract from, or change it in another way. On the date an endorsement becomes effective, the new provisions take precedence over the previous ones.

2. In finance, the signature of an endorser on the back of a check or **note** to indicate **assignment** or transfer. Different endorsements are used for different purposes, and various qualifying statements may be added above the endorser's signature.

a) A *blank endorsement* has only the endorser's signature, without any restrictions, making the instrument payable to the endorser or any other bearer upon delivery and presentation.
b) A *special endorsement* specifies a particular person to whom the instrument is payable ("Pay to the order of John Doe").
c) A *restrictive endorsement* specifies transfer of the instrument for a particular purpose ("For deposit only").
d) A *qualified endorsement* limits the endorser's liability, such as by specifying "without recourse" to refuse lia-

bility if the maker does not pay the instrument when due.

e) A *conditional endorsement* indicates some special condition that is necessary before the endorser will be paid ("Pay to ABC Company upon delivery of 20 cartons of antifreeze").

f) An *accommodation endorsement* is an additional endorsement given by a third party on the back of a note for additional security, thereby extending **credit** to the holder by guaranteeing the debt.

end user See **JARGON: end user.**

equal opportunity A reference to employment conditions free of discriminatory practices in regard to age, race, color, sex, religion, or nationality. The Equal Employment Opportunity Commission, created by the Civil Rights Act of 1964, has worked to end **discrimination** in the business world and has encouraged an environment in which fair and equal opportunities are available to everyone.

equitable lien See **lien.**

equity A company's **net worth** (**assets** minus **liabilities**). In **corporations,** it is referred to as *stockholders' equity* (see **stockholder**); in a sole **proprietorship,** it is called *owner's equity.*

equity of redemption See **foreclosure.**

erasable optical disk See **disk.**

ergonomics Human engineering; the science of the design and arrangement of the physical environment enabling people to interact efficiently and safely with their environment. Businesses are increasingly concerned with workplace design as it affects employee comfort and, in turn, productivity. According to the Occupational Safety and Health Administration

(OSHA), ergonomics is an important factor in preventing or reducing musculoskeletal injuries.

Employees, such as **computer** operators, who make repeated movements, are most susceptible to problems classified as *repetitive-strain injuries* or *cumulative trauma disorders*. Those who are affected may experience muscle soreness or more serious injuries, such as carpal tunnel syndrome and elbow or wrist tendinitis. All are painful injuries that affect the hand, wrist, or elbow. Other common problems are lower back pain and eye strain.

To overcome the problems of workplace injuries, many designers are creating furniture, equipment, and lighting that eliminate or reduce the major sources of environmental stress. Improvements such as adjustable chairs and display-screen (see **cathode ray tube [CRT]**) glare adjustments are examples of efforts to ensure a healthier and safer work environment.

In addition to general improvements in furniture and equipment, task-specific adjustments are being made. Ergonomics specialists believe that furniture, lighting, and other elements in the workplace must be designed not only to adjust to the person (tall, short, and so on) but also to the task (typing, telephoning, and so on).

Employers are trying to reduce workplace injuries further by encouraging more frequent breaks in which employees can stand, stretch, and generally move around or change positions to interrupt harmful activities. The time lost to such relaxation techniques is considered well spent if it successfully prevents an adverse impact on productivity due to injuries.

See also **workers' compensation laws.**

escalation clause A **contract** clause, common in a **lease,** that provides for price or rent increases or decreases. Three basic types of escalation clauses are the cost-of-living, fixed-increase, and direct-expense clauses.

1. A *cost-of-living clause* provides for adjustments that follow the government's cost-of-living index.
2. A *fixed-increase clause* provides for regular increases at specific times, such as annually.
3. A *direct-expense clause* provides for adjustments based on fluctuations in expenses, such as an increase in property taxes.

The term *escalator clause* essentially means the same thing as *escalation clause* but is used more often in reference to labor-management contracts.

escalator clause See **escalation clause**.

escheat See **UNUSUAL WORDS: escheat.**

escrow Something held in **trust** by a third party (*escrow agent*), upon the agreement of two contracting parties, until the required terms and conditions of a **contract** have been met; money or property held by a trustee pending fulfillment of the terms and conditions of escrow instructions. After the conditions of a **contract** have been met, the escrow agent releases the money, document, or other item.

The term *escrow* is used not only in association with **real property** but also in regard to any other property or money that is deposited in this manner.

See also **earnest money**.

ethics Moral principles or values. Various professions as well as individual companies have principles that govern the conduct of members or employees. These principles commonly define matters such as loyalty, confidentiality, honesty, and integrity. Thus an employee bound by such principles would not reveal company secrets or treat clients or customers unfairly. The reputation of a company and its ability to conduct business in the marketplace is dependent on the ethical behavior of each employee.

Eurobank See **Eurocurrency**.

Eurocurrency Monies, such as U.S. dollars, that are deposited by **corporations** or governments in European banks and used in European financial markets as a medium of international **credit**. Eurocurrencies are used to facilitate international trade, to pay deficits, and for currency speculation.

The European banks in which the monies of other nations are deposited are called *Eurobanks*. The U.S. dollars that are deposited in the Eurobanks are referred to as *Eurodollars*.

Eurodollar See **Eurocurrency**.

exchange See **stock exchange**.

Exchange, the See **stock exchange**.

exchange rate The rate or price at which the currency or **commodities** of one country can be readily converted into the currency or commodities of another country. The exchange rate of certain currencies tends to fluctuate; for example, $1 in U.S. currency may equal 1.49 DM in German currency on a certain date and 1.47 DM on another date.

Newspapers, banks, and other institutions have information on exchange rates. Major newspapers usually print various exchange rates daily or weekly, and banks with an international department or officer also can provide this information.

execution 1. In law, the signing and delivery of a written instrument (legal document), such as a **contract** or **agreement**, to make it valid.

2. In **computer** use, the operation of a program or the processing of **data**; the act of carrying out instructions.

See also **execution time**.

3. In investments, the buying or selling of shares of **stock**; the act of carrying out a securities trade.

execution time The time from beginning to end that it takes to complete a procedure, cycle, instruction, or other operation. The term is commonly used in reference to a manufacturing or information-processing operation (see **data processing**).

exit See **JARGON: exit**.

ex officio See **FOREIGN EXPRESSIONS: ex officio**.

exponent A number written as a small raised figure (*superscript*) immediately to the right of a mathematical expression to indicate the operation of repeated multiplication.

Example: $6^3 = 6 \times 6 \times 6 = 216$

The raised number *3* in this example is known as the *power* to which the base is to be raised: *6 to the third power.*

The figures representing powers indicate whether a base is to be squared, cubed, and so on. For example, the second power of x is written as x^2 and may be stated as "x squared." The third power of x is written as x^3 and may be stated as "x cubed."

An exponent may be a positive amount, as x^2, or a negative amount, as x^{-2}.

ex post facto See **FOREIGN EXPRESSIONS: ex post facto**.

F

face value The value or nominal amount written or printed on the face of or within an instrument, such as a **note** or **bond**, excluding **interest** or **dividends.** The nominal amount of a share of **stock** is called *par value*.

The face value of a financial instrument such as a bond may differ from the actual purchase or issue price, which may have been a discounted price. The face value may also differ from the *market value*, which refers to the possible selling price at any given time. At **maturity,** an instrument such as a bond is redeemed for its face value (*maturity value*).

facsimile An exact reproduction of text, **graphics,** and photographic images; the equipment used to transmit documents over a communications **network,** such as the public telephone network or a **local area network (LAN),** to a receiving machine. The common abbreviated form for *facsimile* is *fax*.

Fax machines vary in size from small portable models used by business travelers to full-size office machines. The devices can handle **computer** signals as well as the signals created by another fax machine. For example, with the proper interface (see **JARGON: interface**), fax messages can be sent and received from a personal computer. With the addition of an adaptor called a fax board, a computer can be made to function like a fax machine, thereby enabling material created on or scanned into the computer to be sent directly, without transferring it to a separate fax machine for transmission.

Fax machines have an internal **modem** to handle transmission over the telephone lines. The process of *modulation* involves scanning the images of a document and converting them into signals that can be transmitted to a remote device. Through manipulation of the light source at the destination, in the process of *demodulation*, the signals are converted back into the original images, or into a *facsimile*.

The original document that is inserted into a fax machine for transmission remains with the sender. Specially treated fax paper may be required or plain paper may be used, depending on the equipment's capabilities. The more images that have to be scanned, the longer it will take to complete transmission. But transmission time in any case is usually less than a minute per sheet and often mere seconds (see **baud; modem**).

Fannie Mae mortgage See **mortgage**.

fast track See **JARGON: fast track**.

fax See **facsimile**.

Federal Reserve System See **central bank**.

feedback The return of part of the output (see **JARGON: output**) of a system to its input (see **JARGON: input**); information about the equipment or process being used. In a self-correcting system, feedback is used to control output or to keep it within preestablished limits. An amplifier, for example, uses feedback to reduce distortions that exceed the desired limits.

fee simple See **deed**.

FHA mortgage See **mortgage**.

fiber optics A technique using threadlike transparent fibers of glass or plastic (optical fibers) to transmit information over a communications channel, such as a telephone **network**. The optical fibers are used to transmit either voice or **data** as laser-generated light waves.

Optical fibers are employed in corporate **local area networks (LANs)** and outside telephone company long-distance links. Although they are harder to install and splice, they have many advantages over conventional wires.

1. They can handle a much higher volume of information than conventional lines.
2. They are not affected by outside noise and therefore do not require the shielding that is necessary with metal wires.
3. Since they are more fragile and could break if disturbed, they provide greater security because it is difficult to tap into them unnoticed.
4. They need much less space than bulky copper wire or coaxial cable, which requires insulation and a conductive shield around the central conductor.

Fiber-optic technology is expected to replace current **computer** technology in future-generation computers. With microscopic fibers replacing semiconductor **integrated circuit** chips, it will be possible to process information at speeds far beyond the present limits.

fidelity bond See **bonding**.

fiduciary A company, agent (see **agency**), or other person that holds something, such as money or property, in **trust** for another (the *beneficiary*). For example, a bank or an individual that administers someone's **assets** is a fiduciary. The organization or person charged with this responsibility must invest or maintain the assets wisely and may not use them for personal gain.

field In **data processing,** the space where a single item or category of information is entered in a record; a group of adjacent characters that can be treated as a single unit.

Example: In a **database** consisting of customer and prospect addresses, each item in a particular individual or company address—name, telephone number, zip code, and so on—is a separate field. The collection of all fields (the full address) for a particular person or company is known as a *record*.

In a **database management system** (DBMS), each field is restricted to a certain size or a certain number of characters (*field width*). Certain information must be provided when setting up fields, including the type of data and the field name. The field name, such as *ZIP CODE,* is used as a heading in tables or forms where the actual data, such as 86351, will be entered.

fifth-generation computer See **JARGON: fifth-generation computer.**

file An electronic, paper, film, or other collection of stored documents and other material; the container in which files are kept. Businesses may have a combination of files, including conventional **hard-copy** files; **computer** files, such as hard **disks,** diskettes, and optical disks; and some form of **micrographics,** or reduced-format storage, such as microfilm.

File systems must be adapted to suit the type of business and the type of material being stored. Common systems for both conventional and electronic storage are alphabetical files, geographical files, numerical files, and combination files, such as **alphanumeric.** Booklets that describe the various systems can be purchased from the Association of Records Managers and Administrators (ARMA) in Prairie Village, Kansas.

1. *Alphabetical files* may be simple A to Z name or subject files or more complex hierarchical (classification) files. In the latter case, material is arranged with general al-

phabetical divisions and, usually, two or more specific alphabetical subdivisions under each general division.

2. *Geographical files,* common in sales and marketing departments, consist of international, national, regional, or other large divisions, with numerous subdivisions for cities, states, and other smaller geographical units.

3. *Numerical files* are particularly appropriate when the material to be filed already contains identifying numbers, such as financial **account** numbers. In addition, numerical systems readily allow for ongoing expansion as new digits are added. However, numerical files require the maintenance of a separate alphabetical word index to locate material when only a name or subject is known.

4. *Combination files* may take any form that combines two or more features from different types of files. An order department, for example, might combine numerical designations for customer accounts with geographical sales territory identifications.

Computer storage consists of both active on-line storage and inactive off-line storage (see **JARGON: on line; off line**). Usually, when duplication of computer and hard-copy files occurs, both are given the same *filename,* that is, the same file-folder or computer-document label. Since a computer filename must stay within the allowable **parameters** of the **software,** the conventional label is usually adapted from the computer label.

With detailed indexes to names or numbers, operators in large central file departments are able to retrieve conventional or electronic documents from either active or inactive storage. A company's **records management** policies will indicate the number of years during which files must be maintained or kept in inactive storage before destruction is authorized.

filename See **file**.

file-transfer protocol See **protocol**.

filing system See **file**.

final injunction See **injunction**.

finance charge The amount that lenders charge for consumer **credit,** such as credit card financing. Credit card statements, for example, show the annual percentage rate, such as 19.8 percent; the monthly finance charge rate, such as 1.65 percent; and the dollar amount of the finance charge on purchases and cash advances. Each statement usually includes a detailed explanation of how the finance charge is calculated.

firmware See **software**.

first generation See **JARGON: first generation**.

fiscal period The time that a company designates as its **accounting** period. A *fiscal year* is the calendar or other 12-month annual period during which records of transactions are kept and reported (see **journal; ledger**). At the end of the period, the books of **account** are closed, and the company's profit (see **net income**) or loss (see **net loss**) for the period just ended is reported.

fiscal year See **fiscal period**.

fixed annuity See **annuity**.

fixed asset See **assets**.

fixed capital See **capital goods**.

fixed-rate mortgage (FRM) See **mortgage**.

flexible mortgage See **mortgage**.

flexible-payment mortgage See **mortgage**.

floor trader See **stock exchange**.

floppy disk See **disk**.

flowchart A diagram of symbols that describes an **algorithm**; a diagram of the processes or operations involved in a **com-**

puter or other program. Standard symbols (see list) are used in program and system flowcharts.

1. A *program flowchart* depicts a program or operation as a series of steps.
2. A *systems flowchart* depicts the relationship between events in a **data processing** system.

Common Flowchart Symbols

Program Flowchart		*System Flowchart*	
Processing	▭	Punched card	⌓
Input/output	▱	Perforated tape	∿
Decision	◇	Magnetic tape	○
Program modification	⌂	Transmittal tape	▯
Predefined process	⫿▭⫿	Document	▱
Start/stop/interrupt	⬭	Off-line storage	▽
Connector	○	On-line storage	⊂
Off-page connector	⏢	Display	⌒
Flow direction	⇄ ↕	Manual input	⌐
Annotation	▭---	Sorting and collating	○
		Manual operation	▽
		Auxiliary operation	□
		Keying operation	⬭
		Communication link	⟷

focus group See **JARGON: focus group.**

footnotes See **back matter.**

foreclosure The legal process by which a lender ends all the rights to, **title** to, and interest in the property of a mortgagor or grantee who has failed to meet the obligations of a **mortgage** or **deed** of trust. When a party is in **default,** the property may be sold, as allowed by state statutes, to satisfy the debt.

Foreclosure is most often handled through litigation in the courts, a process that bars *equity of redemption.* This means that the mortgagor is prevented from recovering the property later by paying the full amount due. When handled through litigation, the foreclosure procedure usually requires the filing of a **summons** and **complaint**, as well as arrangements for a hearing, before the property can be sold.

foreign corporation See **corporation.**

format The arrangement or layout of text and **graphics** on a page, including margins, indentions, and spacing between lines and around heads and displayed material. Formatting by **computer** is relatively easy since preferred specifications for a particular type of document, such as a business plan, can be keyed in and saved for future use.

Most organizations have preferred formats for **reports,** correspondence, **minutes,** and other regularly produced documents. The letter illustrated here is set up in a *full-block format.* When a company does not have a standard format, it can get ideas from books of business forms, sold through bookstores or by mail order, that have a wide range of formatted material, such as a sales slip or **quotation** record. Often, these forms are designed for removal and copying in-house without permission.

Some style books, such as *The Prentice Hall Style Manual,* also have a variety of business document models, such as **proposals, meeting** notices, and invitations, to use as a guide

Example: Full-block Format

```
May 19, 1997

Your reference: X193-2
Our reference: 01007658


Ms. Adrian J. Carlton
Manager, Word Processing
Kent & Steel, Inc.
101 East Avenue
Cleveland, OH 44144

Dear Ms. Carlton:

FULL-BLOCK LETTER FORMAT

This letter is an example of the full-block
format that you asked about. Many companies
believe that this format is easy to set up
and that word processing operators can easily
make adjustments in it to suit the size of
the message.

Please let me know, Ms. Carlton, if I can
send you any other information about
formatting. We appreciate your interest.

Cordially,



Jon Abeson, Jr.
Communications Consultant

rt

Enc.: Brochure
```

to setup or for scanning directly into the computer. The model can then be edited on screen to suit the needs of the company.

For examples of other formats, see **acknowledgment, affidavit, attestation, balance sheet, chart of accounts, income statement, minutes,** and **news release.**

for-profit corporation See **corporation.**

Forth See **language.**

FORTRAN Acronym for **For**mula **Trans**lation; see **language.**

Fortune 500 See **JARGON: Fortune 500.**

forward P/E See **price-earnings ratio.**

fourth-generation language (4GL) See **language.**

franchise The license or right that one company (*franchisor*) grants to another company or individual (*franchisee*) to operate a retail establishment, such as Mail Boxes Etc. or Burger King, or to sell or distribute the goods or services of another company, such as Xerox or Michelin, in a specified area; the right granted by a government, such as a municipality, to a public utility company to provide electrical, gas, or telephone services or to a cable company to provide cable service in a certain area; the territory or outlet itself.

Franchises are especially common in the retail field, with operations such as motels, fast-food outlets and other eating establishments, grocery stores, mailing and printing services, car dealerships and rental agencies, discount stores, and greeting-card and gift shops. The franchisor grants the right to use and the franchisee agrees to use the name, products or services, displays, and general operating methods of the franchisor.

fraud False representation or intentional deception that causes injury to another. In law, five elements must be present for something to constitute fraud.

1. A false and material misrepresentation by one person to another while knowing that the representation is false or while being ignorant of the truth
2. The intent by the person making the false representation that it will be relied on by another person
3. The other person's ignorance in not knowing that the representation is false
4. The other person's justifiable reliance on the representation
5. The injury caused by the false representation

Freddie Mac mortgage See **mortgage.**

fringe benefit Something of benefit, such as paid holidays or vacations, insurance coverage, or **pensions,** given to employees in addition to their salaries or wages. The fringe benefits provided by a company are very important to most employees because of the high cost of purchasing such benefits on an individual basis.

front matter The preliminary sections of a book or book-length document, such as a **report.** Front-matter pages are usually numbered with small (lowercase) Roman numerals.

A book may have all or some of the following front-matter material. For samples, refer to the front-matter pages in this dictionary; see **report** for a list of preliminary sections in a business document.

1. A *half-title page* containing only the book title
2. A *title page* containing the title and the names of the author and publisher
3. A *copyright page* stating the notice of copyright and related facts

4. A *dedication page* containing the names of the person(s) to whom the author has dedicated the book (more common in general nonfiction and in fiction material)
5. A *table of contents,* which may contain only chapter titles or both the chapter titles and headings of sections within the chapters
6. A *list of illustrations,* which may be a single list or separate lists for tables and figures
7. A *foreword* of one or more pages consisting of a commentary on the book by someone other than the author, often by an expert on the book's subject or another prominent person
8. A *preface* of one or more pages consisting of the author's statement about the book, including the purpose, its usefulness, and special features
9. The *acknowledgments,* which may be a separate page or a concluding part of the preface and in which the author recognizes the assistance and contributions of others
10. An *introduction,* if not part of the main body of the book, of several pages containing historical or other information that a reader should know before reading the actual chapters

frozen asset See **assets.**

full-duplex system See **duplex system.**

full lot See **odd lot.**

futures A reference to *futures contracts,* which are standard **contracts** for **commodities** or financial instruments that are bought or sold for a particular price upon agreement of delivery at a specified future date. Under the conditions of a futures contract, the buyer must purchase the commodity as agreed and the seller must sell it, unless the contract is sold to someone else before the settlement date. In this respect, futures trading differs from *options trading,* where the buyer may choose whether or not to exercise an option by the agreed-on date.

futures contract See **futures; commodities.**

G

garnishment In a lawsuit that a creditor has won against a debtor, a court order to a third party, such as an employer, to withhold wages, salaries, or other payments that the third party owes the debtor and instead to use that money to pay the required amount to the court or to the creditor. The third party is known as the *garnishee*. Different states have different laws concerning garnishment.

gateway See **Internet; local area network (LAN).**

general journal See **journal.**

general obligation bond See **bond.**

general partnership See **partnership.**

gift deed See **deed.**

gingerbread See **JARGON: gingerbread.**

Ginnie Mae mortgage See **mortgage.**

glass ceiling See **JARGON: glass ceiling.**

glossary See **back matter.**

going-concern value See **goodwill.**

golden handcuffs See **JARGON: golden handcuffs.**

golden parachute See **JARGON: golden parachute.**

goodwill An intangible **asset** consisting of the value of a company's name and reputation; the difference between a company's **book value** and a greater sale price; the excess of a company's going-concern value over its **asset** value. *Going-concern value* is the value of a company to another company or individual. In **accounting** practices, goodwill must be amortized (see **amortization**) over a period not exceeding 40 years.

Gothic type See **typeface**.

grace period The time allowed after a payment due date before one is considered in **default** or before the cancellation of a **contract** occurs. Grace periods are provided for in most loan contracts and insurance policies.

In some long-term loans to multinational companies, the grace period refers to an initial period up to some future date when **principal** payments must begin. Until that date, the payment of principal isn't required. Sometimes the grace period is a negotiating point in such contracts. A company may, for example, prefer a long initial grace period before principal payments must begin rather than receive another benefit, such as a lower **interest** rate.

graded lease See **lease**.

graduated-payment mortgage See **mortgage**.

grandfather clause A provision that exempts someone previously engaged in a business activity or a descendant of such person from new regulations affecting the business.

Example: As a result of a grandfather clause, someone whose family has been engaged in a certain business for a long time may have been exempted from a new rule concerning the type of storefront allowed, whereas newcomers whose families have no history in that business are required to comply with the new regulation.

graphics Pictorial illustration, representation, or visual display of **data**. Graphics, such as charts and diagrams, are used to supplement text discussion in documents, to support presentations and addresses, or to enhance any other type of written or spoken material. Some material, such as an architectural representation of a building, can be presented effectively only in the form of graphics.

Computer graphics are generated from data that are input (see **JARGON: input**) by keyboard or other device, such as a light pen, which is used to draw on the display screen or a graphics tablet. Business graphics **software** enables users to prepare graphs and drawings for **annual reports** and other documents. Examples of special graphics applications are **desktop publishing** and *computer-aided design (CAD)*. The latter is a program used to design two- and three-dimensional models of physical objects, such as mechanical parts for automobiles.

greenmail See **JARGON: greenmail.**

gross income In taxes, total income, before deducting expenses, from all sources except income not subject to tax under Internal Revenue Service regulations.

Compare with **net income.**

gross margin See **gross profit.**

gross national product (GNP) The total value of all final goods and services that are produced in the United States during a specified period, usually a year. The GNP consists of both consumer and government purchases, both private and foreign investments within the country, and the value of exports minus imports (net exports). The GNP growth rate is used to rate the health of the economy. GNP **data** are released by the government on a quarterly basis.

gross profit Total sales or revenue minus the cost of goods sold. The term is sometimes used interchangeably with *gross margin* when the excess is expressed as a percentage.

Compare with **net income.**

groupware See **software; JARGON: groupware.**

guarantee Also called *guaranty* or *suretyship;* a promise to assume responsibility for another person's obligation if that person **defaults;** loosely, a **warranty.**

guaranty See **guarantee.**

H

hacker See **JARGON: hacker**.

half-duplex system See **duplex system**.

halftone A copy of a photograph; a picture or continuous-tone image in which gradations or shadings of tone are created by tiny dots of different density or size. By contrast, a black-and-white *line drawing* has no gray tones and consists entirely of lines; therefore, a line drawing can be photographed for reproduction the same as text matter. Continuous-tone images, however, are photographed through a fine screen to create the halftone.

Although photographs can be scanned into a computer, halftones are usually superior for publication. **Desktop publishing** operators therefore sometimes leave a blank space to paste in halftones later rather than create the pictures digitally.

hard copy A paper copy; printed output (see **JARGON: output**) of a **computer**.

Compare with *soft copy* (see **read-out**).

hard disk See **disk**.

hardware The **computer** equipment; the principal devices in a computer system; the physical equipment and other elements of a computer system, excluding **software** but including elements such as **integrated circuits, disk drives,** cables, expansion boards for enhancing the capabilities of the equipment, and all basic components and **peripherals.**

The following items are the main pieces of hardware in a computer system.

1. Primary unit controlling interpretation and execution of instructions (see **central processing unit [CPU]**)
2. Storage devices (see **disk**)
3. Monitor (see **cathode ray tube [CRT]**)
4. Keyboard (see **Dvorak keyboard; qwerty keyboard; JARGON: input**)
5. Printer (see **printing**)

heavy industry An industry that produces basic metals and other substantial products or raw materials or that manufactures heavy equipment. Examples are the steel, petroleum, automobile, and rubber industries. Heavy industry usually refers to large companies with high output and large employment.

Compare with **light industry.**

hedge Also called *hedging;* transactions made to prevent financial losses resulting from price fluctuations; a financial transaction that offsets or reduces **risk.** Anyone who buys an item at a current price when inflationary increases are expected is hedging against **inflation.** Hedging is common in the investments field.

Example: A manufacturer of ketchup is concerned that there may be future increases in the price of vegetables, especially in the price of the main ingredient of ketchup—tomatoes. To reduce this risk and protect future profits, the manufacturer could buy tomatoes in the **futures** market. The company thereby would have an agreed-on price for the tomatoes to be delivered at a specified future date. It would be hedging against the threat of a future price increase in tomatoes that would adversely affect company profits.

hedging See **hedge.**

heuristic A problem-solving method that relies on experience and speculation, or intelligent trial and error, to select the most appropriate of possible solutions. Heuristic methods, which involve evaluating progress at each step, would be used in a game of chance.

Unlike **algorithms,** heuristic methods do not guarantee correct solutions. A heuristic method is largely a strategy or process of discovery rather than a concrete set of tested rules leading to a desired solution.

hidden asset See **assets.**

high-level language See **language.**

holding company See **corporation.**

holograph See **UNUSUAL WORDS: holograph.**

honorarium A payment given to a professional person for a service, such as delivering an address at a **conference.** An honorarium is given when regular fees are not traditionally or customarily required or paid.

horizontal market See **JARGON: horizontal market.**

hostile takeover See **leveraged buyout.**

housekeeping routine See **JARGON: housekeeping routine.**

hybrid telephone system See **telephone system.**

hype See **JARGON: hype.**

hyperspace See **JARGON: hyperspace.**

hypertext See **JARGON: hypertext.**

hypothesis A statement, theory, formula, or proposition that is being investigated; an assumption believed to be true that is tested against another assumption during research. The one that is believed to be true is called the *null hypothesis;* the one it is tested against is an *alternative hypothesis.*

Example: Market researchers might want to test this assumption: "Sales items that are discounted more than 25 percent sell faster than those that are discounted less than 25 percent." This statement, assumed to be true, is the null hypothesis. But another possibility—the alternative hypothesis—is that items discounted less than 25 percent, say 10 percent, sell just as fast or faster than those discounted more than 25 percent.

I

ideogram See **UNUSUAL WORDS: ideogram**.

ideograph See **UNUSUAL WORDS: ideograph**.

implied contract See **contract**.

implied easement See **easement**.

imprest fund See **petty cash**.

imprimatur See **UNUSUAL WORDS: imprimatur**.

income bond See **bond**.

income statement Also known as *profit and loss statement* and *statement of revenue and expenditures;* one of the key financial statements providing a financial picture of the operations of a business. Whereas a **balance sheet** reports **assets, liabilities,** and **capital** on a certain date, an income statement summarizes income and expenses for a specific **accounting** period, such as a year (see **fiscal period**). The bottom line of an income statement indicates whether a business has experienced a net profit or loss (see **net income; net loss**) during that period.

A long form of income statement is illustrated here. However, businesses also use a short form that lists only the totals for major categories, such as "selling, general, and administrative expenses," but does not list the individual items, such as "telephone expenses," under each major category.

incorporators' meeting The formal organizational **meeting** that founders, or incorporators, hold to form a new **corporation**. The meeting and other steps in incorporation must follow the procedures prescribed by law in accordance with the

Example: Income Statement

Kane Enterprises, Inc.
Income Statement
for the Year Ending December 31, 1997

Gross sales		$5,903,000
Less sales returns, allow., disc.		410,000
Net sales		5,493,000
Less cost of goods sold		3,645,000
Gross profit		1,848,000
Less operating expenses		
Selling, gen., admin. exp.		
Insurance	$ 30,000	
Office salaries	517,000	
Selling expense	266,000	
Heat, light, power	27,000	
Advertising	145,000	
Telephone	77,000	
Office supplies	52,000	
Automobile expense	46,000	
Bad debt expense	29,000	
Travel expense	288,000	
Depreciation expense	61,000	
Miscellaneous expense	52,000	
Total selling, gen., admin. expenses		1,590,000
Research and development costs		103,000
Other operating expenses		16,000
Total operating expenses		1,709,000
Operating profit		139,000
Other income and expenses		
Interest expense	177,000	
Interest income	(126,000)	
Miscellaneous income	(42,000)	
Total other income and expenses		9,000
Profit before taxes		130,000
Provision for corporate income taxes		49,000
Net income		$ 81,000

incremental cost See **marginal cost.**

indemnify In law, to protect and hold harmless; to protect or insure against future damage, loss, or injury; to provide compensation for damage, loss, or injury already suffered.

Example: A **corporation** may indemnify directors and therefore reimburse them for litigation expenses or damages charged against them in a court decision.

Indemnify is a verb; the noun **indemnity** refers to the actual security, obligation, or compensation.

indemnity Security for loss, damage, or injury; one's obligation to compensate another for any loss, damage, or other expense that the party incurs while acting at one's request or for one's benefit; the compensation itself. An *indemnity bond* or *agreement* is designed to protect a person from loss if a **principal** fails to meet his or her obligation.

See also the verb **indemnify.**

indemnity bond See **indemnity.**

indenture See **bond.**

independent contractor A self-employed person, such as a housepainter or landscaper, who is hired to perform a service for another at an agreed-upon rate or fee. Since independent contractors are not employees of the party hiring them, they must pay their own social security and other taxes and must purchase their own insurance and other benefits. In addition, they are expected to provide the necessary tools and materials for a job, and they are responsible for the results of their work and for the payment and supervision of their own employees.

index See **back matter; stock index.**

indirect costs and expenses See **overhead.**

individual retirement account (IRA) See **retirement plan.**

inflation A continuing increase in consumer price levels or a continuing decline in the purchasing power of money. The opposite of **deflation,** inflation commonly occurs when available currency and **credit** increase beyond the proportion of available goods and services. The *rate* of change in prices is measured by the **consumer price index (CPI)** and the **producer price index (PPI).**

information processing See **data processing.**

information superhighway See **Internet; JARGON: information superhighway.**

infrastructure See **JARGON: infrastructure.**

initialism See **abbreviations.**

injunction A command or writ; a court order prohibiting an individual or a **corporation** from taking a specified action that would be injurious to another party. Its intent, therefore, is to prevent future injuries rather than to compensate someone for past injuries.

An injunction may be described as a prohibitory injunction, mandatory injunction, restraining order, temporary injunction, or permanent injunction.

1. A *prohibitory injunction* restrains a party from committing or continuing a specified act.
2. A *mandatory injunction* commands or orders a party to take specific steps to do or undo something.
3. A *restraining order* is granted to restrain a party from doing something temporarily until a hearing can be held to determine whether a temporary injunction should be issued. This order, therefore, would precede a temporary, preliminary, or interlocutory injunction (if granted).
4. A *temporary, preliminary,* or *interlocutory injunction* is granted on the basis of an application alone and is used

to restrain a defendant temporarily while the court decides the case on its merits. This order, therefore, would follow the issue of a restraining order (if any).

5. A *permanent,* or *final, injunction* is granted upon completion of a trial and on the merits of the case.

ink-jet printer See **printing.**

input See **JARGON: input.**

insider trading See **JARGON: insider trading.**

insolvency A financial condition in which a person or business cannot meet its obligations as they mature in the ordinary course of business; an excess of **liabilities** over **assets** at any particular time. A state of insolvency may lead to formal **bankruptcy** proceedings.

installment sale 1. In general, an **agreement** whereby a seller sells an item to a buyer for a fixed **contract** price, usually including a down payment, to be followed by equal payments (installments) made at set intervals over a designated period until the buyer has paid the full amount due. Usually, **title** remains with the seller until the buyer makes the final payment.

2. In real estate, an agreement wherein the seller of **real property** provides part or all of the financing. Some or all of the purchase price must be paid in the year(s) after the tax year of the sale.

intangible asset See **assets.**

intangible property See **abandonment.**

integer A whole number that does not include a fractional part; one of the set of positive or negative natural numbers (*1, 2, 3, . . . -1, -2, -3, . . .*) and zero.

integrated circuit Also called *microchip;* an electronic device that contains an interconnected complex of miniature transistors and other electronic components etched or imprinted on a single slice of semiconductor material, most often a silicon **chip**. A **microprocessor,** for example, which has often been called the ultimate integrated circuit, is a single chip that contains the complete arithmetic and logic unit of a **computer**.

The number of components that a single microchip will hold has steadily increased since the introduction of the integrated circuit in the late 1950s to more than a million by the 1990s. Having a capacity of a million or more components per chip is referred to as *ultralarge-scale integration (ULSI).*

integrated system Any **hardware** or **software** system that provides a common base of shared **data;** different pieces of hardware that can communicate and work together without the need for additional circuits to establish a communications link between the devices; a software program that combines (integrates) two or more sets of data.

With an integrated system, a company can pass data from one function to another without any need for manual intervention as each function takes over.

Example: If a manufacturer produces light fixtures, the same data concerning matters such as available **inventory** and prices, shipping, and financial reporting or **accounting** can be automatically passed from the order department to the shipping department to the accounting department, without each one switching to a different computer system or **database.**

Integrated systems interconnect databases or combine them into a single database, which reduces staff needs and information-management requirements and speeds the handling of individual tasks. This in turn provides better cost and inventory control.

intelligent workstation See **workstation**.

interactive processing See **batch processing**.

interchangeable bond See **bond**, 5. *coupon bonds*.

interest The rate charged or paid for the use of money. Banks, for example, pay depositors interest on their savings **accounts,** and borrowers pay lenders interest on money loaned to them.

Interest earned or paid may be calculated as simple or compound interest.

1. *Simple interest* is a percentage calculated only on the **principal** (principal amount × interest rate): $1,000 × .06 = $60.
2. *Compound interest* is a percentage calculated on the sum of both the principal amount and any previous interest earned or paid. The interest can be compounded on an annual, quarterly, daily, or other basis. Therefore, interest earned in any period, such as annually, is added to the principal amount (principal + interest previously earned × interest rate): $1,000 + $60 = $1,060 × .06 = $63.60; $1,060 + $63.60 = $1,123.60.

The following tables give the interest on $100 at various rates for various days.

Interest on $100 at 5–8 Percent for Various Periods

Days	5%	6%	7%	8%
1	0.0139	0.0167	0.0194	0.0222
2	.0278	.0333	.0389	.0444
3	.0417	.0500	.0583	.0667
4	.0556	.0667	.0778	.0889
5	.0694	.0833	.0972	.1111
6	.0833	.1000	.1167	.1333
7	.0972	.1167	.1361	.1556
8	.1111	.1333	.1556	.1778

Interest on $100 at 5–8 Percent (continued)

Days	5%	6%	7%	8%
9	.1250	.1500	.1750	.2000
10	.1389	.1667	.1944	.2222
20	.2778	.3333	.3889	.4444
30	.4167	.5000	.5833	.6667
40	.5556	.6667	.7778	.8889
50	.6945	.8334	.9722	1.1111
60	.8333	1.0000	1.1667	1.3333
70	.9722	1.1667	1.3611	1.5555
80	1.1111	1.3334	1.5555	1.7778
90	1.2500	1.5000	1.7500	2.0000
100	1.3889	1.6667	1.9444	2.2222

Interest on $100 at 9–12 Percent for Various Periods

Days	9%	10%	11%	12%
1	0.0250	0.0278	0.0306	0.0333
2	.0500	.0556	.0611	.0667
3	.0750	.0833	.0917	.1000
4	.1000	.1111	.1222	.1333
5	.1250	.1389	.1528	.1667
6	.1500	.1667	.1833	.2000
7	.1750	.1945	.2139	.2333
8	.2000	.2222	.2445	.2667
9	.2250	.2500	.2750	.3000
10	.2500	.2778	.3056	.3333
20	.5000	.5556	.6111	.6667
30	.7500	.8333	.9167	1.0000
40	1.0000	1.1111	1.2222	1.3333
50	1.2500	1.3889	1.5278	1.6667
60	1.5000	1.6667	1.8334	2.0000
70	1.7500	1.9445	2.1389	2.3333
80	2.0000	2.2222	2.4445	2.6666
90	2.2500	2.5000	2.7500	3.0000
100	2.5000	2.7778	3.0556	3.3333

Interest on $100 at 13–16 Percent for Various Periods

Days	13%	14%	15%	16%
1	0.0361	0.0388	0.0417	0.0444
2	.0722	.0778	.0834	.0888
3	.1083	.1166	.1251	.1332
4	.1445	.1556	.1668	.1776
5	.1805	.1944	.2082	.2224
6	.2167	.2334	.2499	.2668
7	.2528	.2722	.2916	.3112
8	.2889	.3112	.3333	.3556
9	.3250	.3500	.3750	.4000
10	.3611	.3888	.4167	.4444
20	.7222	.7778	.8334	.8888
30	1.0833	1.1666	1.2501	1.3334
40	1.4445	1.5556	1.6668	1.7778
50	1.8056	1.9444	2.0835	2.2222
60	2.1667	2.3334	2.4999	2.6666
70	2.5278	2.7222	2.9166	3.1110
80	2.8889	3.1110	3.3333	3.5556
90	3.2500	3.5000	3.7500	4.0000
100	3.6111	3.8888	4.1667	4.4444

Interest on $100 at 17–20 Percent for Various Periods

Days	17%	18%	19%	20%
1	0.0472	0.0501	0.0528	0.0556
2	.0944	.0999	.1056	.1112
3	.1417	.1500	.1583	.1668
4	.1889	.2001	.2111	.2224
5	.2361	.2499	.2639	.2776
6	.2833	.3000	.3167	.3332
7	.3306	.3501	.3695	.3888
8	.3778	.3999	.4222	.4444
9	.4250	.4500	.4750	.5000
10	.4722	.5001	.5278	.5556
20	.9444	.9999	1.0556	1.1112
30	1.4167	1.5000	1.5833	1.6668

Interest on $100 at 17–20 Percent (continued)

Days	17%	18%	19%	20%
40	1.8889	2.0001	2.1111	2.2224
50	2.3611	2.5002	2.6389	2.7780
60	2.8333	3.0000	3.1667	3.3332
70	3.3055	3.5001	3.6945	3.8888
80	3.7778	4.0002	4.2222	4.4444
90	4.2500	4.5000	4.7500	5.0000
100	4.7222	5.0001	5.2778	5.5556

interface See **JARGON: interface.**

interlocutory injunction See **injunction.**

internal storage See **memory.**

Internet An international **network** of **computers,** or a network of computer networks, linked by telephone lines or satellites to form a **telecommunications** or electronic superhighway. The Internet links users worldwide to each other via electronic mail and connects them to services, libraries and other **databases,** and a myriad of resources.

Although the terms *Internet* and *World Wide Web* (*WWW; the Web*) are sometimes used interchangeably, the Web is actually a system designed to store, find, and present information over the Internet. Through the Web, users can select images or words on screen by clicking with a **mouse.**

The terms *Internet* and *information superhighway* are also used interchangeably, but they, too, are not really synonymous. The information superhighway, which doesn't yet exist, refers to the connection of all elements of computer, telephone, and cable television systems, as well as the Internet.

With a **modem** and a computer, users can be connected to the Internet in various ways. Companies such as Microsoft and MCI as well as on-line (see **JARGON: on line**) providers such as CompuServe and America Online offer entry avenues; these connections are often called *gateways* to the Internet. Many communities also have local providers that offer a connection.

interpreter See **language**.

interstate commerce The buying, selling, exchange, transportation, and transmission of goods and services over state lines. The U.S. Constitution gives the federal government the power to regulate commerce among the states, and the courts have used a broad interpretation of the term *interstate commerce*.

Compare with **intrastate commerce**.

intervivos trust See **trust**.

intrastate commerce The conduct of business primarily within a single state, with no more than isolated instances of an interchange or movement of goods and services across state lines. **Corporations** chartered in other states must meet a particular state's requirements to engage in intrastate commerce.

Compare with **interstate commerce**.

inventory The aggregate or value of raw materials and other production supplies, work in process, and finished goods awaiting sale. A firm's inventory is determined by physically counting, listing, and valuing all items, including goods in transit and those that have been transferred to another location, such as to a **consignment** house, for sale. A *perpetual* or *continuous inventory* is one in which the record of goods on hand is continually kept in agreement or consistent with the actual goods in stock (in inventory).

involuntary bankruptcy See **bankruptcy**.

irrevocable power of attorney See **power of attorney**.

itinerary A traveler's proposed route, journey, or schedule. Businesspeople who travel usually develop for each segment of a trip an itinerary that includes arrival and departure dates and times, hotel and transportation arrangements, and other information pertinent to the trip.

job lot Merchandise that is sold in one group of like items; a production run in a particular order size; a form of **contract** that authorizes a production run of a particular type or kind of items or of a particular order size. The authorization for job-lot production is called a *job order*.

job order See **job lot**.

job queue See **queue**.

joint bond See **bond**.

joint tenancy Ownership of **real property** or other **assets** by two or more persons (*joint tenants*), each of whom has an equal and undivided interest, with the right of survivorship. Unlike the procedure under **tenancy in common,** in some jurisdictions the interest held by one party under joint tenancy automatically passes to the other owner(s) (survivor[s]) upon the party's death. However, many jurisdictions that oppose this form of ownership permit joint tenants to convey their interest to others or allow them to convert joint tenancy to tenancy in common.

Compare with **tenancy by the entirety.**

joint tenants See **joint tenancy**.

joint venture An undertaking by two or more parties who initially contribute **capital** to a single project, such as developing a new product, after which their association ends. This arrangement differs from a **partnership,** in which the association between the parties continues, as in operating a business.

journal The **accounting** records (traditionally called "books") of original entry; the place where financial transactions are first recorded. A journal may be general or specialized (*subsidiary journal*). Subsidiary journals are used for certain types of transactions, such as sales, that occur repeatedly and can be collected in one place. Other miscellaneous entries not suitable for a subsidiary journal are recorded in a *general journal*. Totals from a journal are posted to a **ledger.**

The following two examples illustrate **computer** entries in a cash receipts journal and a cash disbursements journal.

Example: Cash Receipts Journal

```
              WYATT & PORTER, INC.
                 CASH RECEIPTS
              CASH IN BANK - CHECKING


AS OF 01/31/97                                         PAGE 1

                            G/L    SUB
DATE        PAYOR           ACCT   ACCT   DETAIL      NET AMT
_____    _____   ____   ____   _____     _____

01/01/97    DISCOUNT SALES  4000                     2,000.00

01/01/97    FIXTURES ETC.   4000                     1,000.00

01/01/97    J & J BUILDERS  4000                       100.00

01/01/97    ECKHERT SALES   4000                       250.00
                                                     _____

            BATCH TOTAL                              3,350.00
                                                     _____

            TOTAL                                    3,350.00
                                                     ========
```

Example: Cash Disbursements Journal

```
               WYATT & PORTER, INC.
                 CASH DISBURSEMENTS
               CASH IN BANK - CHECKING

AS OF 01/31/97                                        PAGE 1

                     CHECK   G/L    SUB
DATE       PAYEE     NO.     ACCT   ACCT   DETAIL    NET AMT
-------------------------------------------------------------

01/01/97   SMITH CO.   1200   5000                  1,000.00

01/01/97   TRIBUNE     1201   6000                    500.00

01/01/97   BROWN OIL   1202   6010                    100.00

01/01/97   CHANDLERS   1203   1500                    300.00

01/01/97   THE OFFICE  1204   1510                    250.00
                                                   ---------
           BATCH TOTAL                              2,150.00
                                                   ---------

           TOTAL                                    2,150.00
                                                   =========
```

judgment A judicial decision; an opinion or determination by a court after a trial or hearing. Whereas the decision in a court of law is called a *judgment,* a decision in a court of equity is known as a *decree,* although the term *judgment* is often used in reference to both.

When a judgment by a court involves a monetary award and the debtor refuses or fails to pay it, the other party (creditor) may ask for a writ of **execution.** If the terms of the writ allow, the sheriff may seize and sell the debtor's property to pay the award.

A party against whom a judgment is made may appeal to a higher court. Such action temporarily halts the execution of a judgment until the higher court makes a decision.

judgment lien See **lien**.

judicial precedent See **common law**.

junk bond See **JARGON: junk bond**.

jurat See **FOREIGN EXPRESSIONS: jurat**.

justification 1. In business management, the process of determining whether a new system or other item is necessary and will be cost-effective. Management usually does not order new equipment or other items without first conducting a study to determine factors such as the resulting productivity with the new purchase in comparison with the present situation or with other alternatives.

2. In **computer** use, a **format** option in **word processing** and **desktop publishing** in which both sides of the lines of text are typed even, or flush, against the left and right margins. When the lines along the right margin are of unequal length, the text is not justified and is said to be set *ragged right*.

just-in-time See **JARGON: just-in-time**.

K

Keogh plan See **retirement plan.**
keyboard See **Dvorak keyboard; qwerty keyboard; JARGON: input.**
key telephone system See **telephone system.**
kickback See **JARGON: kickback.**
killer technology See **JARGON: killer technology.**
KSU-less telephone system See **telephone system.**

L

laches See **UNUSUAL WORDS: laches.**

laissez-faire See **FOREIGN EXPRESSIONS: laissez-faire.**

landlord's lien See **lien.**

language A system that enables users to represent and communicate information. Both natural (human) and **computer** languages consist of characters that can be combined to form words or phrases and rules that govern proper usage. A natural language also includes voice sounds to express thoughts and feelings (emotions).

Artificial languages can be described in different ways, such as machine, **programming,** fourth-generation, assembly, high-level, and low-level languages.

1. A *machine language* is any computer language using **binary** instructions that a **central processing unit (CPU)** can understand and use directly. Machine language is considered a low-level language; therefore higher-level languages must be converted to machine language by a program called a *compiler* that translates the language into machine code or by one called an *interpreter* that interprets and carries out instructions one by one.

2. A *programming language* is a computer language with a form of vocabulary and grammatical rules used to write instructions that can be translated into a machine language the computer can understand. A programming language, such as *BASIC* (see item 1 in the next list), is

considered a high-level artificial language, not a natural language.

3. A *fourth-generation language (4GL)* is a user-oriented type of programming language that more closely resembles natural language than does a high-level language. The 4GL helps users develop simpler programs with fewer commands.

4. An *assembly language* is a computer language that is very close to machine language but with commands and functions written in words rather than numbers. This type of language is converted into pure machine language by an assembly program (see **assembler**).

5. A *high-level language,* such as *Pascal* (see item 5 in the next list), is a computer language that uses natural-language instructions (words), which then must be translated to machine-code instructions. The higher the level of a language, the closer it is to a user's natural language.

6. A *low-level language* is any machine or assembly language written in a code that a computer can use. Each line of code is an individual instruction that a **central processing unit (CPU)** can directly act on.

The following are examples of familiar computer languages. Most languages are known by their abbreviated name rather than the complete version.

1. *BASIC* (*B*eginners *A*ll-purpose *S*ymbolic *I*nstruction *C*ode), one of the most widely used and easiest to learn of the languages, is a conversational type of high-level programming language available on personal computers.

2. *COBOL* (*Co*mmon *B*usiness *O*riented *L*anguage), which uses natural-language statements, is heavily used for

data processing activities in business and government, particularly in banking and insurance companies.
3. *APL* (*A P*rogramming *L*anguage), a mathematically structured language capable of handling large numbers, is used in applied mathematics and, more recently, in airline routing and scheduling.
4. *FORTRAN* (*For*mula *Tran*slation) is widely used on both large (*mainframe*) computers and microcomputers for many business and scientific problems.
5. *Pascal* (after Blaise *Pascal*) is a popular high-level programming language used in a variety of teaching and business applications.
6. *Algol* (*Algo*rithmic *L*anguage) is an arithmetic language designed for solving math problems (see **algorithm**).
7. *Forth* (referring to *fourth* generation), originally developed to control a large telescope, is a high-level programming language that can directly control **hardware** devices.

laser printer See **printing**.

last will and testament See **will**.

layaway A form of purchasing based on an **agreement** between a retailer and a customer whereby the retailer holds merchandise, secured by a deposit, until the customer has made enough payments to cover the complete cost of the merchandise. As soon as the balance is paid in full, the retailer releases the merchandise to the customer. The term also refers to the merchandise reserved under the plan.

LCD See **liquid crystal display (LCD)**.

leading See **point**.

lease A **contract** in which the owner of **real property** (*lessor* or *landlord*) gives the right of possession, use, and occupancy, but not **title,** to another person (*lessee*) for a specified time and consideration (*rent*). At the end of the stated period, the lessor has the right to retake possession of the property.

In addition to a standard, or general, rental **agreement**, some leases are designed for special purposes, including the proprietary lease, sublease, graded lease, sale and leaseback, lease with an option to buy, and leasehold.

1. A *proprietary lease,* issued by a cooperative building owner, grants the right of occupancy to a resident or **stockholder** in the cooperative.
2. A *sublease* is a form of **assignment** in which a lessee grants an interest in his or her leased premises, as allowed by the terms of the lease, to a third party but reserves his or her principal interest.
3. A *graded,* or *step-up, lease* is one that specifies rent increases at designated intervals.
4. A *sale and leaseback* form of lease may vary depending on the needs or desire of the parties, but generally, it refers to an agreement involving property that an owner sells and that the new owner immediately leases back to the previous owner.
5. A *lease with an option to buy* has a clause that describes the terms and conditions under which a lessee may purchase the property that he or she is leasing.
6. A *leasehold* is a lease that defines a lessee's interest or estate in **real property** with a fixed term, usually a matter of years. The word *leasehold* is also used to describe a *month-to-month tenancy, periodic tenancy* (for a particular period), or *tenancy at will* (for an indefinite period).

leaseback See **lease.**

leasehold See **lease.**

lease with an option to buy See **lease.**

LED See **light-emitting diode (LED).**

ledger The **accounting** records (traditionally called "books") of final entry; the place to which totals from **journal** entries are transferred. Financial transactions are organized in separate **accounts** in a ledger and are identified by both name and number (see **chart of accounts**). The totals at any given time are used in the preparation of a **balance sheet** or **income statement.**

A ledger may be general or specialized (subsidiary). A *general ledger* contains all accounts; a *subsidiary ledger* is used for maintaining a particular group of related accounts, such as the various customer accounts of a business. When these individual accounts are added together, they equal the total in the general ledger's associated *control account.* The general ledger, therefore, has a control account, such as "customers' accounts," that matches the name of a particular subsidiary ledger.

When a number of similar or related accounts do not exist, a subsidiary ledger is unnecessary. All the various accounts are then set up directly in one ledger, the general ledger.

A *private ledger*, another type of specialized, or subsidiary, ledger, may be used for confidential accounts, such as "management salaries." Although an associated control account in the general ledger for "management salaries" is necessary, it need not reveal the confidential details that appear in the private ledger.

The examples on pages 143 and 144 illustrates **computer** entries in a general ledger.

STANDARD BUSINESS TERMS

Example: General Ledger

WYATT & PORTER, INC.
GENERAL LEDGER

AS OF 01/31/97

ACCT NO	ACCOUNT NAME	FOLIO	BALANCE FORWARD	CURRENT PERIOD	BALANCE
1001	CASH IN BANK - CHECKING		.00		
	JE #1	GJ		1,000.00	
	CHECKS FOR PERIOD	CD1		2,150.00-	
	RECEIPTS FOR PERIOD	CR1		3,350.00	
	INV REG SUMMARY	IR		.00	
					2,200.00
1002	CASH IN BANK - SAVING		.00		
	CHECKS FOR PERIOD	CD2		.00	
	RECEIPTS FOR PERIOD			.00	
					.00
1300	ACCOUNTS RECEIVBLE -		.00		
	INV REG SUMMARY	IR		.00	
					.00
1500	FURNITURE/FIXTURES		.00		
	CHANDLERS	CD1 #1203		300.00	
					300.00
1510	OFFICE EQUIPMENT		.00		
	THE OFFICE	CD1 #1204		250.00	
					250.00
2000	ACCOUNTS PAYABLE - TR		.00		
	MDSE PURCH SUMMARY	MP		.00	
					.00
3000	CAPITAL STOCK		.00		
	JE #1	GJ		100.00-	
					100.00-
3010	ADD'L PAID IN CAPITAL		.00		
	JE #1	GJ		900.00-	
					900.00-
3050	RETAINED EARNINGS		.00		
	PERIOD NET INCOME (CR) OR LOSS (DR)			1,750.00-	
					1,750.00-

Example: General Ledger (continued)

WYATT & PORTER, INC.
GENERAL LEDGER

AS OF 01/01/97   PAGE 2

ACCT NO	ACCOUNT NAME	FOLIO	BALANCE FORWARD	CURRENT PERIOD	BALANCE
4000	SALES REVENUE		.00		
	DISCOUNT SALES, INC.	CR1 01/01/97		2,000.00-	
	FIXTURES ETC.	CR1 01/01/97		1,000.00-	
	J & J BUILDERS	CR1 01/01/97		100.00-	
	ECKHERT SALES	CR1 01/01/97		250.00-	
					3,350.00-
5000	COST OF SALES		.00		
	SMITH CO.	CD1 #1200		1,000.00	
					1,000.00
6000	ADVERTISING		.00		
	TRIBUNE	CD1 #1201		500.00	
					500.00
6010	AUTO EXPENSE		.00		
	BROWN OIL	CD1 #1202		100.00	
					100.00
9999	INCOME TRANSFER		.00		
	PERIOD NET INCOME (DR) OR LOSS (CR)			1,750.00	
					1,750.00
	TOTALS		.00	.00	.00

LED printer See **printing**.

letter format See **format**.

letter of credit See **credit**.

leveraged buyout The takeover or purchase of a company with borrowed funds, often using the company **assets** as **collateral** for the loan.

Example: A group of employees may use a leveraged buyout to prevent a *hostile takeover* in which an outside party, against the wishes of the **board of directors**, would buy enough **stock** to acquire a controlling interest in the company.

liabilities The debts of an individual or a **corporation;** claims against a company's **assets,** excluding owner's **equity**. Liabilities are listed on a **balance sheet** consistent with the **accounting** equation *Assets = Liabilities + Capital (Equity)*.

Current liabilities (due within a year) are listed first on a balance sheet, followed by long-term liabilities (**bonds, mortgages** payable, and so on, due later) and then owners' equity. Contingent liabilities, such as an undecided lawsuit, may be omitted from current or long-term liabilities and instead indicated in a footnote to the balance sheet.

libel In **tort** law, a false and malicious statement that is written or printed with the intent of defaming the character or the reputation of a living person (*defamation*). The statement may be made in various ways, such as in a letter, published article, picture, or sign.

Compare with **slander.**

library classification system A system designed for the classification and arrangement of material in a library. Small office libraries are frequently organized informally with an alphabetical subject system. Larger company libraries, however, may use one of the two major national systems, the Dewey decimal system or the more popular Library of Congress system.

The older Dewey decimal system is used in certain specialized businesses, whereas the Library of Congress system has been adopted in a wide variety of organizations. The following lists give the primary subdivisions in each system.

DEWEY DECIMAL SYSTEM

000	**GENERALITIES**
010	Bibliographies and catalogs
020	Library science
030	General encyclopedic works
040	[Unassigned]
050	General periodicals
060	General organizations
070	Newspapers and journalism
080	General collections
090	Manuscripts and book rarities

100	**PHILOSOPHY AND RELATED**
110	Ontology and methodology
120	Knowledge, cause, purpose, man
130	Pseudo- and parapsychology
140	Specific philosophic viewpoints
150	Psychology
160	Logic
170	Ethics (moral philosophy)
180	Ancient, medieval, oriental philosophies
190	Modern Western philosophy
200	**RELIGION**
210	Natural religion
220	Bible
230	Christian doctrinal theology
240	Christian moral and devotional theology
250	Christian pastoral, parochial, etc.
260	Christian social and ecclesiastical theology
270	History and geography of Christian church
280	Christian denominations and sects
290	Other religions and comparative religion
300	**THE SOCIAL SCIENCES**
310	Statistical method and statistics
320	Political science
330	Economics
340	Law
350	Public administration
360	Welfare and association
370	Education
380	Commerce
390	Customs and folklore
400	**LANGUAGE**
410	Linguistics and nonverbal language
420	English and Anglo-Saxon
430	Germanic languages
440	French, Provençal, Catalan
450	Italian, Romanian, etc.

460	Spanish and Portuguese
470	Italic languages
480	Classical and Greek
490	Other languages
500	**PURE SCIENCES**
510	Mathematics
520	Astronomy and allied sciences
530	Physics
540	Chemistry and allied sciences
550	Earth sciences
560	Paleontology
570	Anthropological and biological sciences
580	Botanical sciences
590	Zoological sciences
600	**TECHNOLOGY (APPLIED SCIENCE)**
610	Medical sciences
620	Engineering and allied operations
630	Agriculture and agricultural industries
640	Domestic arts and sciences
650	Business and related enterprises
660	Chemical technology, etc.
670	Manufacturing
680	Assembled and final products
690	Buildings
700	**THE ARTS**
710	Civic and landscape art
720	Architecture
730	Sculpture and the plastic arts
740	Drawing and decorative arts
750	Painting and paintings
760	Graphic arts
770	Photography and photographs
780	Music
790	Recreation (recreational arts)
800	**LITERATURE AND RHETORIC**
810	American literature in English

820	English and Anglo-Saxon literature
830	Germanic languages literature
840	French, Provençal, Catalan literature
850	Italian and Romanian literature
860	Spanish and Portuguese literature
870	Italic languages literature
880	Classical and Greek literature
890	Literature of other languages
900	**GENERAL GEOGRAPHY AND HISTORY, ETC.**
910	General geography
920	General biography and genealogy
930	General history of ancient world
940	General history of modern Europe
950	General history of modern Asia
960	General history of modern Africa
970	General history of North America
980	General history of South America
990	General history of rest of world

LIBRARY OF CONGRESS SYSTEM

GENERAL WORKS

AC	Collections
AE	Encyclopedias
AG	Dictionaries
AI	Indexes
AM	Museums
AN	Newspapers
AP	Periodicals
AS	Academies and societies
AY	Yearbooks, almanacs, directories
AZ	History of scholarship

PHILOSOPHY, PSYCHOLOGY, RELIGION

B	**Philosophy (general)**
BC	Logic
BD	Speculative philosophy
BF	Psychology, parapsychology, occultism

STANDARD BUSINESS TERMS

BH	Aesthetics
BJ	Ethics, social usages, etiquette
BL	Religion, mythology
BM	Judaism
BP	Islam, Bahaism, Theosophy, etc.
BQ	Buddhism
BR	Christianity
BS	Bible
BT	Christianity: Doctrinal theology
BV	Christianity: Practical theology
BX	Christian denominations

AUXILIARY SCIENCES OF HISTORY

C	**General**
CB	History of civilization
CC	Archaeology
CD	Diplomatics, archives, seals
CE	Technical chronology, calendar
CJ	Numismatics
CN	Inscriptions, epigraphy
CR	Heraldry
CS	Genealogy
CT	Biography

HISTORY: GENERAL AND OLD WORLD

D	**General**
DA	Great Britain
DB	Austria, Hungary, Czechoslovakia
DC	France
DD	Germany
DE	Mediterranean region—classical
DF	Greece
DG	Italy
DH	Low countries: Belgium, Luxembourg
DJ	Netherlands (Holland)
DJK	Eastern Europe
DK	Soviet Union, Poland

150 THE ENCYCLOPEDIC DICTIONARY OF BUSINESS TERMS

DL	Northern Europe, Scandinavia
DP	Spain, Portugal
DQ	Switzerland
DR	Balkan peninsula, Turkey
DS	Asia
DT	Africa
DU	Oceania, Australia, New Zealand
DX	Gypsies

HISTORY: WESTERN HEMISPHERE

E	**America**
F	**U.S. local history, Canada, Latin America**

GEOGRAPHY, ANTHROPOLOGY, RECREATION

G	**General, atlases, maps**
GA	Mathematical geography, cartography
GB	Physical geography
GC	Oceanography
GF	Human ecology, anthropogeography
GN	Anthropology
GR	Folklore
GT	Manners and customs
GV	Recreation, sports, games

SOCIAL SCIENCES

H	**General**
HA	Statistics
HB	Economics
HC	Economic history
HD	Land, agriculture, industry, labor
HE	Transportation and communication
HF	Commerce
HG	Finance
HJ	Public finance
HM	Sociology

HN	Social history
HQ	Family, marriage, women
HS	Societies, clubs
HT	Communities, classes, races
HV	Social pathology, social service, criminology
HX	Socialism, communism

POLITICAL SCIENCE

J	**General legislative and executive papers**
JA	Political science—general
JC	Political theory, the state
JF	Constitutional history—general
JK	Constitutional history—United States
JL	Constitutional history—Canada, Latin America
JN	Constitutional history—Europe
JQ	Constitutional history—Asia, Africa, Australia, Oceania
JS	Local government
JV	Colonies and colonization
JX	International law, international relations

LAW

K	**General**
KD	United Kingdom and Ireland
KDZ	America, North America, OAS
KE	Canada
KG-KH	Latin America
KJ-KK	Europe

EDUCATION

L	**General**
LA	History of education
LB	Theory and practice of education
LC	Special aspects of education
LD	Individual institutions—U.S.

LE	Individual institutions—other Americas
LF	Individual institutions—Europe
LG	Individual institutions—Asia, Africa, Oceania
LH	College publications
LI	Student fraternities and sororities
LY	Textbooks

MUSIC

M	**General**
ML	Literature of music
MT	Music instruction

FINE ARTS

N	**Visual arts (general)**
NA	Architecture
NB	Sculpture
NC	Drawing, design
ND	Painting
NE	Print media
NK	Decorative arts, applied arts
NX	Arts in general

LANGUAGE AND LITERATURE

P	**Philology and linguistics**
PA	Classical languages and literature
PB	Celtic languages
PC	Romance languages
PD	Germanic languages, Scandinavian languages
PE	English language
PF	West Germanic languages, Dutch, German
PG	Slavic, Baltic, American languages and literature
PH	Finno-Ugrian languages and literature
PJ	Oriental languages and literature
PK	Indo-Iranian languages and literature
PL	East Asian languages and literature

STANDARD BUSINESS TERMS 153

PM	American Indian languages, artificial languages
PN	Literature, general literary history and collections, performing arts
PQ	Romance literature
PR	English literature
PS	American literature
PT	Germanic literature
PZ	Juvenile belle lettres

SCIENCE

Q	**General**
QA	Mathematics
QB	Astronomy
QC	Physics
QD	Chemistry
QE	Geology
QH	Natural history, biology
QK	Botany
QL	Zoology
QM	Human anatomy
QP	Physiology
QR	Microbiology

MEDICINE

R	**General**
RA	Public aspects of medicine
RB	Pathology
RC	Internal medicine
RD	Surgery
RE	Ophthalmology
RF	Otorhinolaryngology
RG	Gynecology and obstetrics
RJ	Pediatrics
RK	Dentistry
RL	Dermatology
RM	Therapeutics, pharmacology

RS	Pharmacy, materia medica
RT	Nursing
RX	Homeopathy
RZ	Other systems of medicine

AGRICULTURE

S	**General**
SB	Plant culture
SD	Forestry
SF	Animal culture
SH	Aquaculture, fisheries, angling
SK	Hunting

TECHNOLOGY

T	**General**
TA	Engineering—general and civil
TC	Hydraulic engineering
TD	Environmental technology, sanitary engineering
TED	Highway engineering
TF	Railroad engineering
TG	Bridge constructions
TH	Building construction
TJ	Mechanical engineering and machinery
TK	Electrical engineering, electronics, nuclear engineering
TL	Motor vehicles, aeronautics, astronautics
TN	Mining engineering, metallurgy
TP	Chemical technology
TR	Photography
TS	Manufactures
TT	Handicrafts, arts and crafts
TX	Home economics

MILITARY SCIENCE

U	**General**
UA	Armies

UB	Military administration
UC	Maintenance and transportation
UD	Infantry
UE	Cavalry, armored cavalry
UF	Artillery
UG	Military engineering, air forces, air warfare
UH	Other services

NAVAL SCIENCE

V	**General**
VA	Navies
VB	Naval administration
VC	Naval maintenance
VD	Naval seamen
VE	Marines
VF	Naval ordnance
VG	Minor services of navies
VK	Navigation, merchant marine
VM	Naval architecture, marine engineering

BIBLIOGRAPHY: LIBRARY SCIENCE

Z	**Books, book industries, libraries, library science, bibliography**

lien A form of **encumbrance** on or a claim against someone's **real property** or **personal property** as security for a debt. While a lien exists, a debtor may not sell the property.

Numerous types of liens may be used by creditors to secure the payment of a debt. Common examples are the equitable, judgment, landlord's, and mechanic's lien.

1. An *equitable lien* is created upon the mutual *intent,* but not the actual act, of a debtor and creditor to place a lien on the debtor's property.

2. A *judgment lien* is a lien placed on a debtor's property by a creditor when the debtor fails to pay a court-ordered **judgment** that was rendered in favor of the creditor.
3. A *landlord's lien,* usually backed by statute (see **statutory law**), gives a lessor (landlord) the right to seize the goods of a tenant to satisfy unpaid rent or damage caused by the tenant to the lessor's property.
4. A *mechanic's lien,* also backed by statute in most jurisdictions, gives priority of payment to contractors and others who have furnished work on or material for certain property.

light-emitting diode (LED) An electronic semiconductor device that emits light when current flows through it. Because LEDs use more power than **liquid crystal displays (LCDs)**, they are seldom used for display screens but are commonly used for indicator lights, such as the tiny light on the front of a **disk drive** that flashes or glows when the **disk** is activated.

light industry An industry of any size that produces products considered "light," such as shoes or napkins, in contrast to the raw materials and heavy equipment producers (see **heavy industry**).

limited liability See **corporation; limited liability company.**

limited liability company A company that represents a cross between a **partnership** and a subchapter S **corporation** since it has both the limited liability of a corporation and the tax advantages and flexibility of a partnership.

An investor is said to have *limited liability* in a corporation because the investor is only liable for losses in the amount of his or her investment. The corporation itself is said to have limited liability in that its obligations are usually limited to the amount of its **assets.**

limited partnership See **partnership.**

linear programming A technique for breaking down problems into a form suitable for **computer** processing; a technique for finding an optimal combination, rather than a single best; a procedure used to find the maximum or minimum value of a linear function when there are some conditions or constraints.

Example: A company evaluating its sales returns may want to determine the best combination of quantities of different products that will **yield** the highest profit.

line drawing See **halftone**.

line of credit See **credit**.

liquid asset See **assets**.

liquidated damages The amount specified in a **contract** to be paid by a defaulting party (see **default**) to the other party for a loss resulting from a **breach of contract.** For this provision to be enforced, the amount stipulated in the contract, and agreed to by the parties, must be a *reasonable* estimate of anticipated **damages** at the time of contracting and may not be an amount known to be a false forecast.

liquidation The steps taken to pay off the debts of a business; the process of settling the affairs of a business by using its **assets** to discharge its **liabilities** and distributing any remaining assets to the owners. Liquidation may be voluntary or involuntary. When it is involuntary, it is handled under Chapter 7 of the federal **bankruptcy** law.

liquid crystal display (LCD) A low-power, flat display unit in an electronic device, such as a pocket calculator, activated by long, thin crystal particles that are realigned (changed) as small amounts of electric current pass through them.

The LCDs were originally hard to read because they lacked contrast between the characters and the background. Later models, however, have provided more contrast. Since LCDs do not emit light of their own, the newer models have displays that are backlighted to improve readability, although this feature requires a much higher power level.

Compare with **light-emitting diode (LED)**.

liquid ink-jet printer See **printing**.

liquidity See **capital**.

list price The usual retail price of goods or services before discounts or **markdowns**. The regular price tag on an item in a store gives the list price; a sale tag, often attached in addition to the regular tag, gives the marked-down sales price.

living trust See **trust**.

living will See **will**.

load 1. In **computer** use, a verb referring to the steps taken to bring a program from **disk** memory into random-access **memory** (RAM); the steps taken to transfer information from a **peripheral** storage device into a computer's main memory.

See also **JARGON: download**.

2. In finance, a noun referring to the sales charge that an investor must pay when buying shares in a load **mutual fund**. A *no-load fund* does not charge this fee.

load fund See **load; mutual fund**.

local area network (LAN) The connection of several devices by high-performance cables in a limited area, usually within a single office or building, although the connection can also be between buildings in different locations. Several **computers,** for example, may be connected to the same printer, **database,** or central storage. Through a long-distance communications link, called a *gateway,* a LAN can interact with other LANs, larger **networks,** and large (*mainframe*) computers.

Each **workstation** in a LAN has its own **central processing unit (CPU),** and a personal computer can therefore function as a stand-alone unit unless it specifically has been dedicated to a single task. The advantage of being part of a LAN is that users can share **data** files and large, expensive devices that might otherwise be inappropriate for just one workstation.

Each device in a LAN is called a *node*, and the way that the various workstations are connected is called a *topology*. Three common connections are the bus, ring, and star topologies.

1. In a *bus topology*, the nodes do not form any particular pattern, such as a circle, but are all connected to a central communications cable, or channel, known as a "bus."
2. In a *ring topology*, the nodes are connected by cables in a circular fashion, so that a message must pass through each computer before it reaches its destination.
3. In a *star topology*, all nodes are connected to a central computer, much as the points of a star are connected to its center.

Each LAN must have network-operating **software** for communication between devices to take place.

Compare with **wide area network (WAN)**; see also **metropolitan area network (MAN)**.

logarithm A number that can be expressed as the **exponent** of another number; the power to which a base must be raised to produce a given number. The *base* of a number system refers to the number of digits it contains. Although any positive number except *1* can be used as a base, the most common base is *10* (10 possible digits). Logarithms to the base 10, called *common logarithms,* are the easiest to use since business regularly uses a base-10 number system.

Example: Given that $10^2 = 100$, the logarithm to the base 10 of 100 = 2, or $\log_{10} 100 = 2$.

logo Short for *logotype;* an organization's name, symbol, design, **trademark,** or other representation imprinted on its letterhead, products, and other material for identification and recognition.

logogram See **UNUSUAL WORDS: logogram.**

log on See **JARGON: log on.**

logotype See **logo.**

long sale See **short sale.**

lot See **job lot.**

low-level language See **language.**

M

machine language See **language**.

macroeconomics A study of the broad, overall aspects and aggregate forces of a nation's economy, such as industrial production, total savings, price levels, and unemployment.

Compare with **microeconomics**.

magnetic disk See **disk**.

mailbox The location in random-access **memory** (RAM) for storing **data** addressed to **peripherals** or other **microprocessors**; the **disk**-storage location for holding **electronic-mail (E-mail)** messages until the addressee retrieves them; an electronic **file** where E-mail messages are stored at the destination. An on-screen message alerts the recipient to a waiting message in his or her mailbox.

A *confidential mailbox,* used for security and privacy, can be accessed only by those who know the correct password.

mail order The business of promoting and selling merchandise by mail; ordering and receiving merchandise by mail. A mail-order company is organized primarily to promote selected products by mail, often by sending prospects catalogs or fliers; to process the resulting orders; and to ship the ordered goods by mail.

Many mail-order houses, however, combine conventional mail, **electronic mail (E-mail),** and **telecommunications** for order processing, with 24-hour, toll-free fax (see **facsimile**) and telephone numbers. Some businesses additionally provide **Internet** shopping or television sales programs. Although the term *mail order* is still widely used, very few

mainframe computer See **computer**.

main memory See **memory**.

majority stockholder See **stockholder**.

management information system (MIS) A computerized or other system dedicated to providing management with a variety of current internal and external information needed to make sound decisions. Previously the function of a general **data processing** department in many companies, the MIS is now identified primarily with those research, support, and communication activities that are specifically aimed at supplying useful information to management. The MIS is therefore often directed by a high-level officer rather than a middle manager.

The system consists of not only the MIS **hardware** and **software** but also the people and other resources involved in developing, communicating, and using the necessary information about the organization's operations and performance. It has a complex combination of components including a variety of equipment, **databases**, support staff, communications **networks**, and numerous support activities ranging from scheduling to **programming** to **word processing**.

mandatory injunction See **injunction**.

man-hours See **JARGON: man-hours**.

manuscript See **copy**.

margin 1. In sales, the difference between the selling price of a product and its cost; the percentage of **markup**.

2. In investments, the money or security that a customer deposits with a broker when buying securities on **credit**; the amount that a customer deposits when buying or selling a **futures** contract.

The margin is a percentage of the total dollar amount of securities purchased. The amount that a broker can lend in a particular transaction is regulated by the Board of Governors of the Federal Reserve System (see **central bank**).

Example: A customer buying securities may provide a certain amount of the purchase price in cash and use the securities being purchased as **collateral** for a loan from the broker to cover the rest of the purchase price. When the securities are sold, the loan is then repaid, including the **interest** charged by the broker on the amount borrowed.

marginal cost Also called *incremental cost* and *differential cost;* the increase or decrease in costs resulting from one unit more or less of output. Companies calculate marginal cost to decide whether to increase or decrease the rate of production. Optimum output occurs when marginal cost equals average total cost per unit.

See also **economy of scale.**

markdown A reduction in the original selling price of a product; the actual amount by which a product's price is reduced.

Example: If an office-products store sets a price of $100 on a **file** cabinet (the seller's original cost plus a **markup**) and later reduces the selling price to $80, the markdown is $20.

marketable title A **title** that can be readily sold since either it is free of defects, **liens,** and **encumbrances** or the facts are known and acceptable to a reasonably well-informed purchaser. A principal qualification is that the title be free from reasonable doubt so that it will not put the holder in danger of litigation.

The purchaser, however, must raise any questions he or she has about the title before accepting a **deed.** Once a deed has been accepted, the purchaser's only recourse is to sue on the deed's **covenants** of title (if any).

market research Research conducted to determine potential sales in a particular market before introducing a product or service to that audience or in that area. Market research explores matters such as the characteristics of a market, including the strength of the economy; the company's ability to meet consumer demand and other marketing requirements; and its ability to produce and deliver a proposed product or service.

market share The percentage of total industry sales for which a company is responsible.

Example: If a company has $10 million in sales of ballpoint pens, and the overall industry sales of ballpoint pens totals $200 million, the company's market share is 5 percent.

market value See **face value**.

markup 1. In **retail** businesses, an increase in the selling price of an item over and above the seller's wholesale cost; the actual amount by which a product's price is increased.

Example: If a gift store normally uses a 50 percent markup on items, a vase that cost the store owner $50 would have a markup of $25 ($50 x .50 = $25) to arrive at a selling price of $75 ($50 original cost + $25 markup = $75 sales price).

2. In **desktop publishing** and **printing,** the style instructions that are written on a manuscript that is to be typeset. They include type size (see **point**) and face (see **typeface**) specifications, indications of desired margins, layout of displayed material such as a list, and other matters that define the way a document will look (see **format**) when it is finished.

maturity The conclusion or termination of a financial obligation; the state of a **note, bond,** or other financial instrument being due and payable. The time when the **principal** amount of a financial obligation is due and payable is called the *maturity date*.

maturity date See **maturity**.

maturity value See **face value**.

mean A number that is typical of a group of numbers. An *arithmetic* mean, or *average*, of a group of numbers is the sum of the numbers divided by the number of items in the group.

Example: 5 + 3 + 7 = 15/3 = 5

mechanic's lien See **lien**.

median The middle number(s) in a set of numbers arranged in order. Different rules apply to odd and even numbers.

1. If there is an *odd* number of items, such as *6, 7, 8, 9, 10* (five items), the median is the middle number: *8*.
2. If there is an *even* number of items, such as *6, 7, 8, 9* (four items), the median is the average of the middle two items: *7 + 8 = 15/2 = 7.5*.

mediation See **arbitration**.

meeting The act of gathering or assembling for a particular purpose. The term *meeting* is often used interchangeably with **conference,** although in strict terminology, the latter is a type of meeting in which participants get together to discuss something or exchange ideas. By contrast, a *meeting* is often called not only to discuss something or exchange ideas but, more importantly, to act on something, such as to nominate or vote on new officers and directors (see **board of directors**). A meeting for purposes of taking action, in fact, may be part of the overall proceedings of a large conference.

Formal meetings, such as a **stockholders'** or directors' meeting, are called by notifying the members according to the requirements in the organization's **bylaws** regarding time, method, and content of the notice. To ensure that the legally required number of people attend (*quorum*), as stated in the bylaws, fill-in *proxy* statements may be sent to each person entitled to vote.

Recipients who can't attend may use the proxy to designate another member to cast votes for them. In stockholders' meetings, the legally required quorum is usually determined by the amount of **stock** represented at the meeting, rather than by the number of people present or voting by proxy.

Business is transacted at a formal meeting according to the rules of **parliamentary procedure** adopted by the organization, usually based on some version of *Robert's Rules of Order*. A permanent record of the transactions or proceedings at the meeting is then prepared in the form of official **minutes** (see the sample format in that entry).

memory Internal **computer** storage; a computer's main or primary storage, as opposed to its secondary storage, such as **disk** storage; the space where information is stored in a computer while it is being worked on.

A computer must be able to store the programs that direct its operations as well as the documents and other information on which work is being performed. These programs and **data** are held in the portion of a computer's physical circuitry referred to as its *main memory* or *internal storage*. In small computers, such as a personal computer, internal memory consists of *random-access memory (RAM)* and *read-only memory (ROM)*.

RAM, formerly called *core storage* or *core memory*, is used for holding work temporarily while it is being processed, and ROM is used to store permanent information, such as the **operating-system** program. RAM can be written on (recorded), read, edited, erased, and reused. Since ROM is permanent, however, it can only be read.

The expression *random access* in RAM means that all locations can be accessed with about equal speed, and all locations can be addressed directly by the computer's **central processing unit (CPU)**. When a user wants to provide for larger programs and greater amounts of data, the amount of RAM can usually be expanded by adding additional memory circuits.

From a user's perspective, an important difference between RAM and ROM is that RAM disappears when the computer is turned off—hence the need to save documents on a hard disk or diskette before shutting down the equipment. ROM, however, does not disappear when the computer is turned off. Because of this difference, RAM is sometimes referred to as *volatile memory* and ROM as *nonvolatile memory*.

menu A list of available **computer** options or commands displayed on screen. The menu is often displayed in a horizontal strip, called the *menu bar,* at the top of the screen. Examples of selections in the menu are *File, Edit, View, Insert, Format, Utilities, Macro,* and *Window.*

Depending on the **software** being used, an item on the menu may be selected by pressing *Alt* and typing the first letter or by clicking on the selected (highlighted) item with a **mouse.** After an item on the menu has thus been selected, a *submenu* or *dialog box* will usually appear. This box lists further choices pertaining to the selected item. For example, if a user chooses *Format* from the menu bar, the box that appears on screen will allow the user to focus on the kind of formatting desired, such as *Paragraphs, Sections, Margins, Tabs,* or *Borders.*

After selecting something from the list in the submenu box, such as *Paragraphs,* the user again has the opportunity to indicate specific preferences, such as a 1/2-inch indention and a line space before and after each paragraph. In this way, from the first step of selecting a general item from the menu, the user can proceed to more specific choices in the submenu.

menu bar See **menu**.

menu-driven program See **command**.

merit rating 1. In general, a system of rating employees by means of a periodic performance review to assist in making decisions about raises, promotions, demotions, training needs, and other personnel matters. Since some states impose higher unemployment insurance tax rates on employers with high labor turnovers, companies are encouraged to use rating systems to stabilize employment.

2. In insurance, a pricing system used to determine **premiums** for large businesses; a pricing system that is adjusted according to the loss experience of an insured. A specific **risk** is measured against some standard to judge how the rate for that risk should be adjusted.

metric system The principal system of weights and measures being adopted by countries throughout the world; also known as the *international system* or the *SI system (Système International)*. Although the metric system is legal in the United States, many businesses continue to use the U.S. customary system. The international system, however, is prominent in matters involving international trade.

The metric system has 16 prefixes, such as *kilo,* that when combined with base units, such as *meter,* form multiples and submultiples: *1 kilometer = 1,000 meters.* The following tables list the 16 prefixes and base units, give the appropriate multiplication factors, and illustrate how to find the U.S. customary equivalents when only metric amounts are known.

Metric Prefixes

Prefix	Multiplication Factor	Symbol
exa	1,000,000,000,000,000,000 (10^{18}) (one quintillion)	E
peta	1,000,000,000,000,000 (10^{15}) (one quadrillion)	P
tera	1,000,000,000,000 (10^{12}) (one trillion)	T
giga	1,000,000,000 (10^{9}) (one billion)	G
mega	1,000,000 (10^{6}) (one million)	M
kilo	1,000 (10^{3}) (one thousand)	k
hecto	100 (10^{2}) (one hundred)	h
deka	10 (ten)	da
deci	0.1 (10^{-1}) (one-tenth)	d
centi	0.01 (10^{-2}) (one-hundredth)	c
milli	0.001 (10^{-3}) (one-thousandth)	m
micro	0.000,001 (10^{-6}) (one-millionth)	µ
nano	0.000,000,001 (10^{-9}) (one-billionth)	n
pico	0.000,000,000,001 (10^{-12}) (one-trillionth)	p
femto	0.000,000,000,000,001 (10^{-15}) (one-quadrillionth)	f
atto	0.000,000,000,000,000,001 (10^{-18}) (one-quintillionth)	a

Metric Prefixes Combined with Base Units

Weight
1 *kilo*gram = 1,000 grams
1 *hecto*gram = 100 grams
1 *deka*gram = 10 grams
(1 gram = 1 gram)
1 *deci*gram = 0.1 gram
1 *centi*gram = 0.01 gram
1 *milli*gram = 0.001 gram

Length
1 *kilo*meter = 1,000 meters
1 *hecto*meter = 100 meters
1 *deka*meter = 10 meters
(1 meter = 1 meter)
1 *deci*meter = 0.1 meter
1 *centi*meter = 0.01 meter
1 *milli*meter = 0.001 meter

Volume
1 *hecto*liter = 100 liters
1 *deka*liter = 10 liters
(1 liter = 1 liter)
1 *centi*liter = 0.01 liter
1 *milli*liter = 0.001 liter

Standard Business Terms

Multiplication Factors for Conversion

Length

When You Know	Multiply By	To Find
millimeters	0.04	inches
centimeters	0.39	inches
meters	3.28	feet
meters	1.09	yards
kilometers	0.62	miles
inches	25.40	millimeters
inches	2.54	centimeters
feet	30.48	centimeters
yards	0.91	meters
miles	1.61	kilometers

Area

When You Know	Multiply By	To Find
square centimeters	0.16	square inches
square meters	1.20	square yards
square kilometers	0.39	square miles
hectares (10,000m^2)	2.47	acres
square inches	6.45	square centimeters
square feet	0.09	square meters
square yards	0.84	square meters
square miles	2.60	square kilometers
acres	0.40	hectares

Mass and Weight

When You Know	Multiply By	To Find
grams	0.035	ounce
kilograms	2.21	pounds
metric tons (1,000 kg)	1.10	short tons
ounces	28.35	grams
pounds	0.45	kilograms
short tons (2,000 lb)	0.91	tons (metric)

Volume

When You Know	Multiply By	To Find
milliliters	0.20	teaspoons
milliliters	0.06	tablespoons
milliliters	0.03	fluid ounces
liters	4.23	cups
liters	2.12	pints
liters	1.06	quarts
liters	0.26	gallons
cubic meters	35.32	cubic feet
cubic meters	1.35	cubic yards
teaspoons	4.93	milliliters
tablespoons	14.79	milliliters
fluid ounces	29.57	milliliters
cups	0.24	liters
pints	0.47	liters
quarts	0.95	liters
gallons	3.79	liters
cubic feet	0.03	cubic meters
cubic yards	0.76	cubic meters

Speed

When You Know	Multiply By	To Find
miles per hour	1.61	kilometers per hour
kilometers per hour	0.62	miles per hour

Temperature (Exact)

When You Know	Multiply by	And Add	To Find
°C	9/5	32	°F

metropolitan area network (MAN) A **local area network (LAN)** that connects **computer** users throughout a metropolitan area.

See also **wide area network (WAN)**.

microchip See **chip; integrated circuit.**

microcomputer See **computer.**

microeconomics A study of the behavior or operation of a nation's basic economic components, such as individual companies, households, and consumers.

Compare with **macroeconomics**.

microfiche See **micrographics.**

microfilm See **micrographics.**

microform See **micrographics.**

microform reader See **micrographics.**

micrographics The process of reducing the size of documents and storing them and other material on film. To deal with overcrowded conventional **files** with voluminous **hardcopy** material, companies may use a micrographic process, converting bulky paper items to reduced form so that the hard copies can be destroyed. This process requires the use of *microforms,* which are rolls or sheets of film containing exact duplicates of the original records.

Images on microforms are so small that they must be read with enlarging equipment, called *microform readers.* Most enlarging and reading equipment also includes a **printing** device to make hard copies of selected items as well as display them on screen.

Computer-assisted retrieval (*CAR*), in which **computers** are connected to the micrographics equipment, is a process that can be used to retrieve information quickly from the microforms. But unlike a computer that retrieves information from computer **memory** for editing on screen, a microform reader alone offers no way for users to edit or update the material displayed on the microform reader's screen.

The three common types of microform media are microfilm rolls, microfiche sheets, and ultrafiche sheets.

1. *Microfilm rolls,* the oldest micrographics medium, are continuous rolls of film capable of holding hundreds of pages of hard copy in reduced form.
2. *Microfiche,* which has even smaller images than those on microfilm, is a sheet of film that also can hold several hundred pages of hard copy in reduced form.
3. *Ultrafiche,* which is usually processed in photo labs and is therefore a more expensive alternative, is the smallest of the microform media but has the largest capacity, with a single sheet able to hold thousands of pages of hard copy in reduced form.

micromanagement See **JARGON: micromanagement.**

microprocessor The complex **chip** (see also **integrated circuit**) or set of chips that holds the arithmetic/logic unit, control unit, and various connections to a **computer's** main storage and input-output **peripherals** (see **JARGON: input; output**); the chip that contains the entire **central processing unit (CPU)** of a computer.

Microprocessors are usually compared on the basis of power and speed.

1. *Power* is measured in the number of **bits** of **data,** such as 16 or 32 bits, that can be processed at a given time.
2. *Speed* in measured in megahertz (MHz) of clock speed, such as 33 MHz, which means 33 million cycles per second.

Miller-Tydings Act See **antitrust laws.**

minicomputer See **computer.**

minimum wage The lowest amount allowed by the federal government that an employee can be paid per hour for a specified job. Minimum hourly wages were established by Congress under the Fair Labor Standards Act and can be revised by congressional vote.

minority stockholder See **stockholder.**

minutes An official record of the proceedings of a **meeting.** The records of semiformal and formal meetings, which are usually conducted according to the rules of **parliamentary procedure,** are prepared shortly after the close of each meeting and signed by the organization's secretary and sometimes additionally by its presiding officer.

The individual appointed to take handwritten notes during a meeting, who may or may not be the organization's secretary, usually backs up the handwritten notes with a video- or audiotape recording of the discussion, resolutions, and votes. After the meeting, a transcriber then prepares the text of the minutes in a form adopted by the organization.

The amount of detail and the **format** used for the minutes will vary depending on the level of formality desired and the organization's needs and preferences. In a formal or semiformal meeting, some things must be reported verbatim. Resolutions, for example, must be written exactly as stated at the meeting, with the words *RESOLVED* and *WHEREAS* written in all capitals and the word *That* with an initial capital: *RESOLVED That* . . . .

Page 176 has a common minutes format used for informal business meetings. In this example, the text discussion is minimal, so the headings can be run in with the discussion paragraphs without losing readability. When the text is extensive, however, it is often clearer to place the headings on a line alone above the paragraphs of discussion or in a block alone to the left of the paragraphs.

mobile telephone See **cellular technology.**

mode In **computers,** the part of a system or program dedicated to a particular task or activity; a term that describes

Example: Minutes

COMPANY
Address
Date

CALL TO ORDER: A regular meeting of the
_____ was called to order at
_____. A quorum was present, including the
following: [*Insert Names*].

APPROVAL OF MINUTES: The secretary, _____,
read the minutes of the _____ meeting, and
they were approved as read.

TREASURER'S REPORT: The treasurer, _____,
presented a _____ statement showing that
_____. The treasurer's report was
approved as read.

COMMITTEE REPORTS: The chair of the _____
Committee reported that _____.

OLD BUSINESS: Ms. _____ reminded
members that _____.

NEW BUSINESS: Vice president _____
introduced _____ and moved that
_____. The motion was
seconded by _____ and passed
unanimously.

ADJOURNMENT: There being no further business, the
meeting adjourned at _____.

_____
Secretary

the operating state of a computer system or program. A system, for example, has various modes, such as the access, interpretive, **binary,** and conversation modes. If you are doing **batch processing,** your computer is in a batch mode, rather than in an interactive mode where you can intervene.

Most **software** programs, such as **word processing,** also have a number of modes that a user can select, such as the entry, **format,** insert, and overwrite modes. Therefore, if you are "saving" a document, the program is in the **file** mode. An on-screen message usually displays a program's current mode.

modem Acronym (see **abbreviations**) for **mod**ulator/**dem**odulator; a device that changes signals in **data** transmission, such as by fax (see **facsimile**) or E-mail (see **electronic mail [E-mail]**), from **digital** to **analog** and back again. For example, most **computers** are digital machines, but they can communicate over the telephone lines, which carry analog waves, through the modulation/demodulation process (see description in **facsimile**).

Modems transmit data serially, or one **bit** at a time. The transmission rate, therefore, can be stated in bits per second (bps), such as 9,600 bps. The bps rate is generally synonymous with the **baud** rate at slower speeds. Thus 300 bps is the same as 300 baud. At higher rates, however, the bps rate is more than the baud rate, so that 1,200 bps might equal 600 bauds. Thus it is usually clearer to refer to the transmission speed of modems in bits per second.

modular Having **modules,** or standardized components, designed for easy assembly, as in modular furniture or **hardware;** consisting of standard, easily connected, replaceable, and often interchangeable units.

Example 1: In modular **programming,** a program is divided into smaller programs, or standardized functions, so that each module, or routine, can be programmed, changed, or corrected (see **JARGON: debug**) independently of the other modules and later connected to the others.

Example 2: In modular **accounting** packages, each function, such as **payroll,** is created as a separate program while also being designed to work together with the rest of the programs in the package (accounts payable, general **ledger,** and so on).

Modular systems are popular in budget-conscious small businesses and other companies because they allow the buyers to expand later by adding more parts as funds become available. In this way, a small **computer** system could be expanded with plug-in boards that enhance its capabilities and with other easily connected components to create a larger system. Similarly, a small **file** or storage system could be enlarged later by adding more standardized shelves, drawers, cubes, or other containers.

modular accounting See **modular.**

modular programming See **modular.**

modulator/demodulator See **modem.**

module See **modular.**

money market A market for short-term debt instruments, such as negotiable certificates of deposit, Eurodollar (see **Eurocurrency**) certificates of deposit, **commercial paper,** and Treasury bills and **notes;** a type of **mutual fund** (*money market fund*) that invests in short-term securities and distributes the income from them as **interest** either paid directly to shareholders or reinvested in their **accounts,** which usually have check-writing privileges; a bank account (*money market checking/savings account*) that pays interest rates comparable to money market fund rates, with minimum-balance requirements and limits on the number of checks that can be written.

Money market *bank* accounts are insured by the Federal Deposit Insurance Corporation or the Federal Savings and Loan Insurance Corporation. Most money market *funds*, however, are not federally insured, although some may be covered by private insurance.

money market checking account See **money market**.

money market fund See **money market**.

money market savings account See **money market**.

monitor See **cathode ray tube (CRT)**.

monopoly A form of market dominance in which most trade involving a particular commodity or service is controlled by one person, company, or group to the extent that competition is excluded. In general, monopolies and any attempt to restrain free trade are illegal under the antitrust provisions (see **antitrust laws**) of the Sherman Act and its successor, the Clayton Act. However, certain government-sanctioned monopolies, such as public utility services, are lawful within their assigned areas.

month-to-month lease See **lease**.

moratorium The authorization or right to delay debt payments or the performance of another contractual obligation (see **contract**); authorization to suspend required activity. The term *moratorium* is most often used in reference to assistance offered to a large entity, such as a government or bank, that is experiencing difficulty in fulfilling the terms of an **agreement** or in meeting a debt-payment schedule.

mortgage A conditional **pledge** of **real property** or **personal property** as security for repayment of a loan; a debt instrument in which a borrower (*mortgagor*) gives a **lien** on property to a lender (*mortgagee*) as security for a promissory **note** or, in some states, a **bond.**

A mortgage is a *conditional* conveyance stipulating that it will become void on a specified date provided that all payments have been made as required (*defeasance clause*). The document also describes other terms, such as the amount of the loan (*consideration*), the **interest** rate, the **acceleration clause,** and any prepayment penalty.

Many different types of mortgages exist, including the conventional or fixed-rate, adjustable-rate, flexible or flexible-payment, reverse, FHA (Federal Housing Administration), VA (Veterans Administration), Fannie Mae (Federal National Mortgage Association), Ginnie Mae (Government National Mortgage Association), Freddie Mac (Federal Home Loan Mortgage Corporation), trust, open-end, blanket, purchase-money, graduated-payment, second, balloon, wraparound, rollover, assumable, seller-financed, portable, package, and chattel mortgages.

1. A *conventional* or *fixed-rate mortgage (FRM)* is a loan that has a fixed interest rate during the term of the loan.
2. An *adjustable-rate mortgage (ARM)* is a loan with an interest rate that may be adjusted periodically, such as every six months, during the term of the loan in response to economic indicators, such as a rise in the **prime rate.**
3. A *flexible* or *flexible-payment mortgage* is a loan with a provision specifying that the borrower will pay interest only during the first several years of the term of the loan.

4. A *reverse, reverse-equity,* or *reverse-annuity mortgage* is a scheduled loan on property that the borrower owns and is designed to provide regular income to the borrower, who receives periodic small loan payments over time rather than a single lump-sum payment at the outset.
5. An *FHA mortgage* is a loan issued by a commercial lender, usually at a favorable interest rate and with a low down payment, that is insured by the Federal Housing Administration.
6. A *VA mortgage* is a loan by a commercial lender that is guaranteed by the Veterans Administration and is usually offered at a favorable interest rate with little or no down payment to veterans and qualified widows of veterans.
7. A *Fannie Mae mortgage* is a loan, usually insured by the Federal Housing Administration, that is purchased by the Federal National Mortgage Association (FNMA) from banks for resale to private investors.
8. A *Ginnie Mae mortgage* is a loan insured by the Government National Mortgage Association (GNMA), which underwrites special-assistance loans and buys FHA- and VA-guaranteed mortgages.
9. A *Freddie Mac mortgage* is a conventional residential mortgage purchased by the Federal Home Loan Mortgage Corporation (FHLMC), repackaged, and resold to the public.
10. A *trust mortgage* or a *deed of trust* is a loan in which legal **title** to the property is transferred to a third-party trustee who holds it until the lender has received full payment of the loan from the borrower.
11. An *open-end mortgage* is a loan that allows the mortgagor to reborrow an additional amount up to the

specified limit of the original mortgage after part of
the mortgage has been paid off.

12. A *blanket mortgage,* used by builders and developers,
is a loan that uses more than one property as security.

13. A *purchase-money mortgage* is a loan given by a
seller to a buyer to help the buyer purchase the seller's
property and is usually provided as a second **lien** or
second mortgage (see item 15) for part of the purchase price.

14. A *graduated-payment mortgage* is a loan, especially
designed for those who expect to be able to pay more
later, in which the payment amount increases at specified
intervals but the interest rate remains constant
during the term of the loan.

15. A *second mortgage* is an additional loan, second in
priority to the first mortgage, provided by a second
lender (a) initially when a buyer is unable to get a first
loan of sufficient size to buy the desired property or
(b) later when a buyer wants to use the property as
collateral for a loan needed for another purpose.

16. A *balloon mortgage* is a relatively short-term loan in
which initial payments may consist only of interest
followed by a lump-sum payment of all or any remaining
principal at the end of the loan term, usually
three to five years.

17. A *wraparound mortgage,* common on the West Coast,
is a form of second mortgage in which a new loan is
issued for an amount larger than the first loan, and the
lender assumes the obligation of paying off the first
loan.

18. A *rollover mortgage* is a short-term loan similar to a balloon mortgage in which the borrower is required to secure another mortgage at the end of the term of the loan.
19. An *assumable mortgage* is a loan with a provision allowing for a new buyer to take over, or assume, the mortgage of the previous buyer, who is now the seller.
20. A *seller-financed mortgage* is any loan provided by a seller of property to a buyer to finance the purchase and, unlike the second mortgage (see item 15) or the purchase-money mortgage (see item 13), may cover the entire purchase price.
21. A *portable mortgage* is a loan that homeowners may take (move) with them when they sell property in one location and want to finance new property they are buying in another location.
22. A *package mortgage* is a loan in which the payments not only cover the real property but also include certain household items, such as a dishwasher and a stove.
23. A *chattel mortgage* is a loan in which the lien is on personal property rather than real property.

mortgage bond See **bond**.

motion See **parliamentary procedure**.

mouse A remote-control **computer** input device (see **JARGON: input**) with control buttons; a hand-operated pointing device used for operations such as choosing commands, moving text and other material, and drawing pictures. The small mouselike device is moved by hand over a hard, flat surface to position a highlighted arrow or other symbol where desired on the computer's display screen. The mouse is then activated by clicking its buttons to select or perform the desired operation on the highlighted material.

multiple See **price-earnings ratio.**

multiple listing The listing of **real property** for sale with more than one broker; a notice of real property for sale among a group of real estate brokers who agree to share the listing and split the commission on a sale between the listing broker and the selling broker (if different). Prospective sellers frequently seek a real estate firm that is part of a *multiple-listing service (MLS)* so that notice of their property's availability will reach as many prospective buyers as possible and that the property will be shown by as many brokers as possible.

multiple listing service (MLS) See **multiple listing.**

municipal bond See **bond.**

mutual fund A company that invests shareholders' money in other companies; a fund managed by an investment company for shareholders; a fund that raises money for shareholders by buying and selling **stocks, bonds, commodities,** Treasury bills, and other forms of investment. Funds may be aggressive, thus creating higher **risk** for investors, or conservative, with relatively lower risk, depending on the companies in which a fund invests the shareholders' money.

Mutual funds may be classified as open-end or closed-end funds.

1. An *open-end fund* issues new shares as demand warrants and it redeems (buys back) shares from shareholders on demand.
2. A *closed-end fund* begins with a specified number of shares, rather than creating them as needed, and does not buy back shares from shareholders; instead, the shares are traded on exchanges the same as **stock.**

Mutual funds may also be classified as load or no-load funds.

1. *Load funds,* bought through a brokerage, involve a sales charge (**load**), such as the broker's commission and a management fee; a broker or salesperson offers buying and selling advice in a load fund.
2. *No-load funds,* which are advertised and sold directly to investors by the funds, do not involve a sales charge; since brokers are not involved, no advice is given on buying or selling shares in a no-load fund.

N

NASDAQ Acronym for National Association of Securities Dealers Automated Quotations; see **over-the-counter (OTC) market**.

NASDAQ Composite Index See **stock index**.

National Association of Securities Dealers Automated Quotations (NASDAQ) See **over-the-counter (OTC) market**.

natural language See **language**.

negative easement See **easement**.

negative proof See **proof**.

negligence See **contributory negligence**.

negotiable instrument A signed, written instrument, such as a check or promissory **note,** that represents an order or promise to pay a designated amount of money and can be transferred from one person to another. Under the **Uniform Commercial Code (UCC),** four conditions must be met for an instrument to be negotiable.

1. It must be signed by the maker or drawer.
2. It must promise to pay a certain amount of money.
3. It must be payable on demand.
4. It must be payable to the bearer or to order, by **endorsement.**

Compare with **nonnegotiable instrument**.

net income Also called *net profit;* revenue less expenses. The difference between total income and total expenses is indicated on an **income statement,** which summarizes income and expenses for a given **accounting** period (see **fiscal period**).

See also **net loss**.

netiquette See **JARGON: netiquette.**

net loss The excess of expenses over revenue; the **deficit** indicated on an **income statement** for a given **accounting** period (see **fiscal period**).

See also **net income**.

net profit See **net income.**

network Interconnected elements or units combined to form a communications system capable of sharing **data, hardware,** and **software.** A network may consist only of a number of people who meet, talk by telephone, or write letters to exchange information and help one another. Usually, the term refers to interconnected **computer** terminals (see **workstation**) that enable users to share or exchange information, equipment, and programs electronically.

A network may be limited to a building or several nearby buildings, as in a **local area network (LAN),** or a small geographic area, as in a **metropolitan area network (MAN).** Or it may be unlimited physically or geographically, as in a **wide area network (WAN).**

A WAN uses high-speed, long-distance channels, such as the worldwide telephone system or satellite communications. America Online and CompuServe are examples of WANs. The **Internet,** however, is not only a giant network but a network of networks, consisting of many other WANs all linked together.

See also **JARGON: networking.**

networking See **network; JARGON: networking.**

net working capital See **capital.**

net worth The value of a business calculated as total **assets** less total **liabilities.** An individual's net worth is reflected as his or her personal **equity**; a **partnership's** net worth is reflected as the sum of the partners' **capital** accounts; a **corporation's** net worth is reflected as **stockholders'** equity.

news release Also called *press release;* information sent to newspapers, magazines, television stations, and other print or broadcast media in the hope that they will report the information, thereby providing free publicity to the sender.

News releases must be written in clear, concise, jargon-free language (see **JARGON** entries), with the first paragraph answering the traditional news questions of *who, what, where, when, why,* and *how.* The **format** must include double-spaced paragraphs, written so that the receiving editor can eliminate the final paragraphs if necessary.

A release should begin with a standard release heading that provides a contact's name and number for further information, the date the information is available for release, and the place and date of issue (see example).

```
        Example: News Release Heading



                    [LETTERHEAD]

                                   Contact:

                                   John Jones
                                   212-555-1000




                FOR IMMEDIATE RELEASE


   Los Angeles, Calif. (January 2, 1997): . . .
```

New York Stock Exchange (NYSE) See **stock exchange.**

New York Stock Exchange (NYSE) Composite Index See **stock index.**

nexus See **UNUSUAL WORDS: nexus.**

niche market See **JARGON: niche market.**

Nikkei Stock Average See **stock index.**

node See **local area network (LAN).**

no-fault insurance A form of automobile insurance, adopted in many states, in which all parties in an accident are compensated for any injuries without regard to fault. This type of insurance does not have the conventional requirement that there must be clear evidence of one party's negligence for the other to receive compensation. Under the traditional system, it is often difficult to determine who is at fault; in addition, the process has been criticized for being slow and expensive.

To prevent excessive lawsuits, an insured person under the no-fault system may not sue for general **damages** until special damages exceed a minimum amount. Since all injured persons are compensated up to a specified amount, it eliminates the need for litigation in minor accidents. However, in cases of serious injury in major accidents, compensation above the specified limits can be recovered only by bringing a lawsuit against the negligent party.

no-load fund See **load; mutual fund.**

nominal yield See **yield.**

noncompete agreement An **agreement** between an employer and employee in which an employee who leaves the company agrees not to work for a competitor for a specified period, such as two years. Employers often require this type of agreement when an employee has access to important information that might benefit the competition.

noncumulative preferred stock See **stock.**

noncurrent asset See **assets**.

nonnegotiable instrument A written instrument, such as a **contract,** that cannot be transferred from one party to another without making a formal **assignment.** This differs from a **negotiable instrument,** such as a check, which can be transferred to someone else by simple **endorsement.**

nonparticipating preferred stock See **stock**.

nonprofit corporation See **corporation**.

nonvolatile memory See **memory**.

no-par stock See **stock**.

notary public An individual commissioned (authorized) under state law to handle various public duties, such as administer oaths, attest to and certify certain documents, take **depositions** and **affidavits,** and witness signatures. A document is authenticated by applying a notarial seal to it. In many jurisdictions, private persons as well as attorneys may apply for a notary's license.

note Also called *promissory note;* a maker's written promise to pay a specified amount to the payee on demand or on a future date. To the maker, the instrument is a *note payable;* to the payee, it is a *note receivable.*

The terms of a note specify the amount of **interest** (if any) and payment schedule. When the note is payable to the order of a particular person or to the bearer, it is negotiable. **Title** can be transferred by **endorsement** and delivery.

notebook computer See **computer**.

notes See **back matter**.

not-for-profit corporation See **corporation**.

numerical control The control of machine tools by some form of numerical input medium (see **JARGON: input**), such as magnetic tape. The input medium is usually prepared by a **computer.** When the control is directly initiated by a computer, the process is known as *direct numerical control*. Since the movement of the tools is controlled by digitally coded instructions or direct computer commands, the process eliminates the need for conventional positioning devices.

O

odd lot A quantity of items, particularly **stocks,** that is sold or traded in less than the regular number of units. Stocks, for example, are commonly traded in units of 100 shares (*round lot* or *full lot*).

Odd lots sometimes appeal to buyers or investors who have limited **capital** to invest and cannot afford or do not want a round lot. Although the capital outlay will be less for a smaller odd lot, a broker's commission in stock trading is usually higher for an odd lot than it is for a round lot.

off line See **JARGON: off line.**

offset press See **printing.**

oligopoly See **UNUSUAL WORDS: oligopoly.**

ombudsperson A man or woman who investigates complaints, such as a taxpayer grievance against the Internal Revenue Service, and mediates settlements between the accused and the accuser. In Swedish, the term *ombud* means "commissioner" or "agent," and in Scandinavian countries, the term *ombudsman* originated in reference to a government official who was commissioned to investigate citizen complaints.

In the United States, an ombudsperson is frequently a private party rather than a government official. He or she commonly handles the complaints of consumers, students, and others concerning the actions or policies of a company, school, or other organization, including the government.

on line See **JARGON: on line.**

open account See **credit.**

open end Also *open ended;* having no definite limits regarding time or money, such as an open-end **contract;** a type of financial arrangement, such as an open-end **mortgage,** that allows a debtor to borrow additional funds under an existing loan contract; a type of investment company that sells **mutual funds** (*open-end funds*) to the public, continually creating new shares on demand.

Compare with **closed end.**

open-end fund See **mutual fund.**

open-end mortgage See **mortgage.**

operating ratio A ratio, such as "sales to cost of goods sold," used by businesses to measure their operating efficiency, particularly as compared with a previous **accounting** period (see **fiscal period**) or an industrywide average. The ratio generally relates income and expense items from an **income statement** to each other and to **balance sheet** figures.

operating system The **software,** or master set of programs, that controls the **hardware** of a **computer** or **data-processing** system. The operating system manages a computer's internal functions; controls input, output, and storage (see **JARGON: input; output**); and, in general, handles its interaction with applications programs, such as **word processing.** The operating system, therefore, is the program that enables users to operate their computers and the **peripherals** and to perform a variety of tasks electronically.

operations research The analysis of mathematical or scientific **data** pertaining to a process or operation so that business management can make sound decisions and accurate operational forecasts and can solve problems and improve productivity. Using mathematical models and **computer** simulations, operations research is applied in many areas of business activity, from scheduling to marketing to budgeting.

OPM financing See **JARGON: OPM financing.**

optical character recognition (OCR) The use of light-sensitive devices to identify and encode characters, codes, or symbols.

Example 1: Retail clerks use an OCR device known as a wand to scan product labels and convert them into a form that can be processed by the checkout **computers.**

Example 2: Post offices use optical character readers to provide automated sorting of mail that is prepared according to U.S. Postal Service requirements for OCR addressing. (Instructions on addressing for OCR processing can be found in the *Domestic Mail Manual* or can be secured by inquiring at a local post office.)

optical disk See **disk.**

option See **JARGON: option.**

optional dividend See **dividend.**

options trading See **futures.**

oral contract See **contract.**

oral deposition See **deposition.**

out-of-state corporation See **corporation.**

output See **JARGON: output.**

output contract See **contract.**

outside director See **board of directors.**

outsourcing See **JARGON: outsourcing.**

overhead Also called *indirect costs and expenses;* the operating expenses of a business, such as rent, utilities, insurance, payroll taxes, fringe benefits, and depreciation, that are not directly associated with the production of goods and services, unlike *direct costs,* such as labor and materials, used in production.

over-the-counter (OTC) market The financial market for trading in securities that are not listed on organized **stock ex-**

changes, such as the American Stock Exchange or the New York Stock Exchange. The **stocks** often belong to smaller companies that do not meet the listing requirements of organized exchanges, although some companies simply prefer the OTC trading procedure.

The OTC transactions are conducted over the telephone (instead of on an exchange floor) by way of a computer **network** that connects the various dealers in **stocks** and **bonds.** The trading is largely subject to the rules of the self-governing National Association of Securities Dealers (NASD), and price quotations are provided through the National Association of Securities Dealers Automated Quotations (NASDAQ) system. These quotes are also reported on newscasts and in most major newspapers.

overtime The hours worked beyond, or in addition to, regular working hours; the payment made for work in excess of established working hours. Employees who work at an hourly rate, rather than a salary, are normally compensated for overtime beyond a 40-hour workweek at a rate of one and a half times the normal hourly rate.

owner's equity See **equity.**

P

package mortgage See **mortgage**.

packets See **JARGON: packets**.

page layout See **desktop publishing; word processing**.

page proof See **proof**.

paradigm See **JARGON: paradigm**.

parameter Variable component of **data;** a variable quantity used to express other interrelated variables that can then be viewed as dependent on the parameter; any quantity, which may be known or unknown, that defines or characterizes a system or population. When a parameter is unknown, *statistical inference* is used to estimate it. This process involves estimating characteristics that can't be observed on the basis of information that can be observed.

Although businesses use parameters, such as "unit selling price," in statistical and mathematical studies to aid in decision making, the term is also used loosely as synonymous with *perimeter,* meaning "limit": "The parameters (limits) of the program have been expanded to include telemarketing."

parent corporation See **corporation**.

parliamentary law See **parliamentary procedure**.

parliamentary procedure A form of **meeting** conduct that is based on established rules of order to govern legislative and deliberative assemblies. Ordinary business meetings, meetings of a **board of directors** or **stockholders,** and other semiformal or formal meetings and **conferences** follow a certain pattern in transacting business. Whereas *parliamentary law* refers to the rules, precedents, and customary practices that apply to the conduct of such meetings, **parliamentary procedure** refers to the steps taken to follow parliamentary law.

The most widely used guide to meeting conduct is *Robert's Rules of Order,* first written by General H. M. Robert in 1876. Most newer rules books, such as *The New Robert's Rules of Order* (1989, Signet), or miniguides, such as *How to Run a Meeting* (1994, Plume), are based on General Robert's rules.

One of the most important tools in parliamentary procedure is the meeting motion. By way of formal motions, also called *questions,* proposals can be introduced, debated, and voted on in an orderly and consistent manner. General Robert classified meeting motions as privileged, incidental, subsidiary (secondary), and main (principal) questions.

1. A *privileged motion,* such as a motion to set the time to adjourn, is the highest ranking motion and takes precedence over (must be decided before) all others.
2. An *incidental motion,* such as a motion to withdraw another motion, is prompted by the other motion and has to be decided before action can be taken on the other motion.
3. A *subsidiary (secondary) motion,* such as a motion to table a particular proposal, is applied to another motion being considered and is used as a means of disposing of the other motion.
4. A *main (principal) motion,* such as a proposal to hold a benefit, is a motion used to introduce business. The name is misleading since it is really of lower rank than any of the other three types of motions (the others must be decided first).

General Robert's rules of order recommend that those responsible for meeting conduct under the rules of parliamentary law use certain standard motions, including the following:

1. To *adjourn*
2. To *fix the time to adjourn*
3. To *amend* (to amend something such as the **bylaws**; see **amendment**)
4. To *amend an amendment*
5. To *amend the rules*
6. To *appeal* (to appeal to the chair about something relating to meeting decorum or to other matters)
7. To *call to order* (to call a member to order)
8. To *close debate* (to end discussion of a proposal)
9. To *commit* or *refer* (to assign a task to a person or committee)
10. To *extend the limits of debate* (to allow more time or more subjects to be debated)
11. To *lay on the table* (to table a particular topic or proposal)
12. To *limit debate* (to restrict the time or number of topics allowed)
13. To *object to consideration of a question* (to object to or discourage a discussion believed to be contentious or unprofitable)
14. To call for *orders of the day* (to force a digressing group to return to its scheduled program)
15. To *postpone to a certain time* (to postpone consideration of a subject until another specified time)
16. To *postpone indefinitely* (to postpone consideration of a subject without setting a future time)
17. To call for the *previous question* (to bring debate on a current motion to a close and order an immediate vote on the motion)
18. To *read a paper* (to have something read before voting on it)
19. To *reconsider a question* (to bring back a previously decided motion for further discussion)

20. To *rescind* (to annul a previous action, when it is too late to use the motion to reconsider)
21. To create a *special order* (to suspend all rules that would interfere with considering a question at a specified time)
22. To *suspend the rules* (to do away with the rules temporarily for some reason when it is not in conflict with the constitution or bylaws to do so)
23. To *take from the table* (to bring back a tabled motion for action)
24. To *take up a question out of order* (to consider a topic immediately rather than wait until the time or order in which it is scheduled to be considered)
25. To *withdraw a motion* (to remove a motion from consideration before a vote on it is taken)

In addition to explaining the use of motions, rules-of-order guides offer other information about meeting conduct, such as the steps in holding a first meeting, duties of officers and committees, rules of debate, and voting procedure.

participating preferred stock See **stock**.

partnership A legal association of two or more persons who function as co-owners of a business, with each paying for a portion of the expenses and sharing in a portion of the profit or loss according to the terms specified in the partnership **contract**. The firm's **net worth** is represented by a **capital** account for each partner in an amount equal to the interest of each. In many states, the organization and operation of partnerships are governed by the Uniform Partnership Law and the Uniform Limited Partnership Law.

Partnerships may be classified as general and limited partnerships.

1. In a *general partnership,* the owners, who are all "general partners," are each personally responsible for the debts of the firm, regardless of the amount of a partner's investment. Together, they are responsible for the daily management and operation of the business. Profit or loss is shared equally or according to the proportions specified in the partnership **agreement.**
2. In a *limited partnership,* the "limited partners" are not involved in daily operations and only contribute capital to the business. A limited partner is thus primarily an investor who receives a certain share of the profits but is not liable beyond the limits of his or her capital contribution. A limited partnership, therefore, must have one or more "general partners" to handle the daily management and operation of the firm. Compare with **limited liability company.**

The terms *silent partner* and *limited partner* are sometimes used interchangeably since both refer to owners who do not participate in the management of the business. But *silent partner* also refers to someone who is unknown to the public as a partner. In addition, a silent partner who is not a limited partner is responsible for the debts of the business the same as a general partner.

Partnerships may be dissolved by the withdrawal or death of a partner, by **bankruptcy,** or by court decree.

Compare with **corporation** and **proprietorship.**

par value See **face value.**

par-value stock See **stock.**

Pascal See **language.**

patent An exclusive right granted by the federal government to the creator of an invention to make, use, and sell the invention for a set period. To be granted a patent, an inventor must submit an application, usually prepared by a patent attorney, to the U.S. Patent and Trademark Office in Washington, D.C. According to this office, an inventor may be any person who invents or discovers any new and useful process (method), machine, manufactured article, or chemical composition or any new and useful improvements thereof.

payroll A list of the employees to which a business pays wages or salaries, along with the periodic amounts due to each; any benefits, such as voluntary **pension** contributions or insurance premiums; and the amounts withheld for federal income tax and social security (FICA). The paycheck that is given to each employee is in a net amount after deducting benefits and taxes.

Large **computer**-operated payroll systems include a **database** of employee names and associated **data,** which represents an electronic version of the conventional *payroll journal,* with gross and net computation capability and a check-writing device for preparation of paychecks and file copies.

payroll journal See **payroll.**

PBX telephone system See **telephone system.**

pecuniary damages See **damages.**

pension An employee retirement program (see **retirement plan**) designed to provide regular income after retirement; a sum of money paid regularly to a retired employee based on contributions made from the individual's earnings during his or her term of employment. The employee must meet certain age and service requirements to qualify for a pension.

Organizations that offer pensions set up a fund into which the contributions deducted from an employee's paycheck are deposited. The organization then invests the funds in **stocks** and **bonds** to expand the base of the contributions.

A pension fund may be set up by a **corporation,** labor union, governmental body, or any other type of organization.

P/E ratio See **price-earnings ratio**.

performance bond See **bonding**.

periodic tenancy See **lease**.

peripheral A device, such as a printer or scanner, that is attached externally to the **central processing unit (CPU)** of a **computer**. In general, a computer can be operated without a peripheral, but its addition expands the capability of the system. For example, a user can operate a computer without a **modem,** but if one is added, the user can join a **network** and communicate with other users across the globe.

permanent injunction See **injunction**.

perpetual inventory See **inventory**.

personal computer See **computer**.

personal property Also called *personalty;* movable items, as opposed to immovable **real property** and the things attached to it. Personal property includes tangible items, such as a vehicle or furniture, and intangible items, such as **stocks** or **bonds**.

personalty See **personal property**.

petty cash Also called *imprest fund;* a small amount of money (*petty cash fund*), such as $100, kept in an office for incidental expenses, such as postage stamps or taxi fare. A *petty cash voucher* (see **voucher**) is filled out each time that a payment from the fund is requested. Periodically, as the amount in the fund is used up, a check is drawn and cashed to replenish the fund.

photocopier See **printing**.

photocopying See **xerography**.

pica See **point**.

piggybacking See **telephone system**.

plat A map that shows the location of property in a town or county and depicts the division of a tract of land into actual or planned features, such as blocks, lots, and streets. The record showing owners of **real property** is called the *plat book*. Plat descriptions are used in real estate instruments, such as **deeds.**

Example: Lot Six (6), Block Four (4), Sunset Subdivision, as recorded in Volume 21 of Plats, Page 101, records of _____ County, State of _____.

plat book See **plat.**

plate In **printing,** a sheet of paper, metal, or plastic that is used as a master printing surface; a full-page illustration; a reproduction of a lithograph, woodcut, or engraving. Printing processes involve impressions that are made from some such type of master surface, or plate, also known as an offset master. The plate may consist of either text or **graphics** or both.

pledge An item of **personal property,** such as **stocks** or **bonds,** offered as **collateral** security to guarantee the payment of a debt; goods delivered by a debtor to a creditor until the debt is paid; the act of turning over property to the lender.

The person who delivers his or her property to a lender is the *pledgor;* the one who holds the borrower's property as security until the debt is paid is the *pledgee*. **Title** to an item that is pledged remains with the pledgor.

point 1. In **stocks,** a measure in which 1 point equals $1.

Example: An increase of 10 points in a stock is an increase of $10 a share; a decrease of 5 points is a decrease of $5 a share.

2. In **bonds,** a measure of the percentage change in **face value** in which 1 point equals a 1 percent increase or decrease.

Example: If a bond has a $5,000 face value, a 2 percent, or 2 point, increase is an increase of $100 in the face value; a 1 percent, or 1 point, decrease is a decrease of $50 in the face value.

3. In real estate, the fee charged by a lender that is equal to 1 percent of the **principal.**

Example: On a $50,000 **mortgage,** a charge of 2 points is $1,000; on a $100,000 mortgage, a charge of 3 points is $3,000.

4. In **printing,** typesetting, **desktop publishing,** and **word processing,** a measure of the size of type (see **typeface**) and the space between lines of type (*leading*): 1 inch = 72 points.

Example: A type size of 12 points is equal to 1/6 inch; a type size of 6 points is equal to 1/12 inch.

Another common measurement is the *pica,* which is equal to 12 points: 1 inch = 72 points = 6 picas.

Example: A type size of 12 points is equal to 1/6 inch or 1 pica; a type size of 6 points is equal to 1/12 inch or 1/2 pica.

polling The automatic checking of communication terminals to determine which is ready to receive or send **data.**

Example: Polling can be used in fax transmission (see **facsimile**) to retrieve documents stored in other remote fax machines or to transmit a document to another machine when it calls.

portable mortgage See **mortgage.**

portfolio The collection of **stocks, bonds,** and other investments held by an individual or **corporation.** A portfolio usually consists of a variety of investments designed to reduce or spread **risk** through diversification.

power of attorney A written instrument in which a **principal** appoints another party as his or her agent (see **agency**) to perform certain acts and defines the party's authority in dealing with third parties. A power of attorney may be general, with blanket authorization to act in all matters, or specific, pertaining to only one matter, such as handling a real estate transaction.

An *irrevocable power of attorney* is given when a principal wants an agent to act for him or her in the event of disability or death.

preferred stock See **stock**.

preliminary injunction See **injunction**.

premium The rate that an insurer charges an insured for insurance coverage; the consideration received by an insurer from an insured for assuming the liability or **risk** of the insured. Premium payments are frequently made in installments during the period of coverage.

The premium charged is based on the insurer's expectations of loss or risk and other costs of providing coverage, as well as the rate class in which the insured is placed. A *rate class* is a group of individuals or organizations that have similar characteristics and similar risk expectations.

press proof See **proof**.

press release See **news release**.

price-earnings ratio Also called *multiple* or *P/E;* in investments, the market price of a common **stock** divided by its earnings per share. The figure for earnings may be that of the previous year (*trailing P/E*) or the forecasted earnings for the next year (*forward P/E*).

Example: A stock selling for $30 a share with projected earnings of $3 has a forward P/E of 10. A stock selling for

$20 a share that earned $1 a share last year has a trailing P/E of 20.

Potential investors are interested in the P/E because of what it indicates about a company. For example, a high ratio (over 20) may indicate a young, fast-growing company that pays no **dividends,** whereas a low P/E may indicate a higher-**yield** stock in a more mature company that pays dividends.

price fixing Conspiring with other companies in the same business to fix the prices of **commodities** in **interstate commerce** by raising, depressing, stabilizing, or otherwise affecting them, thereby interfering with free competition and the freedom of trade. Price fixing is prohibited under the federal **antitrust laws.**

prime interest rate See **prime rate.**

prime rate Also called *prime interest rate;* the rate that banks charge their preferred customers. The prime rate is generally lower than the rates charged to other customers and may even be discounted below the prime rate to important customers.

The amount that customers must pay if they do not qualify for the prime rate depends on the lender. If the prime rate is 8 percent, for example, other borrowers may have to pay the prime rate plus 2, 3, or more points. Credit card companies commonly charge customers substantially more than the prime rate.

The prime interest rate is determined by market forces that affect a bank's cost of funds and the rates that borrowers are willing to pay. Generally, when a major bank raises or lowers its prime rate (see **central bank**), the other banks tend to follow that example.

principal 1. In general, one of the main parties in a transaction or **contract,** such as the lessor or lessee in a **lease** or the mortgagor or mortgagee in a **mortgage;** the person who retains an agent (see **agency**) or broker.

2. In finance, the main amount of money in a transaction, such as the sum of money borrowed to finance a business, excluding **interest;** the **face value** of an obligation, such as a **bond,** that must be paid at **maturity,** excluding interest. Periodic payments on indebtedness often include both interest and part of the principal.

See also **amortization; installment sale.**

printer See **printing.**

printing The process of preparing multiple copies of text or **graphics** material by photocopier, printing press, **computer** printer, or other means. The number of copies required and the level of quality desired determine which type of equipment is used.

Photocopier. Photocopiers are often used in offices as a fast and efficient way to make fewer than 100 duplicate copies of material when quality is not critical. Printing presses or high-quality computer printers, such as a laser printer, used in **desktop publishing** operations are preferred when more copies or higher-quality results are desired. Although some high-end photocopiers are capable of producing art-quality color copies in volume, most offices use less expensive, lower-volume, and lower-quality copying equipment.

Offset press. Some businesses purchase small offset presses to handle their printing needs in-house. Most companies, however, send material to an outside commercial printer that has large presses capable of handling jobs of all sizes in both color and black and white.

In offset printing, **camera-ready copy** (finished copy) is prepared and photographed, and an offset master, or **plate,** is made from the film copy (one plate for each color). The printing is done by indirect image transfer. This involves inking the impression on the plate and transferring it to a rubber cylinder, which in turn transfers the inked image to the paper.

Computer printer. Businesses that have a desktop publishing system or a computer system with a sophisticated **word processing** program may prepare material in-house and print it with a black-and-white or color printer connected to the computer. High-quality, high-volume printers may be linked to stand-alone systems, but often such printers are shared by other users in the company.

By the mid-1990s, seven main types of printing technology had evolved, with the associated devices all available by now in color: dot matrix; thermal, or liquid, ink-jet; solid ink-jet; thermal wax-transfer; dye-sublimation, or dye-thermal; laser; and **LED (light-emitting diode)** printers.

1. *Dot matrix printers* are older-technology, relatively slow-speed impact printers that create a low-quality image on paper when the printhead strikes a ribbon.
2. *Thermal,* or *liquid, ink-jet printers* are high-quality, relatively slow-speed printers that create an inked image on paper through a heat-vaporization process.
3. *Solid ink-jet printers* are more expensive and faster types of ink-jet printers that produce high-quality image transfer to paper by melting a solid block of ink.
4. *Thermal wax-transfer printers* are moderate-speed printers, with reasonably high-quality output in general usage and excellent quality in business graphics transparancies, producing images by using heat to fuse wax from film onto paper.
5. *Dye-sublimation,* or *dye-thermal, printers* are very expensive and slow printers that produce near-photographic quality copies by changing solid dyes on ribbons to gas, which then reverts to solid form on chemically coated paper.
6. *Laser printers* are relatively fast (in black and white), high-quality printers that create images by using a laser

to charge the drum (a sensitized device on which images are created), which then attracts a dry, powdered ink (toner) and transfers it to paper.
7. *LED printers,* similar to laser printers in speed, quality, and operation, are electrophotographic devices that use light-emitting diodes to charge the drum, which then attracts toner and transfers it to paper (see light-emitting diode [LED]).

Although most businesses use black-and-white printers, color sales are increasing as the technology improves and as the devices become more affordable for individual **workstations.**

private branch exchange (PBX) See **telephone system.**

private ledger See **ledger.**

privately held corporation See **corporation.**

private-purpose bond See **bond.**

procurement Acquiring materials, supplies, equipment, and other items needed to operate a business. Procurement may be handled by one person or an entire department, depending on the size and needs of the company.

producer price index (PPI) Formerly called *wholesale price index*; a measure of changes in wholesale prices that is released each month by the Bureau of Labor Statistics. To compute the index, the price changes of **commodities** are compared with those in a selected base year.

See also **consumer price index (CPI).**

product line A group of products, often related, that are promoted and sold together, such as outdoor recreational goods.

professional corporation See **corporation.**

profit See **gross profit; net income.**

profit and loss statement See **income statement.**

profit sharing An arrangement in which employees share in the profits of the business. In years when there are profits, employers may make annual contributions to each employee's **account** either in cash or in a deferred plan.

Usually, an employee receives funds from a profit-sharing plan at a certain age or upon retirement, disability, or resignation, at which time the money is taxable. Until then, the company invests the funds in **stocks** or **bonds** to maximize the benefits.

program See **software**.

program flowchart See **flowchart**.

programming The process of designing, writing, and testing a **computer** program containing instructions that tell a **microprocessor** what operations to perform. Programming involves a variety of steps, such as defining the problem, preparing a **flowchart,** using a programming language to make statements that can be converted to machine-readable **binary** language (see **assembler; language**), selecting control modes, and testing the results.

programming language See **language**.

prohibitory injunction See **injunction**.

promissory note See **note**.

proof In **printing,** a preliminary copy of a document used to check for and correct errors before a final version is printed. The two principal types of proofs in business are the page proof and the press proof.

1. *Page proofs* are copies of pages prepared by **computer** in **desktop publishing** or **word processing** or by some form of commercial typesetting. A computer printout or photocopy of the text of each page, often with a blank space where photographs will be inserted later, is given

to customers to read for typographical and other errors (see **proofreading**).

2. *Press proofs,* which are sometimes known by other names, such as *negative proofs, film proofs,* or *blueprints,* are copies of pages appearing exactly as they will be printed in multiple copies, with all text, **graphics,** and photographs included. These proofs are given to customers to check that page-proof errors have been corrected, that the final layout is correct, and that illustrations, captions, and other elements all appear in the right place.

proofreading Checking **proofs** for errors and omissions. To be certain that nothing is overlooked, a proof should be read against the original word for word, carefully examining all text, tables, equations, photographs, titles, running heads, and other material.

Proofreaders mark errors or omissions with standard symbols and abbreviations that printers and typesetters understand. An error should be crossed out in the line of type where it appears and the correction written in the left or right margin of that line.

The following table contains frequently used proofreading marks.

Proofreading Marks

Mark	Meaning	Example
ℊ	Delete.	computers℘
℘̃	Delete & close up.	compute̾rs
stet	Let it stand.	data ~~fields~~ er
no ¶	No paragraph; run in.	files.⁀Containers also
#	Add space.	wordprocessing

212 THE ENCYCLOPEDIC DICTIONARY OF BUSINESS TERMS

Mark	Meaning	Example
out, sc	Something missing; see copy.	Take a width ∧
sp. out	Spell out.	②boxes
⌒	Close up.	tel ecommunications
⊏	Move left.	⊏ the office
⊐	Move right.	⊐ the office
tr.	Transpose.	managaer
‖	Line up; align.	‖report the hours
¶	New paragraph.	account. Yet we
	Question to author.	1897
⦵?	Insert question mark.	Can we begin ∧
!	Insert exclamation mark.	No ∧
/=/	Insert hyphen.	co=owner
⌄/⌄	Insert quotation marks.	He said ∧ Let's begin. ∧
∧;	Insert semicolon.	finished therefore ∧
⌄:	Insert colon.	the following ∧
∧	Insert comma	pens, pencils ∧ and
⊙	Insert period.	at the end ∧
⌄'	Insert apostrophe.	the employees ∧ car
s	Change to s.	/oftware

STANDARD BUSINESS TERMS

Mark	Meaning	Example
Caps	Set in capital letters.	Resolved that
lc	Set in lowercase letters.	INTRODUCTION
bf	Set in boldface type.	Dictionary
ital.	Set in italic type.	A diskette is
s.c.	Set in small capital letters.	a.m. and p.m.
c. & s.c.	Set in capitals and small capitals.	style book
✓✓✓	Correct spacing.	u's є ¥ guide
⌐	Indent paragraph.	⌐To begin, we
rom.	Change to roman type.	programming
\2	Set as superscript.	X\2
/2\	Set as subscript.	X/2\
[/]	Insert brackets.	^1995^
(/)	Insert parentheses.	^1995^
1/M	one-em dash.	page—marked as

property dividend See **dividends**.

proposal A suggestion or plan presented as a means to encourage a particular action or decision. A proposal may be as informal and brief as a one-page letter or memo or as formal and detailed as a 100-page **report**. Funding organizations, such as a research institute or the government, usually require that a grant proposal or other proposal involving monetary support be prepared in a specific **format** or on forms supplied by the organization.

A semiformal or formal proposal, prepared in a report format, may have some or all of the following standard parts, usually presented in this order.

1. The *introduction* describes the proposer's background and expertise, including previous projects undertaken or grants received.
2. The *problem* section explains what the current problem is and how the proposer expects to deal with it.
3. The *objectives* section is a listing of the proposer's goals, including other projects also addressing the same problem and how the proposer plans to handle it differently and contribute to a long-range solution.
4. The *procedure* section describes the steps the proposer will take, special techniques to be used, and the staff and time required to undertake the project.
5. The *evaluation* section explains the proposer's methods for determining later if the project was successful.
6. The *personnel* section identifies everyone who will be involved in the project and gives a description of each person's assignment.
7. The *budget* section lists all expected income, including the funding being requested from the recipient of the proposal, and all expected expenses, including miscellaneous administrative costs.

8. The *addenda* section consists of all supporting material, such as a published article that reinforces the suggestion that the project is necessary.

proprietary lease See **lease.**

proprietorship Also called *sole proprietorship;* an unincorporated form of organization in which one person has sole ownership of the business. Income from the business is taxed directly to the owner, who is solely responsible for the firm's **liabilities.**

A proprietorship can be started without the formality required for incorporation, although the owner must find out whether licenses are required and which state and local taxes must be paid. The owner may raise **capital** by borrowing from banks or other organizations or individuals, using the money as well as regular income as he or she chooses.

A proprietorship form of organization has the advantages of simplicity and flexibility compared to an incorporated organization. However, it is an unstable form of business in that activity may be unexpectedly interrupted by the owner's illness or terminated by his or her death.

Compare with **corporation** and **partnership.**

pro rata See **FOREIGN EXPRESSIONS: pro rata.**

prosumer See **JARGON: prosumer.**

protocol 1. In general, standard procedure or behavior; the required form of ceremony and etiquette; correct conduct.

2. In **computer** and **telecommunications** use, a standard procedure followed in regulating the transmission of **data** between devices. The protocols affect a variety of steps from the coding of data to the speed of transmission.

Through the work of protocol emulators and converters, the protocols used by one device can be modified to those required by another device. A **modem,** for example, converts a computer's **digital** signals to the **analog** signals required for movement over the telephone lines.

Two common types of protocol are the communications and file-transfer protocols.

a. *Communications protocol* refers to the settings selected and the standard procedure followed in transmitting data error-free between remote devices in telecommunications.
b. *File-transfer protocol* refers to the settings selected and the standard procedure followed in transmitting programs and files error-free between remote computers using the telephone lines.

prototype An early model or example; the original type or form that is used as a model for further production; a preliminary model developed for study and testing or as a pattern before duplicates are produced in quantity for sale; archetype; standard example.

proxy Authorization to act for another, such as the authority given to a member of an organization to cast a vote for another absent member at a **meeting;** the person receiving the authorization to act for another.

An authorization to do something is usually provided in writing and includes an expiration date or specifies a particular date to which the authorization applies. A proxy may be in any form desired—letter, postcard, fill-in commercial printed form, or other—but must meet the requirements of the Securities and Exchange Commission (see **stock exchange**) and applicable state statutes in the case of a **stockholders'** meeting.

public corporation See **corporation**.

public domain 1. In real estate, land owned by a government instead of by an individual or **corporation.**

2. In **copyright** and **patent** protection, information available to anyone; the unprotected status of documents and other material that were not copyrighted or patented as required for protection or after the period of protection has expired. Once an item is in the public domain, it can no longer be brought under protection and is available for anyone's use.

Government documents, which are never copyrighted, are always in the public domain and therefore are freely available for reproduction. Works published before February 1989 without copyright notice and those not renewed upon copyright expiration are also in the public domain. But those published after February 1989 are automatically protected without notice for the life of the author plus 50 years.

public easement See **easement.**

publicly held corporation See **corporation.**

public-purpose bond See **bond.**

public service corporation See **corporation.**

public utility corporation See **corporation.**

punitive damages See **damages.**

purchase-money mortgage See **mortgage.**

put The right or option of a holder to sell a specified amount of **stock** within a specified time and at a fixed price, regardless of the current market price; the right or option of a holder to redeem **bonds** before their **maturity** date. Like **calls,** puts are traded in 100-share lots.

put option See **put.**

pyramiding A variety of schemes and strategies to increase profits through an ever-expanding base, including the following:

1. Using unrealized paper profits in investments to purchase additional investments

2. Using financial leverage to create a complex corporate structure, such as a series of companies in which each gains a controlling interest in the one under it
3. Using a strategy of selling distributorships along with company products to widen the marketing base
4. Using a strategy of increasing profits by primarily selling dealerships rather than useful products
5. Using a fraudulent scheme to compensate prior investors from an excessive or widening chain of new investors

Q

qualified endorsement See **endorsement**.

quality control A manufacturing process or system of inspecting and controlling production to ensure that products have acceptable and uniform quality. Repeat sales of many products, such as clothing or **computers,** are dependent on the public's belief that a particular manufacturer's products continue to meet consistently high standards.

quasi See **FOREIGN EXPRESSIONS: quasi**.

quasi contract See **contract**.

queue Also called *job queue* in relation to tasks or computer data; a waiting line of people or vehicles; a group of jobs waiting to be processed; a series or sequence of **data** or programs that are executed by a **computer** one after another. Tasks may be assigned a specific order in which they are processed. Some **software** programs, for example, allow users to give a job number to documents to designate the order in which they will be printed (see **printing**). The time lost to a waiting period between functions is called the *queue time*.

queue time See **queue**.

quit-claim deed See **deed**.

quorum See **meeting**.

quotation 1. In general business, a contractor's bid or a service provider's price estimate for a job or transaction.

2. In investments, the *bid and asked price,* which is the current price range stated as the highest bid and lowest offer for a security or commodity; the highest amount that a buyer is offering (*bid price*) and the lowest price that a seller will accept (*asked price*) after the last transaction and before the close of a trading day.

The difference between the bid and asked price is called the dealer's *spread*. Quotes are made based on round-lot trading (compare with **odd lot**), such as 100 shares of **stock.**

Example: A quote of 10 1/2 to 12 represents a buyer's bid of 10 1/2 per share to a seller (the highest price the buyer will pay), a seller's offer of 12 to a buyer (the lowest price the seller will accept), and a spread of 1 1/2.

qwerty keyboard A computer or typewriter keyboard with a traditional configuration or layout of keys. The name is taken from the first six keys on the upper left: *q, w, e, r, t,* and *y.*

Compare with **Dvorak keyboard.**

R

RAM See **memory**.

random-access memory (RAM) See **memory**.

random sample A small group of people or things selected randomly from a larger group (see **universe**), with each member or item in the group having an equal chance or probability of being selected. The process of selecting members or items in this way is called *random sampling*.

random sampling See **random sample**.

rate class See **premium**.

ratio An expression of a relation in number or degree between two similar things, such as the relation between a company's debt and its **equity;** the relation of two quantities or amounts calculated by dividing one by the other; a quotient of two quantities. A ratio is written numerically as a fraction (x/y) or with a colon ($x:y$), and it is stated as *x to y*.

A business may use ratio analysis, comparing items on financial statements, to make **credit** and investment decisions and to evaluate the financial condition of the company.

raw data Unprocessed, unsorted, and unrefined **data**. For example, a group of random notes collected to use in a business **report** are considered raw data before they are evaluated, organized, edited, and incorporated into the finished document.

read-only memory (ROM) See **memory**.

read-out The *soft-copy output* (see **JARGON: output**) of a **computer**, which is displayed on screen, as opposed to **hard-copy** *output*, which is printed on paper.

real estate closing See **closing**.

real property Land and its buildings, minerals, natural growth, and other attachments or improvements; land and anything natural or constructed that is affixed to it.

Compare with **personal property.**

real time 1. In general, normally occurring time.

2. In **data processing**, a rate of response or processing, such as **computer** processing, that equals the rate of **data** input (see **JARGON: input**); immediate processing of data. For example, when a bank card is inserted into an automated teller machine for an automated transaction, the processing of the request is immediate, or in real time.

record See **field.**

records management A system designed to analyze, control, store, retrieve, and dispose of all types of active and inactive **files** and records. Records management is necessary for businesses to cope with the massive amounts of information they generate each day and to ensure that they comply with regulatory, tax, and other laws.

To deal with burdensome storage-space requirements, many businesses convert inactive **hard-copy** material to **disk** storage or use a form of **micrographics** to store the material in a reduced size either permanently or until destruction of a record is authorized. Federal and state laws, as well as corporate needs and policy, determine how long a business must maintain a particular record before it may be destroyed.

The Association of Records Managers and Administrators in Prairie Village, Kansas, develops records-management standards and other guidelines for businesses that want to set up new records-management programs or reevaluate their existing programs.

recycling Reusing, reprocessing, or readapting discarded products and material, such as converting newspapers into blank sheets ready for a new print run (see **printing**). Businesses regularly dispose of a wide variety of material, including stationery, **file** folders, printed material, aluminum cans, plastic containers, mailing boxes, toner cartridges, printer ribbons, obsolete machines, and fluorescent lamps.

Many community leaders believe that businesses are responsible for a large portion of their waste-disposal problems and requirements and therefore that they should set up in-house recycling programs. This effort would involve placing appropriate items in separate collection bins and taking them to, or having them picked up by, a local recycling center for reprocessing.

Information on recycling is available from associations and magazines dedicated to the subject of waste disposal and from local recycling/waste-disposal organizations. Recycling guides commonly urge businesses to follow three basic rules based on a "3-R system."

1. *Reduce* the amount of material used by eliminating unnecessary and wasteful practices, such as making unnecessary duplicate file copies.
2. *Reuse* materials and products, such as saving and reusing mailing cartons and peanuts or other packing material.
3. *Recycle* what can no longer be used, such as sending empty toner cartridges back to manufacturers that request them.

redeemable bond See **bond**.

redeemable preferred stock See **stock**.

redemption The act of buying back or repurchasing; the repayment of a security or other debt before **maturity**. For example, redemption occurs at the time a government or **corporation** pays investors for the **bonds** that it issued to them. The price that issuers pay investors to buy back a security or debt is called the *redemption price*.

redemption price See **redemption; call.**

red ink See **JARGON: red ink.**

reference list See **back matter.**

registered agent See **resident agent.**

registered bond See **bearer bond.**

registered trademark See **trademark.**

registered office The office that a **corporation** maintains in a state other than the state in which it principally resides and is principally incorporated. A registered office, with a **resident agent,** is established to meet the statutory requirements of the other state and to serve **stockholders** and perform other services in that state.

repetitive-strain injury See **ergonomics.**

report A business document that provides information to the recipients. A report may be as brief as a letter or as long as a book, and it may be formal or informal. Depending on the length and amount of formality desired, a report may have some or all of these parts, usually in the order given here.

1. *Cover:* Although longer, book-length reports commonly have a separate cover, the title page usually serves as the cover for a short report.
2. *Flyleaf:* A blank page is sometimes inserted between the cover and the title page.
3. *Title page:* This page usually lists the report's title and subtitle (if any); the name, job title, and address of the person to whom the report is submitted; the name, job title, address, and telephone/fax number of the person submitting the report; and the date it is submitted.
4. *Transmittal letter:* The main purpose of a transmittal letter is to state briefly the purpose and scope of the report and the sources consulted and sometimes to ac-

knowledge special assistance or a special authorization or request for the report.

5. *Table of contents:* The contents page may list the page numbers of all major headings and subheadings or only the major headings.
6. *List of figures and tables:* Figure captions and table titles may be prepared like a table of contents, with page numbers, in one combined list or as two separate lists, one for figure captions and one for tables.
7. *Abstract:* A condensed summary (see **abstract**) of the report, prepared in paragraph or list style, should state the research results and conclusions.
8. *Introduction:* The body, or text, of a report begins with introductory remarks explaining what the report will cover.
9. *Background:* Many reports give the reader historical **data** or other background facts that are helpful in understanding the topic.
10. *Analysis:* The main part of the body focuses on an evaluation of the data collected for the report.
11. *Conclusions and recommendations:* The final part of the body, often brief, draws a conclusion from the analysis and, when appropriate, makes recommendations.
12. *Appendix:* Supporting material not given in the body but useful to the text discussion may be collected in one or more appendixes (see **back matter**).
13. *Notes:* A report may have bottom-of-page footnotes, end-of-chapter notes sections, a single concluding endnotes section, or some combination of footnotes and chapter notes or endnotes (see **back matter**).
14. *Glossary:* When numerous technical terms are used in a report, an alphabetical list of terms and definitions may follow the endnotes (see **back matter**).

15. *Bibliography or reference list:* The report may have an alphabetical list of sources consulted, cited, or recommended. Bibliographies and reference lists have the same data (see examples in **back matter**) but with the copyright date at the end of a bibliography entry and after the author's name in a reference-list entry.
16. *Index:* Long reports should have a general index or separate indexes, such as both a name and a subject index (see **back matter**).

Although standard reports on virtually any topic may follow the order and content stated here, special types of reports may differ. A **proposal** report, for example, may have additional or different parts, such as a discussion of anticipated personnel and the budget required for a proposed project; an **annual report** may resemble a full-color magazine more than a conventional black-and-white business report.

reprographics The process of making multiple copies, as in photocopying or **printing**; the photographic or electronic reproduction, reprinting, or photocopying of text and **graphics** material.

rescission The act of rescinding, annulling, or canceling a **contract** and restoring the parties to their respective positions before entering into the contract. The contracting parties may mutually decide to rescind their contract before beginning to perform their duties under it, or a court of equity may issue a decree (see **judgment**) that rescinds it. But neither of the contracting parties has the unilateral right to end the contract, and a party who has violated its terms may not seek rescission.

research The process of investigating something or inquiring into a particular matter. Research of printed material may be conducted manually, by studying books and other material in a library, or electronically, by retrieving information through a **network** (see **service provider; Internet; database**).

Sources consulted in research may be documented in footnotes, chapter notes sections, or endnotes (see **back matter**).

resident agent Also called *registered agent;* an agent of a **corporation** that only nominally resides in a particular state where it, therefore, must have an agent who is a resident to meet certain state requirements and to perform certain duties in that state. Statutes may require that a foreign corporation or a company incorporated in the state but primarily residing elsewhere must maintain an office in the state (see **registered office**). An agent who lives in that state is then retained by the corporation to provide whatever services are required there.

resolution See **minutes**.

restraining order See **injunction**.

restrictive covenant See **covenant**.

restrictive endorsement See **endorsement**.

retail The sale of goods and services directly to consumers. Retailing may be handled on-site in a store or by way of a vending machine; it may be handled off-site through a **mail-order** business or a television or electronic shopping service; or it may be handled door-to-door in the consumers' home or place of business.

Compare with **wholesale**.

retirement plan A plan or arrangement made by an employer for an employee or by a self-employed individual to provide income after retirement. Usually, the income is not taxable until the employee or self-employed person retires and begins to receive payments. Until then, the employer receives a tax deduction on the contributions it makes to an employee's retirement account.

Examples of common retirement plans are the *individual retirement account (IRA)* and the *Keogh plan* for the self-employed. The Keogh plan is similar to an IRA, except that contributions may be much higher. Companies may also have their own corporate **pension** programs.

revenue bond See **bond**

reverse-annuity mortgage See **mortgage.**

reverse-equity mortgage See **mortgage.**

reverse mortgage See **mortgage.**

revolving account A charge **account** or a form of **credit** in which the amount of credit available is repeatedly renewed up to a specified amount (*credit line*) each time a periodic repayment is made. Most charge accounts, for example, allow holders to pay a minimum monthly amount that reduces the **principal** owed, thereby making the amount of principal paid once again available for use by the holder.

revolving credit See **revolving account.**

rider See **endorsement.**

ring topology See **local area network (LAN).**

risk 1. In general, the danger or possibility of loss, such as the risk to investors that certain securities they hold may decline in value if economic conditions or other factors change.

2. In insurance, the uncertainty that underwriters (see **underwriting**) assume in providing coverage; a term used in reference to an insured person or organization or to a peril, such as fire.

To determine how much to charge for a policy, insurers analyze the risk associated with a particular type of coverage (*risk classification*). Various factors, such as age and type of business activity, are considered in determining the degree of risk and in controlling or managing the element of risk.

risk capital See **capital.**

risk classification See **risk.**

Robert's Rules of Order See **parliamentary procedure.**

Robinson-Patman Act See **antitrust laws.**

rollback See **JARGON: rollback**.
rollover See **JARGON: rollover**.
rollover mortgage See **mortgage**.
ROM See **memory**.
round lot See **odd lot**.
routine See **diagnostic routine**.
rules of order See **bylaws**.

S

sale and leaseback See **lease.**

sample 1. In general, a specimen, example, or segment of a group, body, or collection; an item that is representative of a class or group of items, such as a sample piece of classic laid stationery.

2. In statistics, a selection of representative elements or group of items from a larger group or population (see **universe**) used to study or estimate the characteristics of the larger group. Analyzing the subset to gain information about the entire collection is known as *statistical inference.*

In *systematic sampling,* the first item is selected randomly, and thereafter, individual items are chosen at specified intervals, such as every tenth item. This type of sampling differs from *random sampling* (see **random sample**), in which every item has an equal chance of being chosen.

sans serif type See **typeface.**

satellite office See **telecommunications.**

savings bond See **bond.**

second mortgage See **mortgage.**

secured loan A loan that is backed by the borrower's **pledge** of **assets** or other **collateral.** In the event of **default,** the lender can then recover the balance due by selling the borrower's pledged assets.

Compare with **unsecured loan.**

Securities and Exchange Commission (SEC) See **stock exchange.**

seller-financed mortgage See **mortgage.**

seminar See **conference**.

serial bond See **bond**.

series bond See **bond**.

serif type See **typeface**.

service mark See **trademark**.

service of process See **summons**.

service provider A company, such as MCI Mail or CompuServe, that offers **Internet** or other **computer** services for third parties.

session See **adjourned meeting**.

sexual harassment See **discrimination**.

share See **stock**.

shareholder See **stockholder**.

shareowner See **stockholder**.

sheriff's deed See **deed**.

Sherman Act See **antitrust laws**.

short sale The sale of securities, such as **stocks,** or **futures** contracts that a seller does not own but intends to purchase after the sale. When a seller already owns the securities or **commodities,** the transaction is called a *long sale*. Sellers who sell short expect that market prices will decline and therefore that the securities or commodities can be bought for less than the sale price.

Example: An investor sells 100 shares of a company **stock** short at $60, and his broker loans him 100 shares and delivers them to the purchaser. When the company stock declines to $50, the investor buys 100 shares and repays the broker for the loan while making a profit of $10 a share ($60 - $50).

sight draft See **bank draft**.

silent partner See **partnership**.

silicon chip See **chip; integrated circuit.**

simple interest See **interest.**

sine die See **FOREIGN EXPRESSIONS: sine die.**

sinking-fund bond See **bond.**

SI system See **metric system.**

slander Spoken remarks about someone, made to a third party, that tend to damage the subject's reputation (*defamation*). Slander may be slander per se or slander per quod.

1. In *slander per se,* the meaning is apparent from the statement itself.
2. In *slander per quod,* the meaning becomes known only from outside, or extrinsic, facts.

slander per quod See **slander.**

slander per se See **slander.**

smart card See **JARGON: smart card.**

soft copy See **read-out;** compare with **hard copy.**

software The **computer** programs, written in a machine-readable **language,** that control the operations of **hardware** or that enable users to perform certain tasks on the computer, such as write a letter. The two principal categories of software are systems and applications programs.

1. *Systems software,* which controls the computer system, or hardware, includes the **operating system;** various *utilities,* such as **backup** and **file** compression; and *compilers* and **assemblers,** which convert human instructions into machine-readable language. Systems software, which is permanently stored in the computer's **memory,** is broadly referred to as *firmware.*
2. *Applications software,* which enables users to accomplish a particular task, includes programs such as **word processing, spreadsheet** and **accounting, database**

management (see **database management system**), **network** communications, page layout (see **desktop publishing**), **graphics, programming,** and game playing (see **artificial intelligence**). Applications software that is designed for a group of users, such as a meeting-scheduler program, is known as *groupware*.

Systems software must be installed in a computer before an applications program can be run.

sole proprietorship See **proprietorship.**

solid ink-jet printer See **printing.**

sound bite See **JARGON: sound bite.**

special endorsement See **endorsement.**

S&P 500 Index See **stock index.**

spin control See **JARGON: spin control.**

split Also called *split up;* in finance, a division of a certain number of shares of **stock** into a greater number while keeping the overall dollar amount the same; an increase in the number of a **corporation's** outstanding shares without a change in the amount of shareholder **equity.** Since each share of a particular stock costs less after a stock split, corporations believe that more individuals will then be able to afford an investment in that stock.

Example: If a company has stock selling at $40 a share, a split of "2 for 1" would double the number of shares while cutting the price per share in half. Therefore, an investor with 100 shares at $40 a share ($4,000) would have 200 shares after the split at $20 a share ($4,000), with the overall amount of $4,000 remaining the same before and after the split.

split up See **split.**

spot market See **commodities.**

spread See **quotation.**

spreadsheet An **accounting**-style worksheet; a **software** program, with an on-screen worksheet consisting of a matrix and rows and columns, that enables users to perform calculations on the **data** they enter. A typical spreadsheet has six main components (see example).

1. *Columns and rows,* which are arranged on screen in a grid
2. *Cells,* which are the points where a vertical column, such as *A* in the example, and a horizontal row, such as *3,* intersect
3. *Cell address,* which is any column letter and row number, such as *B7,* that a computer can identify
4. *Cell reference,* which is the cell address that is highlighted by the cursor block and shows where the user is working in the spreadsheet, such as in *C4:2000,* if the area highlighted is the value *2000* in column *C,* row *4*
5. *Labels,* which are the descriptive headings above the row and column entries, such as *YRS OF SERVICE*
6. *Values,* which are the amounts entered in the columns and rows, such as *2330*

Example: Spreadsheet Layout

	A	B	C
1	NAME	YRS OF SERVICE	CUR MO SALARY
2			
3	J WATTS	12	2330
4	M KING	8	2000

Standard & Poor's 500 (S&P 500) Index See **stock index**.

standing rules See **bylaws**.

star topology See **local area network (LAN)**.

statement of revenue and expenditures See **income statement**.

statistical inference See **parameter; sample**.

statute of frauds A state statute (see **statutory law**) requiring that certain **contracts** to be enforceable must be in writing and signed by the party who is bound by the contract. Examples are contracts for the sale of land or an interest in it, those to be performed after a year of their making, those to answer to a creditor for the debt of another, and those in consideration of marriage. Although all states have such statutes, they may vary from one state to another.

statute of limitations A state statute (see **statutory law**) limiting the time within which one party may bring legal action against another and within which certain crimes may be prosecuted. The time varies depending on the kind of action. The purpose of such limitations is to prevent someone from waiting an unreasonable time to bring action. The concept also recognizes that after a certain period, witnesses and necessary evidence may no longer be available.

statutory deed See **deed**.

statutory law The law created by legislative action. Governmental bodies, such as the U.S. Congress or state legislatures, have either express or implied authority in their constitutions to enact certain laws (*statutes*). These enacted laws supplement and supersede **common law**. Examples are the **statute of frauds** and the **statute of limitations**.

step-up lease See **lease**.

stock In finance, a share of ownership in a **corporation** that entitles the holder to **dividends** and certain rights, such as voting; the aggregate ownership interest in a **corporation;** an investment of one or more shares in a corporation represented by a certificate of ownership (*stock certificate*); the total number of shares of a **stockholder.**

Stock is divided into equal units that are issued (sold) to those who want to invest in the issuing corporation. Each stockholder's interest and record of stock transfers is maintained in the corporation's stock **ledger**.

The two main classes of ownership are common and preferred stock.

1. *Common stock* refers to units of ownership sold by a corporation that usually give stockholders control of management through voting rights; they also provide the right to share in dividends and **assets** that are distributed in cases of **liquidation,** but only after the claims of holders of preferred stock have been satisfied. Common stock is generally more speculative than preferred stock but also tends to offer higher returns.

2. *Preferred stock* refers to units of ownership sold by a corporation that provide for investors a greater degree of security than common stock offers. Preferred stockholders receive their share of the profits and any share of assets distributed at liquidation ahead of common stockholders. Most preferred stock, however, does not provide voting rights.

Different types of preferred stock may be offered, such as participating or nonparticipating, cumulative or noncumulative; redeemable (callable); and convertible preferred stock.

1. *Participating preferred stock* pays a specified dividend as well as additional distributions of earnings in certain cases. The most common of the two types, however, is the *nonparticipating preferred stock,* which pays only

the stipulated dividend regardless of any additional amount that might be paid to common stockholders.

2. *Cumulative preferred stock* allows preferred stockholders priority over common stockholders in receiving any accumulated dividends that were not paid in unprofitable years but were instead held over for payment in a more profitable year. Unpaid dividends do not accumulate with *noncumulative preferred stock* and need not be paid later by the corporation.

3. *Redeemable (callable) preferred stock* gives the corporation the right to **call** in the stockholders' shares and buy them back for cash. Usually, the redemption price is above the stated or **face value** (*par value*) and includes unpaid dividends. *Par-value stock* has an assigned amount, such as $1 per share, used by companies only for **accounting** purposes but not as indicative of market price. Since par value is therefore meaningless to investors, some companies issue *no-par stock,* which does not have an assigned value on the stock certificate.

4. *Convertible preferred stock* may be converted into common stock by the stockholder but not into **bonds,** unless approved by the corporation.

stock average See **stock index.**

stock certificate See **stock.**

stock dividend See **dividend.**

stock exchange An organized market where securities are bought and sold. Trading is conducted by members who act as brokers buying and selling on commission for customers or as dealers buying and selling for their own **accounts** (*floor traders*). The New York Stock Exchange allows trading only in securities listed by it; other exchanges permit trading in unlisted securities as well.

Each exchange has its own rules and regulations concerning membership and trading. Some exchanges report indexes, such as the New York Stock Exchange Composite Index (see **stock index**), that measure stock performance and market trends.

All national stock exchanges and associations are under the supervision of the **Securities and Exchange Commission (SEC)**, a federal agency that regulates and supervises the sale of securities to prevent unfair practices and to protect investors who use the exchanges. **Commodities** exchanges are regulated by the Commodity Futures Trading Commission (CFTC). Like the SEC, the CFTC is a regulatory federal agency, and its primary responsibility is to oversee commodities futures trading. Securities that are not traded on an exchange are traded in an **over-the-counter (OTC) market,** where transactions are handled by telephone and **computer,** using a broker-dealer **network,** rather than on an exchange floor.

The two main exchanges in the United States are the New York Stock Exchange and the American Stock Exchange.

1. The *New York Stock Exchange (NYSE),* located in New York City, is the oldest and largest exchange, with more than 80 percent of all U.S. securities traded on it, including those of very large **corporations.** It is sometimes referred to as the *Big Board* or the *Exchange*.
2. The *American Stock Exchange (AMEX),* also located in New York City, has the second largest volume in the United States, with trading consisting of many **stocks** and **bonds** of small and medium-size companies and many foreign companies, as well as some over-the-counter stocks. It is sometimes referred to as the *Curb,* a reminder of its former name, the Curb Exchange, until 1921.

Smaller U.S. exchanges include the Pacific Stock Exchange (PSE) in Los Angeles, Boston Stock Exchange (BSE), Cincinnati Stock Exchange (CSE), Chicago Stock Exchange (CHX), and Philadelphia Stock Exchange (PHLX).

stockholder Also called *shareholder* and *shareowner;* an individual or company that owns (holds) at least one share of **stock** of a **corporation** as represented by a stock certificate or record of shares held by the owner's broker. An owner may be classified as a minority or majority stockholder.

1. A *minority stockholder* is an owner or one of a group of owners that, together, holds less than 50 percent of the voting shares.
2. A *majority stockholder* is an owner or one of a group of owners that, together, holds more than 50 percent of the voting shares.

State laws, corporate charters, and corporate **bylaws** give stockholders various rights and powers that they may exercise at stockholders' **meetings.** Usually, the consent of all or a majority of stockholders is needed to remove directors, merge with another company, sell or lease **assets,** and dissolve the corporation or liquidate its assets (see **liquidation**).

stockholders' equity See **equity.**

stock index A measure of changes in the value of a security that reflects market trends. Both indexes and averages indicate the value change in representative groups of **stocks.** Broadly, both terms are used to mean "market indicator." Strictly, they differ in that a *stock average* is an arithmetic *mean,* whereas a *stock index* refers to an average expressed in relation to an established base market value.

The principal U.S. indexes and averages are the Dow Jones Industrial Average, NYSE Composite Index, AMEX Market

Value Index, NASDAQ Composite Index, S&P 500 Index, Value Line Composite Index, and Wilshire 5000 Equity Index.

1. The *Dow Jones Industrial Average* ("the Dow") reports price movements in 30 of the largest blue-chip **stocks** traded on the New York Stock Exchange.
2. The *NYSE Composite Index* reports the value change and price movements of all New York Stock Exchange–listed common stocks in four categories: industrials, transportation, utilities, and finance companies.
3. The *AMEX Market Value Index* reports the performance of all common stocks listed on the American Stock Exchange.
4. The *NASDAQ Composite Index* reports the price movements of all over-the-counter stocks listed on the NASDAQ system, a computerized subscription service. The acronym *NASDAQ* refers to the automated quotation system owned and operated by the National Association of Securities Dealers.
5. The *S&P 500 Index* reports the performance of 500 widely held common stocks, known as the Standard & Poor's 500, representing about 80 percent of the value of all issues traded on the New York Stock Exchange.
6. The *Value Line Composite Index* reports the performance of about 1,700 stocks, tracked by the Value Line Investment Survey, that are traded on the New York Stock Exchange and the American Stock Exchange or are traded over the counter (see **over-the-counter [OTC] market**).
7. The *Wilshire 5000 Equity Index* reports price movements of about 5,000 stocks listed on the New York Stock Exchange and American Stock Exchange or traded over the counter.

Other countries also have indexes and averages to measure stock performance and price movements, such as the *Tokyo Stock Price Index (TOPIX)* and the *Nikkei Stock Average,* which is the Dow Jones Industrial Average of the Tokyo market.

stock ledger See **stock.**

stock yield See **yield.**

straight loan A term loan or term **mortgage;** a loan for a specific term, such as three to five years, and usually with a fixed **interest** rate, in which the interest is paid during the term of the loan and the full **principal** amount is due at **maturity,** unless the **contract** is renewed for an additional term. When the loan is due, the borrower must pay it off, refinance it for another term with the present lender, or secure a new loan from another lender so that the current loan can be paid off.

style guide See **back matter; copyedit.**

subchapter S corporation See **corporation.**

sublease See **lease.**

subpoena In Latin, a *subpoena ad testificandum;* a writ or order commanding someone to appear at a judicial proceeding to testify. When the person is required to bring certain objects or documents, the order is called a *subpoena duces tecum.* If the subject of a subpoena ignores the order without reasonable cause, he or she may be held in contempt of court.

subpoena ad testificandum See **subpoena.**

subpoena duces tecum See **subpoena.**

subprogram See **subroutine.**

subroutine Also called *subprogram;* in **computer** use, a small program or routine that is part of a larger program or routine; a set of instructions or sequence of **programming** statements within a longer program. A subroutine pertains to a specific task, such as saving a **file** on **disk,** that will be executed (see

execution) when the main program calls for it. After the task has been completed, the main program resumes.

subsidiary See **corporation**.

subsidiary journal See **journal**.

subsidiary ledger See **ledger**.

summons A legal notice, order, or mandate that requires a defendant to appear in court to answer charges (a **complaint**) brought against him or her. The delivery or communication of the summons to the defendant is called *service of process*.

Compare with **subpoena**.

suretyship See **guarantee**.

syndicate An association of individuals or companies that together promote a common interest, undertake a **joint venture**, or transact specific business that one person or company alone would be unable or unwilling to handle or finance. Investment bankers and **stockholders**, for example, may form a syndicate to market securities.

synergism See UNUSUAL WORDS: synergism.

systematic sampling See **sample**.

Système International See **metric system**.

systems analysis The study of an existing system in order to create a better system for a particular purpose; the study of a problem, process, procedure, or technique to decide the best way to reach a goal or accomplish something desired. When **computer** systems are presently used or desired to achieve an end, the study includes the design, cost, and modification or implementation of the appropriate **software** and **hardware**.

systems flowchart See **flowchart**.

systems software See **software**.

T

tangible property See **abandonment**.

telecommunication(s) Long-distance communication of **data,** voice (see **voice messaging**), or other types of information by electronic transmission, usually over the telephone lines, as in the transmission of an **electronic mail (E-mail)** or **facsimile** (fax) message.

See also **computer; Internet; modem; network; telecommuting; teleconference; telephone system.**

telecommuting Working at home while maintaining a connection to one's business office with a **computer** and a **modem.** Certain types of work, such as field sales, that do not require a regular on-site presence provide the opportunity for employees to have the convenience of working at home and for employers to eliminate or reduce the **overhead** costs of maintaining a full-time in-house office.

Although telecommuting is an increasingly common practice in some types of work, it is not suitable for everyone. For example, the practice is unsuitable for employees who do not like a solitary existence or who have difficulty imposing self-discipline in an unsupervised atmosphere.

teleconference A **conference** in which the attendees are in different locations and exchange information with an audio, video, or **computer** connection. Teleconference systems vary in size and type. A small company, for example, may have two telephones with speakerphones, whereas a large organization may have a conference hall fully equipped with its own video broadcast equipment.

Three broad types of teleconference are the audio, video, and computer teleconferences.

1. An *audioconference* is a teleconference conducted by voice over the telephone lines, as in a long-distance conference call arrangement connecting two or more people. When several individuals in an office participate, speakerphones with a combination microphone and loudspeaker device may be used so that everyone can hear and be heard by everyone else.
2. A *videoconference* is a teleconference in which participants in different locations have both a visual and an audio link, using a picturephone (telephones with a loudspeaker and small televisionlike screen), closed-circuit television (broadcast limited to a small number of receivers linked by cable), or larger video-based system (wide-scale broadcasting to different studios in remote locations connected by broad-based link or satellite).
3. A *computer document conference* is a teleconference in which computers are connected on a **network** allowing participants to work simultaneously on the same document on screen.

Businesses may have custom-designed systems that combine useful features of the different types of teleconferences. Participants may, for example, add a telephone, speakerphone, or picturephone connection to their computer connection to combine an audio or video feature with the computer conferencing capability. A technology called *Cu See-Me* also permits computer users on the **Internet** to see and hear each other by using a local camera-and-sound card.

A remote-participation **meeting** is often selected for the convenience of the participants or as a way to save travel time and expenses associated with conventional meetings. However, the equipment rental or purchase costs in teleconferencing and the availability of facilities are also important factors that must be considered in selecting one type of meeting over another.

telephone system A **digital** or **analog** communications system designed for multiple users or exchanges in an office or throughout a company. Although most systems provide for conventional desktop telephones, *computer-telephony integration,* in which a handset and speakerphone are combined with a **computer,** began to create more interest in the latter half of the 1990s.

Most businesses have some type of in-house telephone system, but an alternative offered by telephone companies is *Centrex.* With this system, a local telephone company provides lines and exchange services for businesses from its own central switch. Centrex is most suitable for companies that have at least 50 extensions.

The five principal in-house telephone systems, some known primarily by their abbreviated form, are the two-line, KSU (key service unit)-less, key, PBX (private branch exchange), and hybrid systems.

1. A *two-line system,* designed for very small businesses, provides a regular telephone with two buttons, one for each line, that is plugged into the wall the same as a conventional single-line telephone.
2. A *KSU-less system,* designed for small businesses with up to five people, has no central apparatus, connects the individual telephones by wiring them together, and includes the same features that would be available on a single telephone.
3. A *key system,* designed for small or medium-size businesses with up to 100 people, has a central apparatus linked to and controlling each specially designed desk

telephone, with each extension user able to answer calls without going through an attendant.

4. A *PBX system,* designed for large businesses of more than 100 people, provides for one or more full-time attendants who answer calls coming from the outside and then transfer them to the right extensions, which consist of regular desk telephones all connected to the central system.

5. A *hybrid system,* designed primarily for medium-size businesses with 30 to 100 people, is a cross between a key system and a PBX system and may have an attendant console but also allows extension users to answer their own calls.

Another option is the use of two or more of the above systems within the same company. With p*iggybacking,* for example, a company might have a key system in one department and a PBX system in the rest of the company.

temporary injunction See **injunction.**

tenancy at will See **lease.**

tenancy by the entirety A form of ownership of **real property** in which a husband and wife acquired **title** to the property jointly after marriage. Neither spouse may convey or **mortgage** his or her interest without the consent of the other. Upon the death of one spouse, his or her interest automatically passes to the other. Tenancy by the entirety is not permitted in all states, and in some cases, divorce effectively converts it to a tenancy in common.

Compare with **tenancy in common** and **joint tenancy.**

tenancy in common Undivided ownership in **real property** by two or more persons, each having a separate **title** and each with an equal or unequal share. A tenant in common may convey or **mortgage** his or her interest without the consent of the other owner. Upon the death of a co-owner, his or her interest passes to the deceased person's heirs, not to the other co-owner.

Compare with **tenancy by the entirety** and **joint tenancy**.

terminal See **workstation**.

term insurance Temporary life insurance coverage that is in effect only for a specified period, such as 5, 10, or 20 years. If death occurs during the stated period, a stipulated amount is paid to the **beneficiary**. But if death occurs after the term has expired, when the policy is no longer in force, nothing is paid. This type of plan differs from a *whole-life plan* under which the policy remains in force for the lifetime of the insured, even after the policy is fully paid.

No cash value is accumulated under term insurance as it is with a whole-life plan. With the latter, not only is cash value accumulated, but the current value can also be borrowed against.

testamentary trust See **trust**.

testimonium clause The closing clause of a written instrument or document (see example), such as a **deed** or **contract**. Not to be confused with the **attestation** clause, it is a declaration by parties signing the document that they are adding their signatures in testimony to the preceding part of the document.

Example: IN WITNESS WHEREOF, the parties to these presents have hereunto set their hands this day and year written above.

thermal ink-jet printer See **printing**.

thermal wax-transfer printer See **printing**.

throughput See **JARGON: throughput**.

time deposit A deposit, such as a certificate of deposit (CD), made to a bank or other financial institution, that the depositor can withdraw only at the end of a specified period or by giving advance notice of intent to withdraw funds.

time draft See **bank draft.**

time-sharing The sharing of time on a central minicomputer or mainframe **computer** by many individuals or companies that are connected to the central unit through a **network.** Businesses may use time-sharing services instead of their own computer facilities for large **data processing** jobs, such as **payroll** processing.

In a multiuser system, a computer assigns time to each user in sequence. Because of the equipment's high speed, however, users generally are unaware that others are using it simultaneously. Although delays may be experienced during peak hours, users tend to accept such inconveniences in return for cost savings and other advantages of using an outside service as opposed to maintaining large, expensive equipment in-house.

title 1. In general, the name given to describe or depict someone or something. The title *Dr.* or *Ambassador,* for example, describes the professional status of a person; the title *Robert's Rules of Order* is the name of a book about **parliamentary procedure.**

2. In **personal property** and **real property,** evidence of ownership. Thus the owner of a car receives a written title that verifies ownership. When a car is financed and the property itself is used as **collateral** for the loan, the property will have a **lien** imposed on it that is reflected on the title document.

Evidence of title to real estate may be indicated in one of four ways.

   a. An **abstract** of title
   b. A certificate of title
   c. Title insurance
   d. Registration with a register of land titles (less common)

A particular locality often prefers one of the procedures over the others.

When a seller of real estate is unable to provide the buyer with a clear title to the property being sold, this problem is known as a *cloud on the title*. The cloud may be an **encumbrance,** an outstanding legal claim or **judgment** against the property, or some other defect. Such a cloud usually may be removed by a quit-claim **deed** or by court action. The purpose of title insurance is to insure against any loss to the property owner resulting from defects in the title.

See also **marketable title.**

Tokyo Stock Price Index (TOPIX) See **stock index.**

topology See **local area network (LAN).**

tort A civil wrong or injury that arises from a breach of some duty, such as the duty of a business to warn against or remove dangerous obstacles in a parking lot or hallway that might cause injury if a customer fell over them. A lawsuit concerning a tort, therefore, relates to a duty that society *expects* others to fulfill, not one described in a written **contract.** Both individuals and **corporations** are liable for torts.

trademark A label, name, symbol, design, or other mark or device that identifies a product (*trademark*) or service (*service mark*) and distinguishes it from other products or services in the marketplace. It expands recognition of the owner not only through the use of the identifying mark on a product but through the use of it on the company's packaging and printed material and in its advertising.

In a state where a trademark is used, **common law** protection applies with the first use of a mark that includes the small raised initials ^{TM} for an unregistered trademark and ^{SM} for an unregistered service mark, placed immediately after the mark itself. After registration has been effected, the raised initial $^{®}$ is used. A business that wants to have stronger protection and expects to use its mark in **interstate commerce** is advised to register it with the U.S. Patent and Trademark Office in Washington, D.C.

Having a registered mark means that the owner may bring suit against others who unlawfully use the same mark. Because the process of registration and any subsequent lawsuit may be complicated, owners usually secure the assistance of an attorney in seeking trademark protection.

trailing P/E See **price-earnings ratio.**

translator See **assembler; language.**

trust 1. In general, a condition of custody or care; a **fiduciary** or guardianship position. Someone who manages another's financial affairs occupies a position of trust. State laws require that brokers and others deposit their customers' money in a separate trust **account,** such as a real estate firm's **escrow** account, rather than commingle customer funds with company funds.

2. In **personal property** and **real property,** the holding of property by one party for the benefit of another party. The property is called the *trust fund, trust estate, corpus,* or *res.* The party supplying the property is called the *trustor* (also *settler* or *donor*); the one who holds the property and administers the trust, the *trustee;* and the one for whose benefit the trust exists, the **beneficiary.**

A trust may be created for virtually any purpose that is not in violation of law or public policy.

Example a: A politician may create a *blind trust* in which he or she is not told where the money is invested. The public is then satisfied that no temptation will arise for the politician to give biased support to the place of investment.

Example b: Rather than prepare a **will,** many individuals set up a *living trust* (*intervivos trust*) while they are living so that, upon death, their estates usually can be disposed of without the need for settlement in court (*probate*). A trust created by will is called a *testamentary trust*.

trust account See **trust**.

trust deed See **deed**.

trust estate See **trust**.

trust fund See **trust**.

trust mortgage See **mortgage**.

turnaround time See **JARGON: turnaround time**.

turnover See **JARGON: turnover**.

two-line telephone system See **telephone system**.

typeface The design or style of a set of type, given a name such as *Times Roman*. Some designs are named after the person who invented them, such as *Baskerville*.

The two general categories of type are the serif and sans serif typefaces, and each individual typeface will fit primarily into one of the two categories, although some styles may appear to be a compromise between the two.

1. A s*erif typeface,* generally considered easier to read, has lines that finish off the top and bottom strokes of the letters. This line is set in a serif typeface called Times.
2. A s*ans serif typeface,* also called *Gothic*, has straighter and plainer letters that omit the top and bottom strokes. This line is set in a sans serif typeface called Helvetica.

See **point** for information about type sizes.

U

ultrafiche See **micrographics**.

ultralarge-scale integration (ULSI) See **integrated circuit**.

underwriting 1. In general, assuming financial responsibility for or guaranteeing against the failure of an act or venture.

2. In insurance, assuming liability for losses. Underwriters assume **risk** in return for a **premium**. They have a variety of functions, such as examining, accepting or rejecting insurance risks, and classifying policies.

3. In investments, guaranteeing the purchase of a (usually) new issue of securities and reselling it to the public either directly or through dealers. The *underwriting spread* is the difference between the cost of buying securities from the issuer and the public offering price. Investment bankers who do the underwriting generally form a **syndicate** to pool the risk.

underwriting spread See **underwriting**.

unemployment compensation See **unemployment insurance**.

unemployment insurance A form of short-term coverage that insures employees against loss of pay during temporary layoffs or when they lose their jobs. The money (*unemployment compensation*) is paid weekly to persons who qualify through federal and state programs. It is funded by a **payroll** tax on employers, based on an employee's rate of pay.

Uniform Commercial Code (UCC) The laws that govern commercial transactions, such as a bank loan or a retail sale. Replacing the Uniform Negotiable Instruments Law, the UCC has been adopted, with some modifications, in all states, the District of Columbia, the Virgin Islands, and Guam.

The objective of the UCC is to bring uniformity to commercial law among all jurisdictions. It aims to simplify, clarify, and modernize the law while allowing the expansion of commercial practices through custom, usage, and agreement among the parties.

unilateral contract See **contract.**

universe The total market; the set of items, people, or **data** from which a statistical **sample** is taken for study. In market research, for example, investigators may select a representative segment of the overall market to study the response to a new product.

unsecured loan A loan that is not secured by a **pledge** of **collateral** and is supported only by the borrower's record or reputation of creditworthiness. Credit-card cash advances, for example, are a form of unsecured loan.

Compare with **secured loan.**

upgrade See **JARGON: upgrade.**

upload See **JARGON: upload.**

uptick See **JARGON: uptick.**

uptime See **JARGON: uptime.**

user friendly See **JARGON: user friendly.**

usufruct See **UNUSUAL WORDS: usufruct.**

254 THE ENCYCLOPEDIC DICTIONARY OF BUSINESS TERMS

V

Value Line Composite Index See **stock index.**

VA mortgage See **mortgage.**

variable annuity See **annuity.**

v-chip See **JARGON: v-chip.**

venture capital See **capital.**

vertical market See **JARGON: vertical market.**

videoconference See **teleconference.**

video display See **cathode ray tube (CRT).**

virus See **JARGON: virus.**

voice-data system A dual voice-and-**data** system; a single **integrated system** that combines both voice and data messages, such as a voice-mail system and an **electronic-mail (E-mail)** system combined to accomplish either voice or data transfer or both.

See also **facsimile; computer; voice messaging.**

voice mail See **voice messaging.**

voice messaging Also called *voice mail;* an electronic system that enables users to receive, store, and route spoken messages through the public telephone system. Voice messages are digitized and stored by a **computer** and are accessed by entering instructions or dialing a code number or password.

While a user is away from his or her telephone, a computer monitors the line, "takes" incoming calls in a way similar to a conventional answering machine, plays any recorded message left by the user, and forwards the caller's message to a voice **mailbox** linked to the computer and the telephone system. Most systems can also route (send) replies to the sender or to other individuals on the voice-mail **network,** and some have a paging system to call the user.

See also **electronic mail (E-mail); voice-data system.**

volatile memory See **memory.**

voluntary bankruptcy See **bankruptcy.**

voucher A document, usually in the form of a slip of paper, that has a record or evidence of an expenditure, such as a **petty cash** voucher; a written authorization that can be exchanged for cash or used as **credit,** such as a retail voucher that a customer can apply toward a future purchase. Companies that use a *voucher system* require that all expenditures be authorized on a voucher.

voucher system See **voucher.**

W

waiver The intentional and voluntary relinquishment, either expressed or implied, of a right; the document that evidences the relinquishment of a right.

Example: **Stockholders** may forgo (waive) their right to receive written notice of a special **meeting.** This type of waiver is ordinarily given in the form of a written (printed) statement sent to each stockholder to be signed and returned to the **corporation.**

warranty An official sanction or assurance, either expressed or implied, given by one party to another and relied on by the other, such as the guarantee given by a seller (*warrantor*) to a buyer (*warrantee*) concerning the condition and quality of goods.

Warranties may concern many matters, such as the merchantability of goods, the fitness or suitability of goods for a specific purpose, the habitability of leased premises (see **lease**), the conveyance (see **deed**) of **real property,** or the statements made by an applicant for insurance coverage.

When a guaranteed performance or the actual condition of something does not meet the promise of the warrantor, the warrantee has a variety of options, such as returning defective goods and asking for a refund or taking legal action against the warrantor for a **breach of warranty.**

warranty deed See **deed.**

waste disposal See **recycling.**

wasting asset See **JARGON: wasting asset.**

Web (World Wide Web) See **Internet.**

whistleblower See **JARGON: whistleblower.**

whole-life insurance See **term insurance.**

wholesale The sale of goods in quantity to other distributors or to merchants, retailers, and large organizations that in turn resell the goods to individual customers. A wholesaler buys the products it distributes directly from producers and, in addition, handles a variety of other functions, from warehousing the goods to transporting them to providing financing for customers.

Compare with **retail.**

wholesale price index See **producer price index (PPI).**

wide area network (WAN) A **network** that is not confined by nearby physical connections, as is the case in a **local area network (LAN),** or limited to immediate geographical areas, as is the case in a **metropolitan area network (MAN).** Instead, WANs consist of high-speed, long-distance channels, such as the telephone lines or satellites, that connect users worldwide through the **Internet** or a commercial service, such as America Online.

will A legal document that describes how a person (*testator*) wants to have his or her property disposed of after death and that goes into effect upon the death of the testator. Each state has its own requirements concerning the preparation and **execution** of a will.

Until a testator dies, the will may be revoked and a new one drawn up. A **codicil** is a supplement to a will that modifies or revokes prior provisions. The phrase *last will and testament* refers to the most recent will.

In lieu of a will, however, many individuals prepare a living **trust,** which is in operation during the person's lifetime, rather than upon the individual's death. A living trust should not be confused with a testamentary trust or a living will.

1. A *testamentary trust,* created by a will, goes into effect upon the testator's death.
2. A *living will* is a document in which the signer requests that he or she not be kept alive by life-support systems in cases of terminal illness.

Wilshire 5000 Equity Index See **stock index.**

word processing The use of a **computer** to create documents, such as a letter or **report;** a type of applications **software** that enables users to create, revise, and print out (see **printing**) documents.

Word processing programs have numerous text-manipulation features, including the following:

1. Formatting (see **format**)
2. Editing, such as rephrasing, deleting, and inserting (see **copyedit**)
3. Transferring or moving blocks of **copy**
4. Checking spelling (*spell-checker*) and grammar (*grammar-checker*)
5. Finding synonyms (*thesaurus*)
6. Merging one file with another
7. Searching for and automatically replacing certain words with other words (*search and replace*)
8. Positioning text and **graphics** on a page (*page layout*)

Some of the more powerful word processing programs have capabilities that approach the sophisticated document-production characteristics of **desktop publishing.**

workers' compensation insurance See **workers' compensation laws.**

workers' compensation laws State statutes (see **statutory law**) that require employers to compensate employees for injuries or illnesses arising out of or sustained during employment. Under the statutes, an employer is deemed to be liable without regard to negligence or fault of the employer.

Workers' compensation insurance is a form of coverage for this liability that is available to employers. It covers medical care, disability, rehabilitation, and death from work-related causes. In a few states, employers must secure coverage through a state fund; in other states, employers may purchase the insurance from private insurers.

working capital See **capital.**

workshop See **conference.**

workstation 1. In general, the place where an individual works with a **computer** and other equipment.

2. In computer use, a computer station, sometimes with its own **peripherals** and sometimes connected to a **network,** used by one person. The two general types of stations are the intelligent workstation and the dumb terminal.

  a. An *intelligent workstation* is an independently functioning (*stand-alone*) personal computer, with its own **central processing unit (CPU)** and **disk drives,** capable of carrying out certain tasks, such as **word processing,** without relying on a central processor or various remote peripherals. Nevertheless, it is usually connected to a **local area network (LAN),** a powerful central microcomputer or mainframe computer, large central storage, and various peripherals, such as a high-speed laser printer (see **printing**).

  b. A *dumb terminal* consists only of a keyboard and a monitor (see **cathode ray tube [CRT]**). Since it cannot function alone, it must be connected to a LAN, and it relies on the system's central processor, disk drives, printer, and other components to produce material.

workup See **JARGON: workup**.
World Wide Web (WWW) See **Internet**.
WORM See **disk**.
wraparound mortgage See **mortgage**.

X

xerography A dry, electrostatic process used in most photocopiers and laser printers (see **printing**). The process involves charging a drum (a sensitized device on which images are created), which then attracts toner (dry powdered ink) that is transferred to and fused by heat onto the paper as text or **graphics** images. Because this process is so common, photocopying is sometimes referred to as *xeroxing*.

x-height In typography, the height of a font's lowercase letters, such as *a, c,* and *e,* that do not have descenders (*y*) or ascenders (*d*). The x-height is not a precise indication of type size. For example, type in different styles, even if all are in a 10-point size, may have different x-heights because of their differing styles.

   See also **typeface; point.**

XMODEM See **JARGON: XMODEM.**

Y

yield An investor's annual percentage rate of return on an investment, such as the rate of return from **dividends** on common or preferred **stock** or the rate of return of **interest** on **bonds**. The bond yield may be calculated as a nominal yield, current yield, or yield to **maturity.**

1. The *yield on stock* is readily determined by dividing the annual dividends received by the price of the stock. If stock that cost $50 paid dividends of $2, the yield is $2/$50, or 4 percent.
2. The *nominal yield on bonds* (also called *coupon yield*) need not be computed since it is stated on the face of the bond certificate of a fixed-income security.
3. The *current yield* is computed by dividing the annual interest payment by the current market price. If a bond cost $900 and paid interest of $90, the current yield is $90/900, or 10 percent.
4. The *yield to maturity* (also called *effective interest rate*) takes into account the cost of the bond, the interest rate, the number of years to maturity, and the amount paid at maturity. Because this yield is difficult to calculate accurately, specially prepared tables available in banks and brokerage houses are usually consulted.

yield to maturity See **yield.**

Z

zero-base budgeting A budgeting method in which all cost and benefit estimates are developed from a zero base (from scratch) for the new budget, and all expenditures must be justified according to need. Zero-base budgeting, therefore, differs from conventional methods that commonly use the previous year's figures as a starting point in deciding what to spend the next year, even though circumstances may have been different in the previous year.

ZMODEM See **JARGON: ZMODEM.**

zoning Dividing a city or county by legislative action into areas, or zones, so that the type of property use and construction on the land can be regulated under *zoning ordinances*. For example, certain areas may be zoned for residential use only, whereas others may be available for commercial or industrial use. Other restrictions, such as the maximum allowable height of buildings or the number of multiple-family structures allowed, also may apply in a particular area.

zoning ordinance See **zoning.**

JARGON

A

abort To discontinue or cut short.

access To enter with the purpose of retrieving something in storage, such as a computer file (see **STANDARD BUSINESS TERMS: computer**).

accessorize To furnish with accessories.

across the board Embracing all categories without exception.

add-on Something that can be added to basic equipment or to an item that is already existing without it.

aftermarket The market for parts and accessories designed to enhance basic equipment that a customer has purchased.

A-list A list of the most important candidates being considered for something.

alpha and omega The first and last letters of the Greek alphabet, used to refer to the beginning and end of something (see **APPENDIX: Greek Alphabet**).

alpha storage The initial stage in venture financing (see **STANDARD BUSINESS TERMS: capital**).

angel A financial backer or investor.

arb Short for **arbitrageur**, someone who buys and sells stocks quickly for profit as companies are preparing to merge (see **STANDARD BUSINESS TERMS: stock**).

at liberty Out of work.

attitude A predisposition toward buying.

Automation Alley Informal term for the Michigan robotics production area between Detroit and Ann Arbor.

B

back to back Coming one immediately after another.

bait and switch pricing An illegal sales tactic in which customers are lured into a shop by the advertising of low prices but then are told that the advertised product is unavailable or sold out, and they are urged to buy a more expensive or lower-quality substitute.

balloon payment A lump sum payable at the end of a loan.

ballpark figure An estimate.

baseland A local area network in which communicating computers are wired together (see **STANDARD BUSINESS TERMS: local area network [LAN]; computer**).

bean counter Someone who makes financial decisions and is frequently disinclined to spend money.

bear A speculator who believes prices will decline.

bells and whistles Nonessential features that are added to a product to make it more appealing.

Big Blue A nickname for International Business Machines (IBM).

blue chip Stock with above-average reliability (see also **STANDARD BUSINESS TERMS: stock**).

boilerplate Standard clauses or covenants (see **STANDARD BUSINESS TERMS: covenant**).

bottom line The final or actual cost or price; the net profit (see **STANDARD BUSINESS TERMS: net income**).

Bowash The Boston–Washington, D.C., corridor.

bucket shop A brokerage that accepts but does not promptly process customers' buy and sell orders, as required by the Securities and Exchange Commission.

bug An unwanted condition or error in a computer program or equipment (see **STANDARD BUSINESS TERMS: software; computer**).

bull A speculator who believes prices will increase.

bumping Downgrading or eliminating someone or something.

burnout A state of mental or physical exhaustion often reached as a result of prolonged stress or frustration.

C

cafeteria plan A flexible benefits package that has alternative options in addition to basic benefits.

candy-store problem A problem for which there are many equally effective (or ineffective) solutions.

cap A limit or upper level beyond which something cannot rise.

causative factor A cause.

change agent Someone who acts to change something.

channel On the Internet and in other communications applications, a named area where users "meet" for discussion (see **STANDARD BUSINESS TERMS: Internet**).

cool and whizzy Computer hardware or software that has many appealing and impressively displayed features (see **STANDARD BUSINESS TERMS: computer; hardware; software**).

corporate raider See **raider**.

crossover Success or activity occurring in more than one area.

crosstalk Unwanted breakthrough or overlap between channels, such as background voices on a telephone line.

cyberspace The intangible place that computer users go while working with equipment **on line;** a computer-generated environment or landscape (see **STANDARD BUSINESS TERMS: computer**).

D

damage control Efforts to minimize damage caused by a mistake or other problem.

dead end A situation with no outlet or opportunity.

debug To find and correct errors in a computer program or equipment (see **STANDARD BUSINESS TERMS: computer**).

digerati People who are intensely involved with computer activity; computer experts (see **STANDARD BUSINESS TERMS: computer**).

dog A product or service that has low sales or low-growth potential.

download To use a modem and the telephone lines to copy computer files from a remote location to your own computer (see **STANDARD BUSINESS TERMS: modem; computer**).

downsize To reduce the size of something.

downtick A small or incremental decrease.

downtime The idle period when activity ceases because of an error or while waiting for repair or servicing.

DRIP A dividend reinvestment program in which shareholders receive dividends in stock (see **STANDARD BUSINESS TERMS: dividend; stockholder; stock**).

dumping Selling large numbers of stock (see **STANDARD BUSINESS TERMS: stock**), which causes the price per share to drop; selling goods below cost to drive away the competition.

dynamic scoring A means of calculating tax cuts by assuming that the reduction will create more economic activity and thus need not be offset by spending cuts.

E

emoticon A symbol that E-mail users can employ to show emotion on a network link, such as *:-)* for a basic smiley face or *:-/* to indicate that the user is skeptical (see **STANDARD BUSINESS TERMS: electronic mail [E-mail]; network**).

end user The customer or client who uses a product or service.

English creep The increasing use of English as an international language.

exit To leave a computer program or operation; now also used informally to mean leaving any activity (see **STANDARD BUSINESS TERMS: computer**).

F

facadism The technique of retaining the fronts of old buildings on new structures.

fallout Consequences.

fast track Rapid advancement or movement of a person or product; the fastest route taken by a person or product.

fifth-generation computer A robotic or other computer programmed to simulate human thinking or other activity in problem solving (see **STANDARD BUSINESS TERMS: computer; programming**).

first generation The earliest or initial technology or equipment.

flanker A spin-off product with a similar name that capitalizes on the name of the original successful product.

flip-flop To change views or to take a different position.

focus group A group of 8 to 12 employees who meet to exchange information about matters of mutual concern, such as the results of a new marketing strategy.

Fortune 500 A list of leading companies published by *Fortune* magazine; big business in general.

frame of reference A theory or viewpoint.

free ride Benefiting from something without paying or contributing to it.

freeze To stop and hold something at its present position.

G

game plan An approach or plan.

gamer Someone who finishes something in spite of pain or setbacks.

-gate A suffix denoting scandal.

gentrification Improving deteriorated urban property and selling it to higher-income people, thereby displacing the former lower-income residents and businesspeople.

gingerbread Elaborate ornamentation, as in or on a house.

glass ceiling An intangible barrier in a company that prevents women and minorities from advancing.

golden handcuffs A contract under which executives will lose attractive benefits if they leave the company (see **STANDARD BUSINESS TERMS: contract**).

golden parachute The guarantee by an acquiring company of a high payment to the executives in other companies that lose in the takeover.

graveyard shift The work shift from midnight to early morning.

green Ecologically and environmentally concerned.

greenmail In finance, the practice of buying enough stock in a company to threaten a hostile takeover, thereby forcing the company's management to buy back those shares at an inflated price if it wants to prevent the takeover (see **STANDARD BUSINESS TERMS: stock**).

groupware A broad range of software, with applications designed to support team efforts and increase productivity (see **STANDARD BUSINESS TERMS: software**).

gym rat A success-oriented competitor who goes to work early and stays late.

H

hacker Someone who breaks into or disturbs other people's computer data (see **STANDARD BUSINESS TERMS: computer; data**).

haircut A cutback in expenditures that doesn't jeopardize the main objective.

hardball A tough approach to something.

high tech Technologically advanced.

hit In databases, a record that has been found (see **STANDARD BUSINESS TERMS: database**).

home page The starting page for a World Wide **Web** site; the starting address for multiple pages of information.

horizontal market A market that has a wide range of customers, such as the market for denim jeans.

host A computer system that provides a service, such as conducting a database search, for peripherals and remote terminals (see **STANDARD BUSINESS TERMS: computer; database; peripheral; workstation**).

housekeeping routine Initial computer instructions that are executed only once, such as clearing storage locations (see **STANDARD BUSINESS TERMS: computer**).

hype To promote something or someone through exaggerated claims.

hyperspace Space that has four or more dimensions.

hypertext A computer-based system that enables users to move around in any way or order among documents and to browse text and some graphics nonsequentially or in a nonlinear fashion (see **STANDARD BUSINESS TERMS: computer; graphics**).

I

infobahn Nickname for the **information superhighway.**

information superhighway A proposed network of computers, telephones, and cable television in all homes and businesses worldwide (see **STANDARD BUSINESS TERMS: computer; Internet**).

infrastructure An underlying foundation or basic framework.

in-house Inside or within a company.

input Information given to a person or machine, particularly information given to a computer (see **STANDARD BUSINESS TERMS: computer**).

insider trading The illegal use of inside knowledge of a company stock to make money (see **STANDARD BUSINESS TERMS: stock**).

interface A connection, such as between computer devices (see **STANDARD BUSINESS TERMS: computer**); improperly used as a verb to mean "meet with" someone.

J

junk bond An industry expression for a lower-rate, high-risk bond offering a high yield, frequently issued to finance a company takeover (see **STANDARD BUSINESS TERMS: bond; yield**).

just-in-time A technique designed to eliminate inventory stockpiles whereby everything arrives "just in time" for production and sale (see **STANDARD BUSINESS TERMS: inventory**).

K

kickback A return of a percentage of money already received, often given as a result of coercion or a secret agreement.

killer technology Technology so radical that everything before it becomes obsolete.

L

log in See **log on**.

log on Also called *log in;* to identify yourself on a network before beginning work; to give a user name and password to gain access and keep track of usage time (see **STANDARD BUSINESS TERMS: computer**).

M

man-hours The hours worked. *Man*-hours is now considered sexist, and *time worked, hours worked, labor-hours,* or some other nongender term is preferred.

Mickey Mouse Petty and unnecessary.

micromanagement The planning of local operations by central management (see **STANDARD BUSINESS TERMS: centralization**).

mommy track The movement of a professional woman from professional activity to domestic life.

morphing Doing two or more jobs.

mouse milking Expending undue effort to achieve a small or minor result.

N

netiquette Accepted standards of behavior on the Internet (see **STANDARD BUSINESS TERMS: Internet**).

net-net The final amount or last word.

networking Communicating with or helping others who have common interests; exchanging information with others (see also **STANDARD BUSINESS TERMS: network**).

niche market A new market that develops between or in addition to existing markets.

O

off line Not electronically connected; not under control of a central processing unit (compare with **on line;** see also **STANDARD BUSINESS TERMS: central processing unit [CPU]**).

on line Electronically connected; under the control of a central processing unit (compare with **off line;** see also **STANDARD BUSINESS TERMS: central processing unit [CPU]**).

operative Referring to a determining or important point or condition.

OPM financing Financing something by using other people's money.

optimize To improve or enhance something.

optimum The most.

option An alternative or a right to something.

output The end product or what is produced.

outsourcing Going to an outside source for labor, services, or parts, rather than using in-house resources, in order to cut costs.

P

packets Groups of data collected for transmission over a network (see **STANDARD BUSINESS TERMS: data; network**).

paradigm An archetype, model, outline, or pattern.

peer-to-peer A computer-to-computer network in which all computers have equal power and share resources equally (see **STANDARD BUSINESS TERMS: computer; network**).

peewee tech Small-company technologies.

poison pill A defense that makes a corporate takeover too expensive for a predator to pursue.

preowned Used.

prioritize To list in order of importance.

promo Advertising designed to sell something or promote someone.

prosumer An older person who continues to be productive but without financial compensation.

protocol A software method of regulating data that enables programs on different machines to communicate with each other (see **STANDARD BUSINESS TERMS: software; data; protocol**).

R

raider Also called *corporate raider;* an investor who tries to take over a company by purchasing a majority of the stock (see **STANDARD BUSINESS TERMS: stock**).

red ink Financial loss.

rep A representative.

rollback A return to lower prices.

rollover Reinvestment.

rug ranking The practice of linking a secretary's career path and pay to the success of his or her boss.

S

sacred cow Something too important to change.

scenario An event or a situation or plan.

scorched earth A self-destructive company strategy to discourage a corporate takeover.

screamer A persistently complaining customer.

shark repellent An effort to discourage an aggressor in a unwanted corporate takeover by making it very expensive and difficult for another to purchase the company.

short list The final candidates most likely to be selected.

slammer A high-pressure salesperson; formerly, slang for "jail."

sleaze factor Evidence of unethical behavior.

smart card A small plastic card containing a microprocessor (see **STANDARD BUSINESS TERMS: microprocessor**).

smart money Those who know best.

snake-check To search thoroughly for hidden consequences.

sound bite A short excerpt of a videotape.

spin control The act of making something seem favorable.

stonewall To be adamant or inflexible.

surfing Navigating electronically on the Internet, searching for particular information or exploring simply to see what is available (see **STANDARD BUSINESS TERMS: Internet**).

systematize To put in order or arrange according to a plan.

T

teflon A quality something or someone has of being immune to external influences; capitalized in reference to the nonstick coating on products.

throughput A rate of data processing or transfer measured in characters or bytes per second from **input** to **output**; the amount of work processed in a given period; computer performance in sending data through all components of the system (see **STANDARD BUSINESS TERMS: data processing; bytes; computer; data**).

time frame Time.

top of the line The leading or best product.

trojan horse Something appearing to provide normal activity but actually designed for illegal or secret activity.

turnaround time The time required to perform a task or to fill an order or receive, complete, and return something.

turnover A change in personnel or products, with new ones entering and previous ones leaving.

U

upgrade To move up or to improve something.

upload The process of transmitting a local computer file "up" through a network to a remote system (see **STANDARD BUSINESS TERMS: computer; network**).

uptick A small or incremental increase.

uptime The time when equipment is either operating or available for operation.

user friendly Anything that is easy to learn and use.

V

v-chip A new technology that would enable television viewers to block violent programs.

vertical market A market that has a limited range of customers, such as the market for medieval crossbows.

viable Being capable of working or developing.

virus An uninvited program deliberately inserted into a computer system to harass users and disrupt activity or data in the computer (see **STANDARD BUSINESS TERMS: data; computer**).

W

wanna-be Someone who wants to be something or to attain a particular position.

wasting asset An asset (see **STANDARD BUSINESS TERMS: asset**) that declines in value.

Web Short for "World Wide Web," a worldwide electronic system managed by the World Wide Web Organization and designed to facilitate use of the Internet (see **STANDARD BUSINESS TERMS: Internet**).

whistleblower Someone who reveals another person's or organization's wrongdoing.

white knight A corporation that comes to the aid of another in a takeover fight (see **STANDARD BUSINESS TERMS: corporation**).

window An opening or opportunity.

-wise A suffix attached to words to mean "in regard to," as in *budgetwise* or *saleswise* (see list in **PREFIXES AND SUFFIXES: SUFFIXES**).

workup Routine diagnostic procedures (see **STANDARD BUSINESS TERMS: diagnostic routine**).

X

XMODEM A common computer file-transfer **protocol** (see **STANDARD BUSINESS TERMS: computer**).

Z

ZMODEM A rapid file-transfer **protocol** on the Internet (see **STANDARD BUSINESS TERMS: Internet**).

FOREIGN EXPRESSIONS

A

a bon marché *(Fr.)* At a bargain price.

ab ovo usque ad mala *(Lat.)* From beginning to end.

à compte *(Fr.)* On account (see **STANDARD BUSINESS TERMS: credit**).

ad hoc *(Lat.)* For this; for this special purpose.

ad infinitum *(Lat.)* Indefinitely; forever.

ad referendum *(Lat.)* For reference; for further consideration.

ad valorem *(Lat.)* According to value.

aficionado *(Sp.)* A devotee; one who fervently pursues an interest.

a fortiori *(Lat.)* With stronger reason; much more.

a la carte *(Fr.)* According to a menu with items priced separately.

a la mode *(Fr.)* In fashion.

amicus curiae *(Lat.)* A friend of the court.

anno Domini *(Lat.)* In the year of the Lord.

a priori *(Lat.)* Reasoned from self-evident propositions, from what goes before, or from cause to effect.

apropos of *(Fr.)* Concerning; pertinent to; with regard to.

atelier *(Fr.)* A workshop; studio.

attaché *(Fr.)* A diplomatic official.

au contraire *(Fr.)* On or to the contrary.

au fait *(Fr.)* Socially correct; fully informed; to the point.

aussitôt dit, aussitôt fait *(Fr.)* No sooner said than done.

autobahn *(Ger.)* A German road or highway.

avant-propos *(Fr.)* A preface (see **STANDARD BUSINESS TERMS: front matter**).

avec plaisir *(Fr.)* With pleasure.

B

belles lettres *(Fr.)* Serious literature.

bête noire *(Fr.)* Something or someone feared or disliked.

bolshoi *(Rus.)* Large; great.

bona fide *(Lat.)* In good faith; genuine.

bon appétit *(Fr.)* Good appetite; enjoy your meal.

bravura *(Ital.)* A display of daring or brilliance.

C

cache *(Fr.)* Something hidden.

camaraderie *(Fr.)* Goodwill.

carpe diem *(Lat.)* An admonition to enjoy the moment.

carte blanche *(Fr.)* Unconditional power; complete freedom.

causa sine qua non *(Lat.)* An indispensable cause or condition.

cause célèbre *(Fr.)* An issue arousing widespread controversy; celebrated legal case.

caveat *(Lat.)* Let him or her beware; a warning.

caveat emptor *(Lat.)* Let the buyer beware.

caveat lector *(Lat.)* Let the reader beware.

certiorari *(Lat.)* To be informed; a writ from a higher court to a lower one asking for a case transcript.

chacun à son goût *(Fr.)* Everyone to his own taste.

Foreign Expressions

chef de cuisine *(Fr.)* A head cook.

chef d'oeuvre *(Fr.)* A masterpiece.

chicano *(Sp.)* A Mexican-American; individual of Mexican origin living in the United States.

cloisonne *(Fr.)* An enameled decoration.

cogito ergo sum *(Lat.)* I think, therefore, I exist.

communiqué *(Fr.)* An official report; communication (see **STANDARD BUSINESS TERMS: report**).

connoisseur *(Fr.)* An expert; informed person with discriminating taste.

contra *(Lat.)* Against.

corpus *(Lat.)* Body.

corpus juris *(Lat.)* Body of law.

corpus juris civilis *(Lat.)* Body of civil law (see **STANDARD BUSINESS TERMS: civil law**).

cortege *(Fr.)* A train of attendants; procession; funeral procession.

costa *(Sp.)* Coast; coastal area; shore.

coterie *(Fr.)* An exclusive group.

coup d'état *(Fr.)* Sudden overthrow.

critique *(Fr.)* A critical review.

curriculum vitae *(Lat.)* Résumé; short account of career and experience.

D

debacle *(Fr.)* Sudden collapse.

debonair *(Fr.)* Suave; urbane.

de facto *(Lat.)* In fact; in deed; actually.

de gustibus non est disputandum *(Lat.)* There is no arguing about tastes.

Dei gratia *(Lat.)* By the grace of God.

de jure *(Lat.)* By right; lawful.

démarche *(Fr.)* A plan of action; change in a course of action.

denouement *(Fr.)* Climax; outcome.

Deo gratias *(Lat.)* Thanks (be) to God.

Deo volente *(Lat.)* God willing.

de rigueur *(Fr.)* Customary; fashionable; strictly necessary; proper.

de trop *(Fr.)* Too much; too many; superfluous.

ding hao *(Ch.)* Very good; fine; excellent.

Dominus vobiscum *(Lat.)* The Lord be with you.

dossier *(Fr.)* Documents pertaining to a particular subject.

double-entendre *(Fr.)* Two meanings.

E

ecce homo *(Lat.)* Behold the man.

effendi *(Turk.)* A man of property; authority; education.

élan *(Fr.)* Vigorous spirit or enthusiasm; flair.

en famille *(Fr.)* Informally; in one's family.

ennui *(Fr.)* Boredom.

en plein jour *(Fr.)* Openly; in full daylight.

en poste *(Fr.)* In a diplomatic post.

en rapport *(Fr.)* In sympathy or agreement.

entourage *(Fr.)* Attendants.

entre nous *(Fr.)* Between us; confidentially.

entrepôt *(Fr.)* A distribution point; warehouse; transshipment center.

e pluribus unum *(Lat.)* One out of many.

ergo *(Lat.)* Therefore; hence.

erratum/errata *(Lat.)* Error/errors

ersatz *(Ger.)* Imitation; substitute.

et alii *(Lat.)* And others.

et uxor *(Lat.)* And wife.

et vir *(Lat.)* And husband.

ex cathedra *(Lat.)* From the chair; with the authority derived from one's office.

ex gratia *(Lat.)* As a favor.

ex more *(Lat.)* According to custom.

ex officio *(Lat.)* From office; by virtue of or because of an office.

ex parte *(Lat.)* On one side only; by or for one party.

ex post facto *(Lat.)* After the act.

ex relatione *(Lat.)* On information of; on behalf of another.

F

fait accompli *(Fr.)* An accomplished fact or deed.

faux pas *(Fr.)* A blunder; social error.

fiat *(Lat.)* A command; dictate; order.

finis *(Lat.)* The end; the conclusion.

force majeure *(Fr.)* An irresistible force; event that cannot be reasonably controlled or anticipated.

G

gauche *(Fr.)* Tactless.

gomei kaisha *(Jpn.)* Partnership; association.

gourmet *(Fr.)* A connoisseur of food and drink.

gratis *(Lat.)* Free of charge.

H

habitué *(Fr.)* A regular; someone who frequently goes to a particular place.

haute couture *(Fr.)* Houses or designers that create high-class fashions; fashionable items that are created.

hoc anno *(Lat.)* In this year.

homme d'affaires *(Fr.)* A man of business; business agent.

humanum est errare *(Lat.)* To err is human.

I

id est *(Lat.)* That is.

imbroglio *(Ital.)* A state of great confusion; difficult situation; complicated misunderstanding.

impasse *(Fr.)* Deadlock.

incommunicado *(Sp.)* Isolated; cut off from contact.

infra *(Lat.)* Below.

in loco parentis *(Lat.)* In the place of a parent.

in medias res *(Lat.)* In or into the middle of a sequence of events.

in perpetuum *(Lat.)* Forever.

in propria persona *(Lat.)* In one's own person.

in rerum natura *(Lat.)* In the nature of things.

in situ *(Lat.)* In its place; in the original terms.

in statu quo *(Lat.)* In the state in which it was before.

inter alia *(Lat.)* Among other things.

in toto *(Lat.)* Altogether; entirely.

ipso facto *(Lat.)* By that very fact; intrinsically.

ipso jure *(Lat.)* By the law itself.

J

jurat *(Lat.)* Portion of affidavit where officer administering oath certifies it was sworn to before him or her (see **STANDARD BUSINESS TERMS: affidavit**).

jure divino *(Lat.)* By divine law; by divine right.

jus *(Lat.)* Law; laws collectively.

jus canonicum *(Lat.)* Canon law.

jus civile *(Lat.)* Civil law (see **STANDARD BUSINESS TERMS: civil law**).

jus commune *(Lat.)* Common law (see **STANDARD BUSINESS TERMS: common law**); common right.

jus gentium *(Lat.)* International law.

jus proprietatis *(Lat.)* Right of property.

justitia omnibus *(Lat.)* Justice for all.

L

laissez-faire *(Fr.)* A governmental or personal policy of non-interference.

le style, c'est l'homme *(Fr.)* The style is the man.

le tout ensemble *(Fr.)* The whole (taken) together.

liaison *(Fr.)* An affair; connection.

lis pendens *(Lat.)* Litigation pending; a pending lawsuit.

locus in quo *(Lat.)* The place in which.

locus sigilii *(Lat.)* The place for the seal.

M

mala praxis *(Lat.)* Malpractice.

mea culpa *(Lat.)* My fault; acknowledgment of personal fault or error.

mélange *(Fr.)* A mixture; medley.

melee *(Fr.)* A free-for-all; confused struggle.

métier *(Fr.)* Trade; profession; business; experience.

mi casa es su casa *(Sp.)* My house is your house.

mikado *(Jpn.)* (title of) Emperor of Japan.

milieu *(Fr.)* Environment; setting; background.

millennium *(Lat.)* A period of 1,000 years (see also **APPENDIX: Time-Period Designations**).

mise en scène *(Fr.)* A stage setting; environment.

modus operandi *(Lat.)* A method of operating.

mon ami *(Fr.)* My friend.

monde *(Fr.)* The world; the fashionable world; society.

mutatis mutandis *(Lat.)* The necessary changes having been made.

N

nee *(Fr.)* Born.

nemine contradicente *(Lat.)* No one contradicting.

nemine dissentiente *(Lat.)* No one dissenting.

nolens volens *(Lat.)* Whether willing or not.

nolle prosequi *(Lat.)* Unwilling to prosecute or follow up.

nolo contendere *(Lat.)* I will not contest it.

nom de guerre *(Fr.)* A pseudonym.

nom de plume *(Fr.)* A pen name; pseudonym.

non prosequitur *(Lat.)* He or she does not prosecute or follow up.

non sequitur *(Lat.)* It does not follow; something that does not follow logically from that which was just expressed.

nouveau riche *(Fr.)* The newly rich.

nuance *(Fr.)* A subtle distinction.

nul tort *(Lat.)* No wrong done.

O

obiit *(Lat.)* He or she died.

obiter dictum *(Lat.)* A judge's incidental, nonbinding expression of opinion.

objet d'art *(Fr.)* A work of art.

oeuvre *(Fr.)* The lifework of a writer, composer, or artist; substantial body of work.

okimono *(Jpn.)* Decorative objects.

opere citato *(Lat.)* In the work cited.

opus *(Lat.)* Work; labor.

P

panache *(Fr.)* Dash; high spirits; verve.

par avion *(Fr.)* By airplane.

par excellence *(Fr.)* The best of a kind.

pari passu *(Lat.)* With equal pace.

pasha *(Turk.)* A man of high rank or office.

penchant *(Fr.)* A strong or habitual inclination.

per annum *(Lat.)* By the year.

per diem *(Lat.)* By the day.

per se *(Lat.)* In itself; essentially; as such.

persona grata *(Lat.)* Fully acceptable.

persona non grata *(Lat.)* Personally unacceptable.

pièce de résistance *(Fr.)* An outstanding accomplishment.

pied-à-terre *(Fr.)* Part-time or temporary lodging.

pis aller *(Fr.)* The last resort.

pleno jure *(Lat.)* With full authority.

plus ça change, plus c'est la même chose *(Fr.)* The more it changes, the more it's the same thing.

post mortem *(Lat.)* Afterward; after death.

potpourri *(Fr.)* A mixture; medley.

précis *(Fr.)* A summary.

prima facie *(Lat.)* At first sight.

primus inter pares *(Lat.)* First among equals.

pro *(Lat.)* For.

pro bono *(Lat.)* Donated; given voluntarily; without cost; for the public good.

pro forma *(Lat.)* Done in a perfunctory way; as a matter of form.

pro rata *(Lat.)* According to the rate or proportion.

protégé *(Fr.)* Someone trained by a person of experience or prominence.

pro tempore *(Lat.)* For the time being; temporarily.

Q

quasi *(Lat.)* As if; resembling.

quid pro quo *(Lat.)* Something for something.

quod erat demonstrandum *(Lat.)* Which was to be proved.

quod vide *(Lat.)* Which see.

quo jure? *(Lat.)* By what right?

quo warranto *(Lat.)* By what right or authority.

R

raconteur *(Fr.)* A storyteller.

raison d'être *(Fr.)* Reason for existing or being.

recherché *(Fr.)* Choice.

reich *(Ger.)* A state or an empire.

rendezvous *(Fr.)* The place for a meeting; the meeting itself (see also **STANDARD BUSINESS TERMS: meeting**).

répondez s'il vous plaît *(Fr.)* Reply, if you please.

ricochet *(Fr.)* Rebound.

risqué *(Fr.)* Suggestive.

rococo *(Ital.)* Elaborate; ornate.

S

salon *(Fr.)* An elegant home or room; fashionable gathering of notables in the home of a prominent person.

sans doute *(Fr.)* Without doubt.

sans gêne *(Fr.)* Without embarrassment.

sans pareil *(Fr.)* Without equal.

sans peine *(Fr.)* Without difficulty.

sans souci *(Fr.)* Without worry.

savoir faire *(Fr.)* Know-how; knowledge.

scilicet *(Lat.)* To wit.

secundum *(Lat.)* According to.

semper fidelis *(Lat.)* Always faithful.

semper idem *(Lat.)* Always the same.

semper paratus *(Lat.)* Always ready.

sigillum *(Lat.)* A seal.

s'il vous plaît *(Fr.)* If you please.

sine die *(Lat.)* Without day; without a day specified for a future meeting (see **STANDARD BUSINESS TERMS: meeting; parliamentary procedure**).

sine qua non *(Lat.)* Something essential; precondition.

sub nom *(Lat.)* Under the name.

sub verbo *(Lat.)* Under the word.

summum bonum *(Lat.)* The greatest good.

suo jure *(Lat.)* In one's own right.

suo loco *(Lat.)* In one's rightful place.

supra *(Lat.)* Above.

suum cuique *(Lat.)* To each his own.

T

table d'hôte *(Fr.)* A meal served to all guests at a certain time for a certain price.

Tao *(Ch.)* Pathway of virtuous conduct; the right way; rational basis of human conduct.

tempora mutantur *(Lat.)* Times change.

tempus fugit *(Lat.)* Time flies.

tête-à-tête *(Fr.)* A private conversation.

tong *(Ch.)* A meeting place; secret organization.

tour de force *(Fr.)* A feat of skill, ingenuity, or strength.

tout de suite *(Fr.)* Immediately; all at once; consecutively.

trompe-l'oeil *(Fr.)* A style of art so real as to deceive the eye.

U

ultra vires *(Lat.)* Beyond the power of.

ut infra *(Lat.)* As below.

ut supra *(Lat.)* As above.

V

veni, vidi, vici *(Lat.)* I came, I saw, I conquered.

verbatim *(Lat.)* Word for word.

verbatim et literatim *(Lat.)* Word for word and letter for letter.

versus *(Lat.)* Against.

videlicet *(Lat.)* That is; namely; it is easy to see.

vis-à-vis *(Fr.)* In relation to; compared with; face-to-face with.

voilà *(Fr.)* There! Look! See!

vox populi *(Lat.)* Voice of the people.

W

weltanschauung *(Ger.)* A comprehensive concept of the world; worldview.

wen *(Ch.)* Literature; letters; culture.

Wissenschaft *(Ger.)* Learning.

UNUSUAL WORDS

A

a • be • ce • dar • i • an *(adj.)* Referring to the alphabet; alphabetically arranged; rudimentary; elementary.

ab • jure *(vb.)* To disclaim formally; renounce; retract; repudiate.

a • boz • zo *(n.)* A rough draft or sketch.

ac • a • deme *(n.)* An academic environment; college; university; place of instruction.

a • cal • cu • li • a *(n.)* The inability to perform simple arithmetic tasks manually.

ac • cep • ti • la • tion *(n.)* In civil law, a formal verbal acknowledgment by a creditor that his or her claim has been satisfied, with or without payment (see **STANDARD BUSINESS TERMS: civil law; acknowledgment**).

ac • cou • tre • ment *(n.)* Equipment; outfit; furnishings.

a • cu • i • ty *(n.)* Acuteness; sharpness; keenness of perception.

a • cu • men *(n.)* Keen perception; acuteness of mind; shrewdness, especially in business matters.

a • cu • mi • nate *(adj.)* Pointed.

ad • duce *(vb.)* To cite or bring forward as proof.

ad • min • i • cle *(n.)* Something that provides support; in law, corroborative or explanatory proof.

ad • um • brate *(vb.)* To foreshadow; symbolize; hint at something to come.

ad • ven • ti • tious *(adj.)* Added; appended; not inherent; extraneous.

ad • ver • sar • i • a *(n.)* Comments or notes; a miscellaneous collection of notes or remarks.

ag • i • o • tage *(n.)* The exchange business; speculation with stocks (see **STANDARD BUSINESS TERMS: stock; stock exchange**).

a • le • a • to • ry *(adj.)* Dependent on luck or chance in regard to either profit or loss; unpredictable.

al • go • rism *(n.)* The system of Arabic numerals; arithmetic.

al • i • quot *(adj.)* Contained in a larger quantity an exact number of times, as *3* and *4* are aliquot parts of *12*.

al • lo • graph *(n.)* A signature or writing made for someone else, in contrast to an *autograph,* which is one's own signature.

al • lo • nym *(n.)* A name used by an author that actually belongs to someone else, in contrast to a *pseudonym,* which refers to a fictituous name.

am • ba • gious *(adj.)* Roundabout; circuitous.

am • bi • dex • trous *(adj.)* Able to use both hands with equal ease.

a • mo • tion *(n.)* The removal of a specified object; ousting someone, such as a corporate officer, from his or her office (see **STANDARD BUSINESS TERMS: corporation; board of directors**).

am • phi • gae • an *(adj.)* Found throughout the world; cosmopolitan.

an • a *(n.)* A collection of memorable sayings or anecdotes.

an • a • lects *(n.)* Selected miscellaneous written passages.

an • a • stat • ic *(adj.)* Relating to a printing process with raised letters (see **STANDARD BUSINESS TERMS: printing**).

an • i • mad • ver • sion *(n.)* A critical or adverse comment or observation; censure.

an•o•pis•tho•graph•ic *(adj.)* Having writing or printing on one side only (see **STANDARD BUSINESS TERMS: printing**).

a•poph•a•sis *(n.)* Allusion to something while simultaneously declaring that it is unnecessary to mention it, as in "Needless to say . . ."

ap•o•thegm *(n.)* A short saying; aphorism; adage; maxim; universal truth or precept.

ar•bi•tra•geur *(n.)* See **JARGON: arb.**

ar•che•type *(n.)* The original model, form, or pattern; prototype (see **STANDARD BUSINESS TERMS: prototype**).

ar•ri•viste *(n.)* Someone who will use any means to achieve success.

ar•ro•gate *(vb.)* To claim or seize something that one isn't entitled to have; appropriate.

ar•ti•fice *(n.)* A ruse; craftiness; stratagem; insincerity.

as•ce•sis *(n.)* Self-discipline; self-restraint.

as•sev•er•ate *(vb.)* To affirm, assert, or declare earnestly.

ath•e•nae•um *(n.)* A library; reading room.

au•to•di•dact *(n.)* Someone who is self-taught.

au•tog•no•sis *(n.)* Self-knowledge; an understanding of one's own psychodynamics.

B

bis•sex•tile *(adj.)* Having 366 days (leap year); having an extra day (see also **APPENDIX: Time-Period Designations**).

bre•vi•ate *(n.)* A brief statement; summary; abstract.

C

ca • chet *(n.)* A seal or stamp of official approval; prestige.

ca • co • e • py *(n.)* Bad pronunciation.

ca • cog • ra • phy *(n.)* Bad handwriting.

ca • col • o • gy *(n.)* Bad diction or pronunciation.

cam • a • ril • la *(n.)* A clique; a group of unofficial and often secret or scheming advisors.

cam • bist • ry *(n.)* The science of exchange in international finance.

cam • er • a • lis • tics *(n.)* The science of public finance.

car • tog • ra • phy *(n.)* Mapmaking.

cat • a • chre • sis *(n.)* The misuse of words.

cat • e • chet • i • cal *(adj.)* Using questions and answers.

ca • thol • i • con *(n.)* A universal remedy; cure-all; panacea.

cau • se • rie *(n.)* Informal, light conversation or composition.

cav • il *(vb.)* To quibble; raise frivolous or trivial objections.

cen • trif • u • gal *(adj.)* Moving away from a center or axis.

cen • trip • e • tal *(adj.)* Moving toward a center or axis.

chaf • fer *(n.)* Articles of merchandise; wares.

chrem • a • tis • tics *(n.)* The study of wealth; a theory of wealth as measured in money.

cir • cum • fo • ra • ne • ous *(adj.)* Going from market to market.

cla • vis *(n.)* A key or glossary designed to help in interpretation.

co • ac • er • vate *(vb.)* To collect; accumulate; amass.

co • ad • ju • van • cy *(n.)* Cooperation.

co • e • val *(adj.)* Of the same age or era; contemporary.

col • lo • cate *(vb.)* To arrange in a place or position; to set side by side.

col • o • phon *(n.)* The emblem or imprint of a publisher; an inscription of facts about a work's production.

com • i • ty *(n.)* Mutually courteous behavior; mutual consideration; friendly civility.

com • pen • di • ous *(adj.)* Concise; brief expression of a comprehensive matter.

con • cat • e • na • tion *(n.)* A united or connected series or chain.

con • ge • ries *(n.)* A collection; aggregation; agglomeration.

con • sue • tude *(n.)* Social usage; custom; habit; custom imbued with legal force.

cop • u • la *(n.)* A link; tie; coupler.

cum • brous *(adj.)* Unwieldly; cumbersome.

cunc • ta • tion *(n.)* Delay; procrastination.

D

de • cad • ic *(adj.)* Relating to the decimal system.

de • fal • ca • tion *(n.)* The misappropriation of money, property, or other item by the person holding it in trust (see **STANDARD BUSINESS TERMS: fiduciary**).

de • men • ti *(n.)* An official or formal denial of the truth of a report.

de • mit *(vb.)* To resign; give up or relinquish an office or membership; withdraw.

de • mog • ra • phy *(n.)* The statistical study of population.

de • mot • ic *(adj.)* Popular; common; pertaining to the common people.

de • sid • er • a • tum *(n.)* Something desired that is essential and causes concern if it is unavailable.

des • i • nence *(n.)* An ending; termination.

di • a • tribe *(n.)* A bitter, abusive denunciation.

di • glot *(adj.)* Bilingual.

di • ur • nal *(adj.)* Daily (see also **APPENDIX: Time-Period Designations**).

drag • o • man *(n.)* An official embassy interpreter, primarily of Arabic, Persian, or Turkish; guide for tourists.

dra • goon *(vb.)* To harass; persecute; coerce vigorously.

dry • as • dust *(n.)* A dull, pedantic, uninteresting speaker or writer.

du • bi • e • ty *(n.)* Dubiousness; uncertainty.

E

ec • type *(n.)* A copy from an original; imitation; reproduction.

el • ee • mos • y • nary *(adj.)* Charitable; philanthropic.

e • len • chus *(n.)* Refutation; cross-examination.

e • mol • u • ment *(n.)* A salary; fee; compensation for services.

en • chi • rid • i • on *(n.)* A handbook; manual; reference source.

en • fi • lade *(n.)* An arrangement in opposite and parallel rows; suite of rooms with an open vista.

e • ris • tic *(adj.)* Controversial; quarrelsome.

es • cheat *(n.)* The reversion of land to the state.

es • o • ter • ic *(adj.)* Known to or understood by a select few.

es • trade *(n.)* A platform; dais.

ex • e • ge • sis *(n.)* Explanation; critical interpretation.

ex • ig • u • ous *(adj.)* Meager; narrow; paltry; skimpy.

ex • or • di • um *(n.)* The beginning; introduction; introductory part of composition or discourse.

ex • o • ter • ic *(adj.)* Known by many; readily comprehensible; popular.

F

fa • cient *(n.)* An agent; doer.

fe • lic • i • tous *(adj.)* Appropriate; befitting; suited to the occasion.

fe • ra • cious *(adj.)* Productive.

fu • ga • cious *(adj.)* Short-lived; fleeting.

fun • gi • ble *(adj.)* Interchangeable; similar; replaceable.

G

ge • o • des • ic *(adj.)* The shortest distance between two points on a plane or arc.

glot • to • gon • ic *(adj.)* Relating to the origin of language.

gnome *(n.)* An aphorism; proverb; maxim; terse expression of a general truth.

gra • va • men *(n.)* A grievance; the basis of a grievance or charge.

grim • thorpe *(vb.)* To remodel or restore a building without proper knowledge or without being faithful to the original.

H

heb • dom • a • dal *(adj.)* Weekly; once a week (see also **APPENDIX: Time-Period Designations**).

he • gem • o • ny *(n.)* Leadership; dominance.

hes • per • i • an *(n.)* Western (world); occidental.

het • er • o • nym *(n.)* A word spelled like another word but pronounced differently and with a different meaning, as *lead* (guide) and *lead* (metal).

hol • o • graph *(n.)* A personally written and signed document, such as a handwritten will.

hom • o • graph *(n.)* A word that is spelled like another word but differs in sound and meaning, such as *present* (*vb.:* to give something) and *present* (*n.:* a gift).

hom • o • nym *(n.)* A word, which may be a **homophone** or a **homograph,** that is spelled and pronounced like another word but differs in meaning, such as *plane* (*n.:* an aircraft) and *plane* (*n.:* a smoothing tool).

hom • o • phone *(n.)* A word that is pronounced like another word but differs in spelling and meaning, such as *meet* (*vb.:* to encounter) and *mete* (*vb.:* to allot or apportion).

hor • ta • to • ry *(adj.)* Exhortatory; urging a certain course.

hy • per • bo • le *(n.)* Extravagant exaggeration.

hy • po • bu • li • a *(n.)* Difficulty in acting or making decisions.

I

id • e • o • gram *(n.)* A picture or symbol, rather than a word, that represents something; an **ideograph.**

id • e • o • graph *(n.)* See **ideogram**.

il • la • tion *(n.)* An inference; conclusion; the act of inferring or reaching a conclusion.

im • mis • ci • ble *(n.)* Incapable of being mixed or blended, like oil and water.

im • pri • ma • tur *(n.)* A license to print or publish; imprint; sign or mark of approval.

in • de • fec • ti • ble *(adj.)* Faultless; defectless; unfailing; not subject to failure or decay; lasting.

in • ex • pug • na • ble *(adj.)* Invincible; impregnable; fixed; stable.

in • ter • ca • late *(vb.)* To interpolate; insert an extra day or month in a calendar; insert between layers.

i • soch • ro • nous *(adj.)* Being equal in duration, interval, or metrical length.

i • so • gen • e • sis *(n.)* Similarity in origin or development.

J

ja • wab *(n.)* A building erected to balance or correspond to another.

je • june *(adj.)* Dull; lacking interest or significance.

ju • ral *(adj.)* Relating to the law or to rights or obligations.

L

la • bile *(adj.)* Changeable; adaptable; unstable; fluctuating.

lach • es *(n.)* Negligence; undue delay.

le • gist *(n.)* Someone who specializes in law or a branch of it.

lem • ma *(n.)* An assumption; preliminary proposition; auxiliary proposition.

li • cen • ti • ate *(n.)* The title conferred upon receiving a license from an institution; a European degree that falls between a baccalaureate and a doctorate; one licensed to practice a profession.

li • ti • gious *(adj.)* Contentious; prone to be involved in lawsuits; marked by litigation.

li • to • tes *(n.)* An expression of the affirmative by using the negative, as in "He's *not* a bad writer."

log • o • gram *(n.)* A letter, character, sign, or symbol used to represent a word, such as % (*percent*).

lon • gil • o • quence *(n.)* long-windedness.

M

mac • ro • scop • ic *(adj.)* Large enough to be seen by the naked eye; the opposite of *microscopic*.

ma • gis • te • ri • al *(adj.)* Authoritative; dignified; weighty; domineering; pompous.

mal • ver • sa • tion *(n.)* Corruption or breach of trust in an office or position of trust.

man • u • duc • tion *(n.)* Introduction; something that guides or leads.

ma • tu • ti • nal *(adj.)* Early; occurring in the morning; early in the day.

mel • io • rate *(vb.)* To make better; soften.

met • age *(n.)* The official measuring of contents or weight; the charge for metage.

mil • len • ni • um *(n.)* A period of 1,000 years; the 1,000th anniversary.

mis•o•cai•ne•a *(n.)* An abnormal or intense hatred of new ideas.

mon•o•lith•ic *(adj.)* Massive; uniform.

mort•main *(n.)* The perpetual and inalienable possession of title to land by a charitable or business corporation.

mulct *(n.)* A fine; penalty.

mu•ni•ment *(n.)* Evidence that can be used to defend a claim or title; title deeds and papers; statutory grants; charters; judgments.

N

ne•ol•o•gism *(n.)* A new word, phrase, or usage.

ne•o•ter•ic *(adj.)* Modern; recent; new.

ne•science *(n.)* Ignorance; lack of knowledge or awareness.

nex•us *(n.)* A connection or link; a group or series that is connected.

ni•mi•e•ty *(n.)* An overabundance; excess; redundancy.

no•dus *(n.)* A difficult situation; complication.

no•e•sis *(n.)* Intellectual activity; cognition.

no•mic *(adj.)* Generally valid; customary; ordinary; conventional.

nous *(n.)* Mind; reason; alertness; common sense.

O

ob•jur•gate *(vb.)* To decry; reproach; denounce harshly.

ob•ro•gate *(vb.)* To modify or repeal a law by passing a new law.

ob • sig • na • tion *(n.)* A formal ratification, such as by an official seal.

oc • ci • dent • al *(adj.)* Western (world).

ol • i • gop • o • ly *(n.)* A condition in which a few sellers dominate the market, and because competitors are few, the actions of any one affects the others.

or • is • mol • o • gy *(n.)* Terminology; the science of defining technical terms.

or • tho • e • py *(n.)* The customary pronunciation of a language.

or • thog • ra • phy *(n.)* Correct conventional spelling.

ox • y • mo • ron *(n.)* A figure of speech consisting of two contradictory terms, such as *bittersweet*.

P

pan • dem • ic *(adj.)* Occurring over a wide area; affecting a majority of the people; universal.

pan • op • tic *(adj.)* All-seeing; all-inclusive.

pa • roe • mi • a *(n.)* A proverb; adage.

pec • u • late *(vb.)* To embezzle; appropriate wrongfully something in one's care.

pe • riph • ra • sis *(n.)* Circumlocution; roundabout manner of expression; use of a longer phrase when a simpler one will do.

per • spic • u • ous *(adj.)* Clear; easily understood; intelligible.

phon *(n.)* A unit for measuring the level of loudness.

pho • neme *(n.)* The smallest unit of speech that distinguishes one utterance from another.

pho • no • gram *(n.)* A character or symbol, such as & used for *and*, used to represent a word, syllable, or **phoneme.**

ple • o • nasm *(n.)* Repetition; redundancy; superfluity.

pleth • o • ric *(adj.)* Excessive; profuse.

post • pran • di • al *(adj.)* After a meal, usually dinner.

prax • is *(n.)* Actual practice; exercise; use; habit; custom.

pre • pran • di • al *(adj.)* Before a meal, usually dinner.

pre • scrip • tive *(adj.)* In law, unchallenged; customary; attained by long use.

pre • ter • nat • u • ral *(adj.)* Exceptional; outstanding; supernatural; abnormal.

pris • tine *(adj.)* Original; primitive; uncorrupted.

pro • em *(n.)* Introductory piece; opening; preface.

pro • lep • sis *(n.)* Anticipation; presupposition; preconception.

pro • me • the • an *(adj.)* Inventive; creative; resembling Prometheus.

pro • trep • tic *(n.)* An exhortation; pep talk.

prox • i • mate *(adj.)* Very near; close; imminent; approximate.

Q

quid • di • ty *(n.)* A trifling point; quibble; essential nature of something.

quo • tid • i • an *(adj.)* Daily; commonplace.

R

ra • dix *(n.)* The primary source or cause of something; originating cause.

ra • ti • oc • i • nate *(vb.)* To reason; deliberate; consider.

rec • to *(n.)* A right-handed page.

re • i • fy *(vb.)* To make an abstraction mentally concrete or material; materialize.

ru • bric *(n.)* A heading or caption at the beginning of a section, chapter, or other part; name; title.

S

scho • li • um *(n.)* Also *scholion*. A marginal notation; explanatory remark.

sed • u • lous *(adj.)* Persevering; characterized by diligence and care.

se • mei • ol • o • gy *(n.)* The science of signs and symbols and of sign language; semantics.

se • ri • a • tim *(adj.)* Following serially; point by point.

sim • u • la • crum *(n.)* Image; representation; imitation.

so • dal • i • ty *(n.)* An association based on common interests; community.

sol • i • dus *(n.)* A diagonal slash mark, as in *2/3*.

sto • chas • tic *(adj.)* Conjectural; random.

sub • ven • tion *(n.)* Assistance; aid, especially financial; support; endowment; subsidy.

sump • tu • ar • y *(adj.)* Regulating and limiting expenditures; controlling extravagance.

syl • lo • gism *(n.)* A form of deductive reasoning that consists of a major and minor premise and a conclusion; deduction.

sy • ner • gism *(n.)* Cooperative activity; acting or working together.

T

tax • on • o • my *(n.)* The technique of scientific classification; orderly classification.

tec • ton • ics *(n.)* The science or art of construction; architectonics.

tele • ge • nic *(adj.)* Especially suitable for broadcasting on television.

ten • den • tious *(adj.)* Biased; having a tendency toward a particular viewpoint.

ter • gi • ver • sate *(vb.)* To keep reversing one's attitude or opinion; shift; equivocate.

ter • ra • que • ous *(adj.)* Consisting of land and water.

top • o • nym *(n.)* A place name; noun derived from a place name, as in *damask* (Damascus).

tra • duce *(vb.)* To slander or malign; betray.

trope *(n.)* Figure of speech; the use of language in a nonliteral sense, as with a metaphor.

U

un • to • ward *(adj.)* Unfortunate; unfavorable; awkward; unruly.

u • su • fruct *(n.)* The right to enjoy the use of something owned by someone else.

V

ver • so *(n.)* A left-handed page.

ver • tex *(n.)* The farthest point; highest point; terminating point.

W

wid • get *(n.)* A colloquial term for any small mechanical device; gadget.

X

xen • o • phile *(n.)* Someone attracted to foreign things, such as manners and styles, or people.

xen • o • phobe *(n.)* Someone fearful of foreign things or people.

CLICHES

A

A-1 The best; excellent.

ace in the hole An advantage held in reserve for later use.

acid test A crucial or severe test.

Actions speak louder than words. What you do is more important than what you say.

all in a day's work A routine matter.

all in the same boat All sharing the same risk or experience.

all wet Wrong.

armed to the teeth Fully or excessively equipped.

arm's length A distance deliberately maintained.

at one's fingertips Readily available.

avoid like the plague To avoid at all costs.

ax to grind Something to achieve.

B

backhanded compliment A compliment that seems like a criticism.

back to square one Starting over.

back to the drawing board The need to redo or redesign something.

back to the wall Being in a desperate position; under attack.

bag of tricks All of one's available resources.

bark up the wrong tree To pursue the wrong thing.

bear the brunt To assume the burden or responsibility; take the main load.

beat around the bush To be indirect or evasive.

bed of roses An enviable or desirable situation.

beg the question To accept as fact something in doubt or not yet proven.

being all things to all people Trying to please everyone.

beside the point Irrelevant.

better late than never An excuse for being late.

bide time To wait for a good opportunity.

bird's-eye view A broad view.

bite off more than one can chew To undertake more than one can handle.

bite the bullet To prepare reluctantly for a difficult task; make a difficult decision.

blaze a trail To lead the way in a new venture.

blessing in disguise A misfortune that turns out to be useful or beneficial.

blow hot and cold To be inconsistent.

blow off steam To vent anger or frustration.

bone of contention A topic or matter of dispute.

both feet on the ground Practical; sensible.

burden of proof The need to demonstrate or prove an assertion or charge.

burn a candle at both ends To overwork mentally or physically; use resources and energies to excess.

burn the midnight oil To work late.

bury the hatchet To settle a disagreement or dispute.

business as usual Doing the same thing in the same way; continuing to do something in the face of difficulty.

by leaps and bounds Quickly; at an impressive rate.

by the book Strictly by the rules.

by the same token For the same reason.

by word of mouth Informally; by telling others in conversation; dissemination by speech rather than by writing.

C

call a halt To discontinue activity, usually temporarily.

call into question To challenge; question.

captain of industry An influential businessperson; a leader in the business community.

catbird seat A position of advantage.

change of heart A reversal of opinion.

checkered career A history of both success and failure.

chew out To reprimand.

clean as a whistle Neat; clean; pure.

clear the air To remove obstructions or complications; be candid.

close shop To stop work; discontinue business operations.

conventional wisdom Generally accepted ideas.

cream of the crop The best of the lot; the choicest ones in a group.

cross a bridge when one comes to it To deal with a problem later.

cut and dried Routine; established.

D

dead letter Something or someone who no longer has any influence or has become unimportant.

dead to rights Certain; without possibility of error.

deep-six To discard.

die is cast, the It's too late; a decision has been made.

dot the i's and cross the t's To be thorough; pay attention to the details.

draw the line at To refuse to cross a boundary or go beyond a certain point.

E

eleventh hour At the last minute; latest possible time.

entertain high hopes To have high expectations.

Every man has his price. There is a limit to everyone's principles; everyone's support can be bought.

explore every avenue To be thorough, diligent, and resourceful in searching for a solution.

F

face the music To confront something unpleasant; cope with a difficult situation.

fair shake Fair treatment.

false alarm A warning that proves unnecessary; an expectation of something that does not happen.

far cry Long distance; a big difference.

fat cat A wealthy person.

feel the pinch To suffer from adverse conditions; suffer a hardship; suffer from financial constraints.

few and far between Infrequent.

fight tooth and nail To fight or work hard.

fill the bill To meet the need; serve the purpose.

finishing touch The final details; last bit of work.

first magnitude, of the Prominent; outstanding.

fly-by-night Undependable; referring to an operation that sets up and departs quickly.

fly in the face of To challenge; defy.

fly in the ointment An obstacle.

food for thought Something to think about.

force to be reckoned with Something of strength or significance that must be taken into account or dealt with.

foregone conclusion Something already decided.

fourth estate The press; the media.

from A to Z From beginning to end; from first to last.

from the word go From the outset; from the beginning.

full steam ahead Proceeding with all available power; at top speed; without hesitation.

G

get a handle on To find a way to cope with something difficult.

get down to brass tacks To deal with the essentials of something.

get it down pat To get it right; learn how to do it right.

get sacked To be fired.

get to the bottom of To find the underlying reason; find out why something happened.

give a wide berth to To avoid; steer clear of.

give short shrift to To make quick work of.

give the benefit of the doubt To decide favorably even though evidence isn't available or doesn't support the decision.

go against the grain To do something that seems unnatural or illogical.

go for broke To risk everything.

going in circles Not accomplishing anything.

good old boy An accepted member of a cohesive or traditional group, especially one that excludes or discriminates against others.

grist for the mill Something that can be used.

H

half the battle A lot accomplished; a successful start.

handwriting on the wall A forewarning; something bad about to happen.

hang in the balance To be undecided; have an uncertain outcome.

hard and fast Rigid.

have a bone to pick To have something to discuss, question, or argue about.

hit the nail on the head To reach the right conclusion.

hive of industry A busy place, especially one that is commercial.

hoi polloi The masses; the common people.

hold forth To discuss at length or in depth.

holding the bag Left with a responsibility.

I

in a nutshell Briefly; concisely.

in a word Briefly.

ins and outs Ramifications of or changes in a situation.

in the long run Over a long period.

J

jaundiced eye A prejudiced, generally antagonistic view.

John Hancock One's signature.

K

keep the ball rolling To sustain something; take action.

keep one's head above water To stay solvent.

kill two birds with one stone To achieve two objectives with a single effort.

know the ropes To know how to do something; understand something.

L

lay one's cards on the table To be candid; reveal what one has or wants.

leave no stone unturned To be persistent and thorough in a quest.

leave out in the cold To exclude.

letter-perfect Perfect; just right.

let the chips fall where they may. Don't worry about the consequences; do what one thinks must be done regardless.

live and learn To profit from mistakes.

lock, stock, and barrel Everything.

long shot An attempt with little chance of success.

lost cause Hopeless effort or quest.

M

maintain the status quo To keep things as they are.

make or break To succeed or fail.

Midas touch The ability to make money at anything.

moment of truth A time of crisis; severe test; time for a decision.

month of Sundays A long time.

more than one bargained for Beyond what one expected or wanted.

movers and shakers The decision makers; influential people.

muddy the water To confuse things; make trouble.

N

net result The outcome; basic reason.

nose to the grindstone Hard at work; busy working.

no-win situation A situation in which one won't benefit regardless of what one does.

O

off and running On the way; making good progress.

off the beaten track Isolated; inaccessible.

old-boy network An unofficial association of men who because of common interests or past connections tend to help each other to the exclusion of others.

on the fence Neutral; undecided; uncommitted.

open and aboveboard Fair; without anything underhanded.

open book Transparent; with motives easily perceived.

open question An undecided issue.

out on a limb In a dangerous position; exposed.

over a barrel At a disadvantage.

P

pack it in To quit; give up.

paper over To conceal.

paper tiger Something less formidable than it appears.

pave the way for To prepare for.

pay through the nose To be charged an exorbitant price; be overcharged.

pick someone's brain To question someone to get information; glean information from someone.

plain as day Obvious.

play fast and loose To fail to keep a promise that was made or implied.

play one's cards right To make good decisions or moves.

point of no return The time when or place where it is too late to go back or change something.

pull it off To succeed.

put a good face on it To do or say something to make a bad situation seem better.

put all one's eggs in one basket To rely on one thing; risk everything on a single venture.

put it on the back burner To postpone it; wait until later.

putting the cart before the horse Taking steps in an illogical order.

put one's best foot forward To present the best possible image of oneself.

put one's money on the line To back up one's opinions with an investment.

Q

quick study Someone who learns quickly.

R

rank and file Ordinary people.

read between the lines To determine what is really meant rather than what is actually written; surmise.

read something into it To attach significance to something when nothing significant is evident; assume something more than what was said or done.

red herring Something done or said to divert people from the truth or from a matter that one does not want known.

red-letter day A memorable or important day.

roll with the punches To adjust to the situation.

rubber check A check returned for insufficient funds.

rule of thumb A general guide.

run its course To go to completion.

run of the mill Ordinary; usual.

S

save face To avoid embarrassment.

second to none The best; as good as or better than the competition.

see eye to eye To agree; mutually understand.

seize the bull by the horns To take bold action under difficult circumstances.

separate the men from the boys To reveal who is tough and mature.

ship of state The nation.

short end of the stick, at the At a disadvantage.

shot in the dark A conjecture.

sight unseen Without inspection.

sit tight To wait; wait patiently.

sixth sense The ability to understand things that other people ordinarily miss.

soft soap Flattery.

sound as a dollar Reliable.

sour grapes A negative attitude; suggestion that something unattainable isn't desirable anyway.

split hairs To argue over fine points or trifling matters.

square deal A fair and honorable arrangement.

stem the tide To stop, divert, or change something.

stickler for the rules Someone who is overly fussy about established procedure.

string along To deceive.

T

take with a grain of salt To be skeptical; to not take something seriously.

talk it up To promote or advance something.

thorn in one's side An annoying or bothersome person or thing.

throw light on To clarify; explain.

tighten one's belt To economize.

tip of the iceberg Only a small part of something.

track record One's accomplishments.

turn the tables To reverse something.

turn the tide To change one's fortune.

20/20 hindsight A clear understanding after the fact.

CLICHES

U

up to snuff Equal to a certain level of quality.

W

wave of the future A significant trend.
whole ball of wax The entire situation.
whole new ball game A changed or different situation.
whys and wherefores Questions and answers.
with flying colors With success.

ABBREVIATIONS

General Business Abbreviations

A

aa Always afloat; author's alteration(s)

a&a Additions and amendments

aac Average annual cost

aae Average annual earnings

aap Advise if able to proceed

aar After-action report; against all risks

abi Abstracted business information

ac Average cost

a/c Account; account current

acn All concerned notified; assignment control number

a/c pay. Accounts payable

a/c rec. Accounts receivable

acv Actual cash value

ad, a/d After date

a&d Accounting and disbursing; ascending and descending

A.D. (Latin: *Anno Domini*) In the year of our Lord

ada Average daily attendance

adcon Advance concepts; advise all concerned

ad&d Accidental death and dismemberment (insurance)

ade Automatic data entry; average daily enrollment

adeda Advise effective/earliest date

ad fin. (Latin: *ad finem*) To the end

ad id. (Latin: *ad idem*) Both the same; likewise

ad inf. (Latin: *ad infinitum*) To infinity

ad init. (Latin: *ad initium*) At the beginning

ad int. (Latin: *ad interim*) In the interim or meantime

ad lib. (Latin: *ad libitum*) At one's pleasure; freely to the degree desired

ad loc. (Latin: *ad locum*) To or at this place

adm Action description memo; average daily membership

adsap Advise as soon as possible

adsc Average daily service charge

Adt Atlantic daylight time

ad val. (Latin: *ad valorem*) According to value

advof Advise this office

aec Additional extended coverage; at earliest convenience

aep Accrued expenditure paid

afc Average fixed cost

agb Any good brand

agi Adjusted gross income; annual general inspection

a&h Accident and health (insurance)

a.h.v. (Latin: *ad hunc vocum*) At this word

a&i Abstracting and indexing; accident and indemnity (insurance)

aia Advise if available

aka Also known as

alc (French: *a la carte*) On a menu with items priced separately

alcon All concerned

ald A later date; acceptable limit for dispersion

alf Automatic letter facer

all. Above lower limit

a.m. (Latin: *ante meridiem*) Before noon

am. cur. (Latin: *amicus curiae*) Friend of the court

amo Advance material order; airmail only

amr Automatic message routing

an. Above named; arrival notice (shipping); (Latin: *ante*) before; (Latin: *anno*) year

anon. Anonymous; nameless

anvo Accept no verbal orders

ao Access opening; area of operations; accuracy only

ao, a/o Account of

aob Annual operating budget; any other business; at or below

aod As of date

aok All okay

aor Area of responsibility

a/or And/or

aos Acquisition of signal; add or subtract

ap Above proof; access panel; action potential; additional premium; advanced placement; attached processor; author's proof; average product

a/p Authority to pay; authority to purchase

apc Average propensity to consume

apr, APR Annual percentage rate

aps Average propensity to save

aq Accomplishment quotient; achievement quotient; any quantity

ar Achievement ratio; all rail; allocated reserve; average revenue

ar, a/r All risks

a/r At the rate of

ARM Adjustable-rate mortgage

aro After receipt of order

art. Advanced research and technology; automatic reporting telephone

as. At sight

a/s After sight; alongside

asap As soon as possible

ASC All Saver Certificate

Asl, ASL American sign language

asr Answer and receive; available supply rate

Ast Atlantic standard time

@ At

At Atlantic time

A/t American terms

ata Actual time of arrival; air to air

atar Above transmitted and received

atiob As this is our best

ATM Automated teller machine

ato According to others

a to oc Attached to other correspondence

atp (French: *á tout prix*) At any price

aureq Authority is requested

av Assessed valuation; audiovisual

ava Audiovisual aids

avc Average variable cost

a/w Actual weight; all-water; all-weather

awiy As we informed you

B

b. Born; brother

b/a Billed at; budget authorized

ba&f Budget, accounting, and finance

b/b Bail bond

b&b Bed and board; bed and breakfast

bc Back course; bad check; between centers; budgeted cost; building center; bulk carrier

bc, b/c Bills for collection

b/c Broadcast

b&c Buildings and contents

B.C. Before Christ

bd Bank draft

b/d Barrels per day; brought down (accounting)

bdi Both days included

b/e Bill of exchange; bill of entry

bf Backfeed; boldface

b.f. (Latin: *bona fide*) Genuine; in good faith; without fraud or deception

b/f Brought forward (accounting)

b&g Buildings and grounds

b&i Bankruptcy and insolvency

b/l Basic letter; bill of lading; blueline; blueprint

bll Below lower limit

bo Blackout; branch office

bo, b/o Back order

b/o Brought over (accounting); budget outlay

bop Balance of payments; best operating procedure

b/p Bills payable; bill of parcels
br Bank rate; bill of rights; builder's risk
b/r Bills receivable
BRM Business reply mail
bs Backspace
b/s Bill of sale; bill of sight
bta Best time available; better than average
btf Balance to follow
b/tf Balance transferred
BTW By the way (E-mail)
bv Book value
b.w. (German: *bitte wenden*) Please turn over
b/w Black and white

C

c About; calorie; candle, carat; cent; century; chapter; child
©, copr. Copyright
ca About; civil authorities; current assets
c/a Capital account; current account
cad. Cash against documents; contract award date
caf Clerical, administrative, and fiscal; cost and freight; cost, assurance, and freight
cap. Capital letter; client assessment package
caps. Capital letters
catv, CATV Cable television; community antenna television
cav. (Latin: *caveat*) Warning; writ of suspension
cav. emp. (Latin: *caveat emptor*) Let the buyer beware
CB Citizen's band (radio)

cbd Cash before delivery

cbx, CBX Computerized branch exchange; computerized business exchange

cc Chief complaint; color code; command and control; computer copy; copy

c/c Center to center; current account

c/d Carried down (accounting); cash against documents; certificate of deposit

c&d Collection and delivery

CD Certificate of deposit; compact disk

cdst Central daylight saving time

cdt Central daylight time

ce copyeditor

ceo, CEO Chief executive officer

cf. (Latin: *conferre*) Compare

c/f Carried forward (accounting)

c&f Clearing and forwarding; cost and freight

cf&c Cost, freight, and commission

cfi Cost, freight, and insurance

cfo Cost for orders

cfo, CFO Chief financial officer

ci Coefficient of intelligence

ci, c&i Cost and insurance

c/i Certificate of insurance

cia Cash in advance

c/l Carload lot; cash letter

c&lc Capital and lowercase (small) letters

c/m Current month

c/o Care of; carried over (accounting); cash order; complains/complaints of

c.o.d., C.O.D. Cash on delivery

coh Cash on hand

cola, COLA Cost-of-living adjustment; cost-of-living allowance

co-op Cooperative

cos Cash on shipment

cpa Closest point of approach; cost planning and appraisal

cpa, CPA Critical path analysis

CPA Certified public accountant

cpi, CPI Consumer price index

CPLS Certified professional legal secretary

CPS Certified professional secretary

cr. Credit

c/r Company risk; correction requirement

CRIS Carrier Route Information System

cs Capital stock; center section; current series

c&sc Caps and small caps (capital and small capital letters)

cst Cargo ships and tankers; central standard time

ct Central time; central timing

c/t Certificate of title

cv Capital value; carrier vehicle; collection voucher

c.v., C.V. Curriculum vitae

cwo Cash with order

cx Correct copy

cx, CX Central exchange

cy Calendar year; current year

D

d Daughter; day; degree; died

da Days after acceptance; delayed action; discharge afloat; do not answer; documents against acceptance; documents attached; doesn't answer

da, d/a Deposit account

dad. Dispense as directed

daf Discharge afloat

dalpo Do all possible

dap Data analysis package; data automation proposal; do anything possible; documents against payment

das Delivered alongside ship

dat Day (date) after tomorrow

db Day book; delayed broadcast; distribution board; double bed

db. Debit

d/b Documentary bill

dba Doing business as/at

dbb Dinner, bed, breakfast

dbi Database index

dc Data collection; dead center; deck cargo; digital computer; direct credit; down center

dc, d/c Deviation clause; double column

d/c Drift correction

dco Draft collection only

dd Days after date; deferred delivery; delayed delivery; double draft; dry dock

dd, d/d Due date

d/d Dated; delivered at dock; demand draft; developer/demonstrator; domicile to domicile

de Deflection error; direct elimination; direct entry; double entry

d/e Date of establishment

ded Date expected delivery

dep Do everything possible

df Damage free; dead freight; decontamination factor; disposition form

d/f Defogging; direct flow

dia Date of initial appointment; due in assets

dis Delivered into store

diw Dead in water

dj Disc jockey; dust jacket

D-J Dow-Jones (industrial average)

dl Day letter; driver's license

dl, d/l Data link; demand loan

dlo Difference in longitude; dispatch loading only

dlo, DLO Dead-letter office

dlp Date of last payment

d/m Date and month; day and month; density/moisture

dn, d/n Debit note

dnl Do not load

dnr Does not run; do not renew

do. Days off; direct order; ditto; dual ownership

do., d/o Delivery order

d/o Disbursing officer

doa Date of arrival; date of availability; direction of approach; disposal of assets

dob Date of birth

dos Date of sale

dp Data processing; deal pending; departure point; distribution point

d/p Delivery papers; documents against payment

dpa Deferred payment account

dpp Deferred payment plan

dr. Differential rate

d/r Deposit receipt

ds Days after sight; dead-air space; debenture stock; double strength

d.s., dss Documents signed

dso Direct shipment order

ds&r Data storage and retrieval; document search and retrieval

dss Dry surface storage

dst Daylight saving time

dta Daily travel allowance

dtc Design to cost; direct to consumer

dtp, DTP Desktop publishing

d/tr Documents against trust receipt

dudat Due date

d/v Declared value

D.V. (Latin: *Deo volente*) God willing

dw Deadweight; delivered weight; double weight

d/w Dock warrant

dyb Do your best

dyu Do your utmost

E

eac Estimate at completion

ead Equipment allowance deduction; estimated availability date

eaf Emergency action file

eal Estimated average life

eaon Except as otherwise noted

eat. Earnings after taxes

ecd Estimated completion date

ecr Energy consumption rate

e&d Exploration and development

edd Estimated delivery date; expected date of delivery

edt Eastern daylight time

ee Errors excepted

eeo Equal employment opportunity

eer Energy efficiency ratio

e.g. (Latin: *exempli gratia*) For example

e/i Endorsement irregular

ein, EIN Employer identification number

el Each layer; educational level; extra line

e.m.p. (Latin: *ex modo prescripto*) As or in the manner prescribed

eo (Latin: *ex officio*) End of operation; by authority of his or her office

eoa Effective on or about; examination, opinion, advice

eod Every other day

eoe Equal opportunity employer

e&oe Errors and omissions excepted

eom End of message; end of month; every other month

eooe Error or omission excepted

eoq End of quarter

eot End of transmission

eov End of volume

eps Earnings per share; emergency power supply

epte Existed prior to entry

e/r Editing/reviewing; en route

Esl, ESL English as a second language

Esq. Esquire

est Eastern standard time

et Eastern time; educational therapy; elapsed time; electric/electronic typewriter

eta Estimated time of arrival

et al. (Latin: *et alibi*) And elsewhere; (Latin: *et alia*) and others

etc. (Latin: *et cetera*) And so on; and so forth

et seq. (Latin: *et sequens*) And following

et ux. (Latin: *et uxor*) And wife

ev Earned value; exposure value

e/w Equipped with

ex. af. (Latin: *ex afinis*) Of affinity

ex cath. (Latin: *ex cathedra*) From the seat of authority

ex int. Ex (without) interest

ex off. (Latin: *ex officio*) By authority of his or her office

ex p. (Latin: *ex parte*) On one side only

F

f Family; farthing; father; female

f. Folio; following page

F Fahrenheit
faa Free of all average
fac Fast as can
faq Fair average quality; free at quay
FAQ Frequently asked questions (E-mail)
fas Free alongside ship
fb Freight bill
f/b Feedback; front to back
fc Fixed cost; follow copy
fc, f/c Free and clear
f&c Fire and casualty (insurance)
f&d Freight and demurrage
ff Far afield; folded flat; form feed
ff. Following (after a numeral)
f/f Face-to-face; flip-flop
ffa Free for all; free from alongside; for further assignment
ffwd Fast forward
fga Foreign general average; free of general average
fic Freight, insurance, carriage
FICA Federal Insurance Contributions Act
fifo First in, first out
filo First in, last out
fka Formerly known as
fl. (Latin: *floruit*) Flourished
f/n Freight note
fna For necessary action
fo Fade out; free out; full out terms
fo, f/o Firm offer
f/o For credit of; for orders

fob Free on board
foc Free of charge; free on car
fod Free of damage
foq Free on quay
fow Free on wharf
fp Fire policy; fixed price; floating policy; fully paid
f/s Financial statement; first stage
ft Free of tax; free trade; full terms
f&t Fire and theft (insurance)
fv. (Latin: *folio verso*) Back of the page
fx Foreign exchange
FY Fiscal year
fyeo, FYEO For your eyes only
fyi, FYI For your information
fyr, FYR For your reference

G

g/a General average; ground to air
gaq General air quality
gar Gross annual return
GATT General Agreement on Tariffs and Trade
gav Gross annual value
g/av General average
gbo Goods in bad order
gdp, GDP Gross domestic product
gep, GEP Gross energy product
gi Government issue; gross income; gross inventory

GmbH (German: *Gesellschaft mit beschrankter Haftung*) Incorporated, limited liability company

Gmt Greenwich mean time

gne, GNE Gross national expenditure

gni, GNI Gross national income

gnp, GNP Gross national product

gtc Good till canceled

gtw Good this week

g/w Gross weight

H

h.a. (Latin: *hoc anno*) In this year

hb, h/b Handbook

hc Hard copy

h-d Heavy duty; high density

h/f Held for

hi fi High fidelity

h.l. (Latin: *hoc loco*) In this place

ht Half title; halftone; high tension

I

i&a Indexing and abstracting

iae In any event

iatr Is amended to read

iaw In accordance with

ibid. (Latin: *ibidem*) In the same place

ico In case of
icw In connection with
id. (Latin: *idem*) The same
ID, I.D. Identification
id. ac (Latin: *idem ac*) The same as
i.e. (Latin: *id est*) That is
ifo In favor of; in front of
iia If incorrect, advise
i/l Import license
IMHO In my humble opinion (E-mail)
inf. (Latin: *infra*) Infinity; below
i/o In and/or over; input/output; instead of
i&o Input and output
IOU I owe you
iow In other words
i/p Input
i&p Interest and principal
IQ Import quota; intelligence quotient
ISBN International Standard Book Number
it. Information technology
iv Invoice value
iv, i/v Increased value
i.v. (Latin: *in verbo*) Under the word

J

j. Journal
j/a Joint account
jds Job data sheet

je Job estimate
j/f Jigs and fixtures

L

l. Line
lc Lowercase (small letters)
l.c. (Latin: *loco citato*) In the place cited
lcl Less than carload lot
lifo Last in, first out
lmsc Let me see correspondence
loc Letter of credit
loc. primo cit. (Latin: *loco primo citato*) In the place first cited
lr Letter report; long range
l.s. (Latin: *locus sigilli*) Place of the seal
ltd. Limited

M

m (Latin: *meridies*) Male; married; masculine; noon
M Money supply
ma Machine account; mental age; monthly account
mag. op. (Latin: *magnum opus*) Major work
maitre d' (French: *maitre d'hotel*) Head waiter
mbo, MBO Management by Objectives (technique)
m/d Market day; memorandum of deposit; month(s) after date
Messrs. (French: *Messieurs*) Gentlemen
m/f Male or female

m&f Male and female

Mgr. (French: *Monseigneur*) Form of address to princes and prelates

Mlle. (French: *Mademoiselle*) Miss

Mlles. (French: *Mademoiselles*) Misses

m.m. (Latin: *mutatis mutandis*) With the necessary changes

Mme. (French: *Madame*) Madam

Mmes. (French: *Mesdames*) Ladies

ms, m/s Months after sight

MS., ms. Manuscript

MSS., mss. Manuscripts

mst Mean solar time; mountain standard time

mt Mountain time

N

n, n. Note; number

n. Net

na Not authorized

na, NA, N/A Not applicable; not available

n/a No account (banking)

NAFTA North American Free Trade Agreement

n.a.n. (Latin: *nisi aliter notetur*) Unless it is otherwise noted

n.b., N.B. (Latin: *nota bene*) Note well

n/c No charge

nd Next day; no date; no decision; no discount

ne Not exceeding

nes Not elsewhere specified

nf, n/f, N/F No funds

nfa No further action

ng No go; no good; not given; not good

nl New line; no liability; not licensed; not listed

nmi No middle initial

n/n No number; not to be noted

n/o In the name of; no orders

noa Not otherwise authorized

nohp Not otherwise herein provided

nol. con. (Latin: *nolo contendere*) Do not want to contend

nol. pros. (Latin: *nolle prosequi*) Do not want to prosecute

non obs. (Latin: *non obstante*) Notwithstanding

non seq. (Latin: *non sequitur*) It does not follow

no op. No opinion

nop Not otherwise provided for

nos Not otherwise specified

np Notary public; note payable

np, n.p. No place; no publisher

np, n/p Net proceeds

ns New series; not specified

NS, N.S. New style

nsf Not sufficient funds

n/t New terms

ntp No title page

O

o/a On account; on or about

oac On approved credit

ob. (Latin: *obiit*) Died

oc Office copy; on camera; open charter
o/c Overcharge
o/d On demand; overdraft
oe Omissions excepted
oka Otherwise known as
omc, OMC Owner may carry (real estate)
oo, o/o On order
o/o Order of
op Old prices; open policy; out of print
op. cit. (Latin: *opere citato*) In the work cited
os, o.s. Old series
os, o/s Out of stock
os, OS Operating system
o/s Out of service
OS On sample; one side
OS, O.S. Old style
ot Overtime
ow One way
owc, OWC Owner will carry (real estate)

P

p. Page
pa Particular average; pending availability; private account
pa, p/a Power of attorney
p/a Per annum
P.A. Professional associates; professional association
pabx, PABX Private automatic branch exchange
pass. (Latin: *passim*) Here and there

pax., PAX Private automatic exchange
pbx, PBX Private branch exchange
pc Percent; petty cash; prices current
pc, p/c, pct. Percent(age)
pc, PC Personal computer
pd Per diem
p.d. (Latin: *per diem*) By the day
pe printer's error
PERT Program Evaluation and Review Technique
p/f Portfolio
p&i Principal and interest
pin., PIN Personal identification number
pl. Plural; plate
p&l Profit and loss
PLC Public limited company (British)
P.M. (Latin: *post meridiem*) Afternoon and night
pn, p/n Part number; promissory note
p/n Please note
po, P.O. Postal (money) order; purchase order
p/o Part of
PO Post office
por Payable on receipt
pp Parcel post
pp. Pages
ppd. Prepaid
pph Per person hour
pro tem. (Latin: *pro tempore*) For the time being
P.S. (Latin: *post scriptum*) Written after
Pst Pacific standard time

Pt Pacific time

pto Please turn over

px, PX Please exchange; post exchange; private exchange

Q

q&a Question and answer

q.e. (Latin: *quod est*) Which is

q.e.d. (Latin: *quod erat demonstrandum*) That which was to be proved or demonstrated

q.v. (Latin: *quod vide*) Which see

R

r Recto

r&d, R&D Research and development

r/e Rate of exchange

roa Received on account; return on assets

roi Return on investment

rom. Roman (type style)

rop Run of paper; run of press

rp Return premium; reply paid

Rsvp, R.s.v.p. (French: *répondez s'il vous plaît*) Please reply

r&t Rail and truck

rv, RV Recreation vehicle; reentry vehicle

S

s Son; substantive; second

/s/ Signed

sa Subject to approval; safe arrival; (Latin: *sine anno*) without year ; (Latin: *sub anno*) the year

sae Self-addressed envelope

sanr Subject to approval—no risks

sare Self-addressed return envelope

sase Self-addressed stamped envelope

sb Small business; switchboard

s/b Statement of billing

sc Separate; small caps (small capital letters); statistical control

sc. (Latin: *scilicet*) To wit; namely

s/c Single column

scc Specific clauses and conditions

sd standard deviation

s.d. (Latin: *sine die*) Without a day being named

se Single entry; standard error; straightedge

s.e.e.o. (Latin: *salvis erroribus et omissis*) Excepting errors and omissions

seq. (Latin: *sequens*) The following; (Latin: *sequitur*) it follows

sf Sinking fund

sgd. Signed

s/h Shorthand

s.h.v. (Latin: *sub hoc voce*) Under this work

SIC Standard Industrial Classification

sit. Stopping in transit

SI unit (French: *Système International unit*) International System of Units

s/l Self-loading

s&l Savings and loan

slr Self-loading rifle; single-lens reflex

SM, sm Service mark

smat See me about this

sm. caps Small capitals (small capital letters)

smsa, SMSA Standard metropolitan statistical area

s/n Serial number; service number; stock number

so. Seller's option; senior officer; ship's option; shop order; standing order; supply office(r)

so., s/o Shipping order

s-o Shutoff

s/o Son of

sob. See order blank

sop., SOP Standard operating procedure

sp Self-propelled; selling price; single purpose; special purpose; standard practice; starting point; stop payment

srac Short-run average cost

srm Standard reference material

ss Sample size; single signal; single source; social security; solid state; stainless steel; steamship; supersonic

ss. (Latin: *scilicet*) Namely; (Latin: *supra scriptum*) written above

s/s Same size

st Stock transfer; surface tension; survival time

s&t Science and technology

sto Standing order

s to s Ship to shore; station to station

sup. (Latin: *supra*) Above

s.v. (Latin: *sub verbo*) Under the word

s-w Shortwave

s/w Seaworthy; standard weight

s&w Salaries and wages; surveillance and warning

swm Standards, weights, and measures

swoc Subject word out of context

T

ta Target area; teaching assistant; time and attention; travel allowance

t/a Trading as

taw Twice a week

tb Time base; trial balance

t&b Top and bottom

tba To be announced; to be approved; to be assigned; to be audited

tbb To be billed

tbd To be determined

tbo To be ordered

tc Total cost; true course

tcb Take care of business

td Technical director; time delay; time of departure

td, t/d Time deposit

t/d Table of distribution

tf Till forbidden (advertising)

t/f True/false

t&h Transportation and handling

tl Time limit; time line; time loan; total load; transmission line; truck load(ing)

t/l Total loss

TM, tm Trademark

to. Telephone order; turn off

t/o Takeoff

toc Table of contents

tod Time of day; time of delivery

tp Title page

tr. Transpose

t/r Transmit/receive

ts Time sharing; typescript; type specification

U

uc Uppercase (capital letters)

ucb Unless caused by

ufa Until further advised

ufn Until further notice

u&lc Upper and lowercase (capital and small letters)

uo Undelivered orders

u/o Used on

us. Under seal; undersize; uniform sales

u.s. (Latin: *ut supra*) As above

usc Under separate cover

u.s.w. (German: *und so weiter*) And so forth

ut Universal time

u/t Untrained

u/w Underwater; under way; underwriter; used with

ux. (Latin: *uxor*) Wife

V

v. Verse; verso
v., vb. Verb(al)
v., vs. Versus
vg Very good
v.i. (Latin: *vide infra*) See below
vid. (Latin: *vide*) See
vip Very important person; very important people
viz. (Latin: *videlicet*) Namely
vr Variable response
v.s. (Latin: *vide supra*) See above
vv Vice versa

W

wa Will advise; with average (insurance)
war. With all risks
wats, WATS Wide-area telephone/telecommunications service
w/b Westbound
wc Working capital; workers' compensation
w/c With corrections
w/e Weekend
wf Wrong font
wip Work in process; work in progress
wo Wait order; work order; write out; written order
wo, w/o Without
woh Work on hand

wp Will proceed; word processing; working paper; working party

w/p Without prejudice

wpi, WPI Wholesale price index

ww Warehouse warrant; waterworks; wrong word

WYSIWG (pronounced wiz · ee · wig) What you see is what you get (desktop publishing)

X

xch Exchange

xp Express paid

xref Cross-reference

xs Cross section; extra strong

Y

y/o Years old

yob Year of birth

yod Year of death

ytd Year to date

ytm Yield to maturity

Z

z, zn. Zone

zo Zero output

Technical Business Abbreviations

A

a Arc; atto- (*prefix:* one-quintillionth)
a, amp. Ampere
A Absolute
Å Aangstrom
abamp Absolute ampere
abm, ABM Automated batch mixing
abp, ABP Actual block processor
ac Alternating current; automatic analog computer
acc, ACC Accumulator
ace. Automatic circuit exchange
acf Advanced communication function
acm Area-composition machine; automatic coding machine
acr Abandon call and retry
acu Address control unit; automatic calling unit
a/d Analog to digital
adc, ADC Analog-to-digital converter
ADDR Address
ade Automatic data entry
ADJ Adjust
adl, ADL Automatic data link

adp Automated data processing
ADR Adder
ADV Advance
aex Automatic electronic exchange
af Audiofidelity; audiofrequency; autofocus
agw Actual gross weight
agz Actual ground zero
ah, a-h, Ah, amp. hr. Ampere-hour
ahm, a-hm Ampere-hour meter
ahp Air horsepower; aviation horsepower
ai Azimuth indicator
alcom Algebraic compiler; algebraic computer
alphanumeric Alphabetical and numerical
altran Algebraic translator
am., AM Amplitude modulation
a/m Auto/manual
a/m, A/m Ampere per meter
amp Average mean pressure
amp. Amplification; amplifier; amplitude
amp-turns Ampere-turns
amr, AMR Automatic message routing
amu Atomic mass unit
anacom Analog computer
aoi Angle of incidence
aor Angle of reflection
aos Add or subtract; angle of sight
a/p After perpendicular; angle point
aper. Aperture
apu Auxiliary power unit

ar Achievement ratio; aspect ratio; auditory reception
ar, AR Address register
arcos Arc cosine
aru Analog remote unit; audio response unit
asc Automatic sequence control; automatic switching center; auxiliary switch closed
ASCII American Standard Code for Information Interchange
asm Auxiliary-storage management
asr, ASR Answer-send-receive
at., a-t, At Ampere-ton; ampere-turn
atl Analog threshold logic
at. m Atomic mass
at/m, At/m Ampere turns per meter
AUTOVON Automatic voice network
avdp. Avoirdupois
aw Atomic weight
a/w Actual weight
az., azi., azm Azimuth

B

b Bit
ba, BA Binary add; bus available
bac, BAC Binary asymmetric channel
BAM Basic access method
bar. Barometer; barometric; base address register
bar., BAR Buffer address register
BASIC Beginner's All-Purpose Symbolic Instruction
bau Basic assembly unit; British absolute unit

bbl. Barrel
bbp Building-block principle
bbs Bulletin board system
bc Binary code; binary counter; bioconversion
bcd Binary-coded data; binary-coded decimal
bd. Baud
bdl. Bundle
bev, BeV Billion electron volts
bex Broadbank exchange
bfr. Buffer
bhp Boiler horsepower; brake horsepower
bi Buffer index
bi., BI Binary
bit., bit Binary digit
biu Basic information unit
bix Binary information exchange
bjf Batch-job format
bl Baseline
bl. Bale
bm Board measure
bm, BM Buffer mark; buffer modules
bmep Brake mean effective pressure
bn, BN Binary number (system)
bof, BOF Beginning of file
bot, BOT Beginning of tape
bpi Bits per inch; bytes per inch
bps Bits per second; bytes per second
bpu Base production unit
br., BR Branch

bs Binary subtraction

bs, BS Backspace (character)

bsc Basic message switching center; binary synchronous communication

bsd Bit storage density

btl Beginning tape level

btu Basic transmission unit

btu, Btu, BTU British thermal unit

bu Base unit

bu. Bushel

C

c Calorie (large); carbohydrates; centi- (*prefix:* one-hundredth); coefficient; computer; cycle; speed of light

C Calculated weight; candle; Celsius; centigrade

cad. Cartridge-activated device

cad., CAD Computer-aided design

cad./cam., CAD/CAM Computer-aided design/computer-aided manufacturing

cal, CAL Computer-aided learning; Conversational Algebraic Language

cal. Calorie (small)

cam. Central-address memory; computer-addressed memory

cam., CAM Computer-aided manufacturing

CAN Cancel (character)

cap., CAP Computer-aided production

car., CAR Computer-assisted retrieval

CARR Carriage

caw Cam-action wheel; channel address word
c-b Circuit breaker
ccb Command control block; convertible circuit breaker
ccc Central computer complex; command control console; computer-command control
ccr Command control receiver; computer character recognition; control circuit resistance
ccv Closed-circuit voltage
Cd Coefficient of drag
cdb Current data bit
cdc Call-directing code
ce Circular error; compass error
cea Circular error average
cep Circle of equal probability; circle of error probability
cet Cumulative elapsed time
cf Centrifugal force
cff Computer forms feeder
cfp Computer forms printer
cg Centigram
cg, c of g Center of gravity
cgf Center-of-gravity factor
cgh Computer-generated hologram
cgl Center-of-gravity locator
c-h, chr Candle-hour
char., CHAR Character
ci Coefficient of intelligence
cic Command input coupler
ciu Computer interface unit
cl Centiliter

cla Communication line adaptor
cll Circuit load logic
clp, CLP Command language processor
CLS Close
clu Central logic unit
cm Center of mass; centimeter
cm, c/m Communications multiplexor
c/m Control and monitoring; cycles per minute
cml Circuit micrologic; current mode logic
CMND Command
CMP Compare
cmw Critical minimum weight
c/n Carrier to noise (ratio)
cnl Circuit net loss
coax. Coaxial
cof Coefficient of friction
c of e Coefficient of elasticity
compac, COMPAC Computer program for automatic control
cos., cos Cosine
cot. Card or tape reader
cot., cot, cotan. Cotangent
cp Candlepower; center of pressure; central processor
c/p Control panel
cpa Critical-path analysis
cpe Circular probable error
cph Characters per hour; cycles per hour
cpi Characters per inch
cpl Characters per line; common program language

cpm Cards per minute; characters per minute; counts per minute; critical path method; cycles per minute

cp/m Control program/microcomputers

cps Central processing system; characters per second; critical path scheduling; cycles per second

cpu, CPU Central processing unit

crf Control relay forward

crm Critical reaction measure; crucial reaction measure

crt, CRT Cathode-ray tube

crtu Combined receiving and transmitting unit

c/s Call signal; cycles per second

csect Control section; cross section

csl Computer-simulation language; computer-sensitive language

cst Channel status indicator; channel status table

csu Central statistical unit; circuit-switching unit; constant-speed unit

ct Contrast threshold; control transformer; current transformer

ctk Capacity-ton kilometer

ctm Capacity-ton mile; communications terminal modules

CTRL Control

ctu Centigrade thermal unit; central terminal unit

ctw. Counterweight

ctx Computer telex exchange

cub. Control unit busy; cubic

cum Central unit memory

cv Coefficient of variation

cw Continuous wave; cubic weight

c/w Chainwheel; counterweight

cwp, CWP Communicating word processor

cwt Centum weight; counterweight; hundredweight
cx Control transmitter
cx, CX Central exchange
cyc. Cycle
CZm Compass azimuth

D

d Day; deci- (*prefix:* one-tenth)
da Deka- (*prefix:* ten); density altitude; drift angle
dag Dekagram
dal Dekaliter
dam Dekameter
dam., DAM Direct-access method
datacom Data communications
dav Data above voice
db, dB Decibel
dbam, DBAM Database-access method
dbase Database
dBu Decibel unit
d-bug Debug(ged)(ging)
dc Digital computer; direct current; directional coupler; drift correction
dcd Differential current density
dd Digital data; digital display
ddc Direct digital control
dde Direct data entry
ddis Data display

ddl Data definition language; data description language; digital data link

ddm Data demand module

dds Digital display scope; digital dynamics simulator

decit Decimal digit

del., DEL Delete (character)

de/me Decoding memory

d/f Defogging; direct flow

dfa Digital fault analysis

dfd Data function diagram

dfg Digital function generator; diode function generator

dg Decigram

dgs Designated ground zero

dhp Developed horsepower

dian Digital analog

didad Digital data display

di/do. Data input/data output

dig., r-o Digital readout

div Data in voice; digits in voice

dks Dekastere

dl Deciliter

dl, d/l Data link

dlu Digitizer logic unit

dm Decimeter; delta modulation; demand meter

DMA Direct memory access

d-max. Density maximum

dmb Dual-mode bus

dmc Digital microcircuit

dmpi Desired mean point of impact

dms Digital multiplex switching
DNS Domain Name Servers (Internet)
dohc Double overhead cam; dual overhead cam
dos, DOS Disk operating system
dov, DOV Data over voice
dp Data processing; dewpoint; diametral pitch; diffusion pressure
dr. Dram
dri Data rate indicator; data reduction interpreter
drs Data-reduction system
drt Data-review technique
ds, DS Data set
dscb Data set control block
ds&r Data storage and retrieval
d to a Digital to analog
dtr Distribution tape reel
dtr, DTR Data terminal ready
duv, DUV Data under voice
dv Dependent variable
dvl Direct voice line
dvm Digital voltmeter
dvom Digital volt ohmmeter
dw Deadweight
dwc Deadweight capacity
dwt Deadweight ton; pennyweight

E

eb Electron beam
ecm Extended core memory

ecr Energy consumption rate
edac, edc Error detection and correction
edc Electronic digital computer
edp, EDP Electronic data processing
eer Energy-efficiency ratio
efi Electronic fuel injection
ehd Electrohydrodynamics
ehf Extra high frequency; extremely high frequency
ehp Effective horsepower
ekv Electron kilovolt
ekw Electrical kilowatt
elf. Extra low frequency; extremely low frequency
elv Extra low voltage; extremely low voltage
e/m (Specific) Electron mass
emf Electromotive force
ems Expected mean squares
emux Electronic multiplexer
emv Electron megavolt
eo, EO End of operation
e-o Electro-optical
eob, EOB End of block (character)
eof, EOF End of file
e of m Error of measurement
eoj, EOJ End of job
eolb, EOLB End-of-line block
eom, EOM End of message
eor, EOR End of record; end of run
eot, EOT End of tape; end of transmission
erf Error function

erp Effective radiated power
esc, ESC Escape (character)
esd Echo-sounding device; estimated standard deviation
esl Expected significance level
etb, ETB End-of-transmission block (character)
etx, ETX End of text (character)
ev Exposure value
ev, eV Electron volt
evt Effective visual transmission
ez Electrical zero
e/z Equal zero

F

f, F Farad; feedback
f, F, fath Fathom
f, ft. Feet; foot
F Fahrenheit
f-b Full-bore
f/b Feedback; front to back (ratio)
fbm Board foot measure
fc Foot-candle
fca Frequency control and analysis
fde Field decelerator
fdm Frequency division multiplexing
fe, FE Format effective
ff, FF Form feed
ffwd Full-speed forward
fhp Fractional horsepower

fl Flow line; fluid loss; focal length
fL Foot-lambert
fl. dr. Fluid dram
flf, FLF Flip-flop (computer)
fl. oz. Fluid ounce
fl. pt. Fluid pint
fl./rt. Flow rate
fm, FM Frequency modulation
fnp Fusion point
FORTRAN Formula Translation (language)
fov Field of view
f&r Feed and return; force and rhythm
fs, FS File separation
f/t Freight ton
ftbm Foot board measure
ft.-c Foot-candle
ft.-lb. Foot-pound
ft.-lbf Foot-pound force
FTP File transfer protocol (E-mail)
fwt. Featherweight

G

g Gram; gravity (acceleration of)
G Gauss; giga- (*prefix:* one billion)
gal. Gallon
galv. Galvanometer
Gb Gilbert
gc Geographical coordinates; gigacycle; gyrocompass

g cal. Gram calorie
GDT Graphic display terminal
gev, GeV Gigaelectronvolt
gew Gram equivalent weight
g-force Gravity force(s)
g gr. Great gross
ghx Ground heat exchange
GHz Gigahertz
g ion Gram ion
giq Giant imperial quart
gj Gigajoule
gm-aw Gram atomic weight
gmv Gram molecular volume
gmw Gram molecular weight
gor Gas-oil ratio
gpu Ground power unit
gr. Grain; gross
g-r Gamma ray
grtm Gross-ton mile
gs Ground speed
gsd Grid sphere drag
gtm Gross ton mile
gtw Gross ton weight
GV, Gv Gigavolt
gvw Gross vehicle weight
gw Ground wave
gw, Gw, GW Gigawatt
g/w Gross weight
gwh, GWh Gigawatt hour
gz Ground zero

H

h Hecto- (*prefix:* one hundred); height; hour
h, ha Hectare
H Henry
ha Hour angle; hour aspect
hc Hydrocarbon
hdtv, HDTV High-definition television
hepa High-efficiency particulate air (filter)
hf Hyperfocal
hf, HF High frequency
hhp Hydraulic horsepower
hi-T High torque
hl Hectoliter
hm Hectometer
hp High pressure; horizontal parallax; horsepower
hph, hp-h Horsepower-hour
HSP High-speed printer
hv High velocity; high voltage
hz, Hz Hertz

I

ia Impedance angle; international angstrom
iae Integral absolute error
ibw Information bandwidth
ic Input circuit; integrated circuit
i/c Intercom
icff Intercommunication flip-flop

id Inside diameter

idac Interim digital-analog converter

idp Information data processing; input data processing; integrated data processing

if. Information feedback; intermediate frequency

i gal. Imperial gallon

ihp Indicated horsepower

ihph Indicated horsepower hour

ildf Integrated logistic data file

ilf Inductive loss factor

im Impulse modulation; intensity modulation

imp. gal. Imperial gallon

in. Inch

INDN Indication

INDR Indicator

inr Impact noise rating; impact noise ratio

INT Initial

i/o Input/output

i&o Input and output

iob Input-output buffer

i/p Input

IP Internet protocol

ipa Intermediate power amplifier; internal power amplifier

ipfm Integral pulse frequency modulation

ir Infrared

i&r Information and retrieval

IRC Internet relay chat

ISDN Integrated Services Digital Network

ise Integral square error

is&r ~~Information storage and retrieval~~
ixc Interexchange

J

J Joule
jds Job data sheet
j/f Jigs and fixtures

K

k Carat (karat); Kelvin; kilo- (*prefix:* one thousand); knot
k, K About one thousand (computer storage capacity)
kb Keyboard; kilobit; kilobyte
kbar Kilobar
kbe Keyboard entry
kbtu Kilo British thermal unit
kc Kilocycle
kcal Kilocalorie
ke Kinetic energy
kev One thousand electron volts
kev, keV Kiloelectronvolt
kg Kilogram
kG Kilogauss
kg cal. Kilogram calorie
kg-f Kilogram-force
kgm Kilogram meter
khp Kilohorsepower

khz, kHz Kilohertz

kilohm, kΩ Kilo-ohm

kj, kJ Kilojoule

kK Kilokelvin

kl Kiloliter

km Kilometer

kmw Kilomegawatt

kmwhr Kilomegawatt-hour

kn Kilonewton; knot

kPa Kilopascal

kr Kiloroentgen

krad Kilorad

ksia Thousand square inches absolute

kt Karat (carat); kiloton

kv, kV Kilovolt

kva, kVa Kilovoltampere

kV/a Kilovolts per ampere

kvah Kilovolt-ampere-hour

kvam Kilovolt ampere meter

kvar Kilovar; kilovolt ampere reactive

kvarh Kilovar hour

kvm Kilovolt meter

kvp Kilovolt peak

kw, kW Kilowatt

kwh, kWh, kwhr Kilowatt hour

kwm Kilowatt meter

kwr Kilowatt reactive

L

l Line; liter; locus
L Lambert
LAN Local area network
lb Line buffer
lb. Pound
lb. ap., lb. avdp. Apothecaries' pound
lb. cal. Pound calorie
lbf, lb.-f Pound-force
lb. ft. Pound foot
lb. in. Pound inch
lbl., LBL Label
lbs. Pounds
lbs. t Pounds thrust
lc Liquid crystal; low calorie; low carbon
lcd Lowest common denominator
lcd, LCD Liquid crystal display
lcf Least common factor; lowest common factor
lcm Large-core memory; least common multiple; lowest common multiple
l-d Low density
lf Line feed; low frequency
lft Linear feet; linear foot
lg Large grain; long grain; low grade
lg. tn. Long ton
lha Local hour angle
lhr Lumen hour
li Line item; longitudinal interval

linac Linear accelerator
lin. ft. Linear feet; linear foot
ll, l/l Lower limit
l/l Line by line
llr Line of least resistance
lm Lumen
lms Least mean square; lumen second
lmt Length, mass, time
lna Low-noise amplifier
lob. Line of balance
loc Locus of control
lo-d Low density
log. Logarithm
lop. Line of position
los Line of sight; loss of signal
lp Latent period; light perception; linear programming; low pressure
lpcw Long-pulse continuous wave
lq Linear quantifier; lowest quartile
lsb Least significant bit
lsc Least significant character
lsd Last significant data; last significant digit; least significant difference; least significant digit
lsg List set generator
lt Line terminator; long ton; low temperature; low tension; low torque
ltm Low thermal mass
lv Low viscosity; low voltage
lvr Line voltage regulator
lw Long wave

M

m Mega- (*prefix:* one million); meter; milli- (*prefix:* one-thousandth)

M Money (supply); thousand

ma, mA Milliampere

mÅ Milliangstrom

mad. Mean absolute deviation

mae Mean absolute error

mamp Milliampere

MAN Metropolitan area network

mar. Memory address register; minimal angle resolution

mas Milliampere second

mb Macrobiotic; megabyte; memory buffer

mb, mbar Millibar

mbps Megabits per second; million bits per second

mbr Memory buffer register

mb/s Megabits per second

mc Magnetic center; master control; megacycle; metric carat; millicycle

mcg Microgram

mc hr. Millicurie hour

mci Megacurie

mcvf Multichannel voice frequency

m-d, modem Modulator-demodulator

mdn. Median

mdt Mean downtime

m/e Mechanical/electrical

mean max. Mean maximum

mep Mean effective pressure

mev, meV Million electron volts

mf Medium frequency

mf, mF Millifarad

mftL Millifoot lamberts

mg Megagram; milligram

mG Milligauss

mgn Micrograin

mgw Maximum gross weight

mh Magnetic heading

mh, mH Millihenry

mhz, mHz Megahertz; millihertz

mi. Mile

mic Micrometer

μ Micro- (*prefix:* one-millionth)

μa Microampere

μbar Microbar

μF Microfarad

μg Microgram

μH Microhenry

μin Microinch

μm Micrometer

μs Microsecond

μv, μV Microvolt

μw, μW Microwatt

mil. Mileage; million

mil. m/t Million metric tons

mis, MIS Management information system

mJ Megajoule; millijoule

mK Millikelvin

ml Machine language; milliliter

ml, mL Millilambert

mlr Main line of resistance; multiple linear regression

mm Megameter; millimeter; millimicron

mmx Memory multiplexer

mnls Modified new least squares

moa Minute of angle

moe Measure of effectiveness

mΩ Megaohm

mot Mean operating time

mp Manifold pressure; melting point

mpg Miles per gallon

mph Miles per hour

mpx Multiplex

mr, mR Milliroentgen

mrad Megarad; millirad

mre Mean radial error

mrt Mean radiant temperature

ms Mean square; metric system; millisecond

msc Most significant character

msd Most significant digit

mse Mean square error

mt Machine translation; maximum torque; mean time; megaton; metric ton

mte Maximum thermal energy

mux Multiplex(er)

mv Mean variation

mv, mV Megavolt; millivolt

mva Mean vertical acceleration; megavolt ampere

mw Molecular weight
mw, mW Megawatt; milliwatt
mwh, mWhr Milliwatt hour
mwr Mean width ratio
mx Multiplex

N

n Nano- (*prefix:* one-billionth)
N Newton
na Nanoampere
nc, NC Numerical control
ndw Net deadweight
nF Nanofarad
nhp Nominal horsepower
nls New least squares; nonlinear system
nm Nanometer; nuclear megaton
Nm Newton meter
nmi Nautical mile
nrl Normal rated load
nrp Normal rated power
ns Nanosecond
nsd No significant deviation; noise suppression device
n/t Net tonnage
ntc Negative temperature coefficient
ntm Net ton mile
nw, nW Nanowatt
n/w, nwt Net weight
nzg Nonzero test

O

oc Open circuit
ocr, OCR Optical character reader; optical character recognition
odt On-line debugging technique
olc On-line computer
olrt On-line real time
ols Ordinary least squares
o/p Output
opn., OPN Open
os Oil solvent
os, OS Operating system
oz. Ounce
oz. ap. Apothecaries' ounce
oz. avd. Avoirdupois ounce
ozf, oz.-f Ounce-force
oz. t Ounce troy

P

p Pico- (*prefix:* one-trillionth); probability
pa Paper advance; picoampere; power amplifier
Pa Pascal
p/bhp Pounds per brake horsepower
pc Pitch circle; point of curve; printed circuit; program counter; pulsating current
p/c Processor controller; pulse counter
pd Pitch diameter; pulse duration
pdm Pulse-delta modulation

pe Photoelectric; probable error; program element

pf Performance factor; pulse frequency

pf, pF Picofarad

pfm Power factor meter; pulse frequency modulation

pfr Peak flow rate

p/l Payload

pm Primary memory; pulse modulation

p-m Permanent magnet; phase modulation

p/m Parts per million; pounds per minute

pmm Pulse mode multiplex

po Power oscillator

pos Product of sums

pot. Point of tangency; potentiometer

ppb Parts per billion

pph Pulses per hour

ppm Parts per million; pulse position modulation

PPP Point-to-point protocol

pr Percentile rank

ps Pressure sensitive

ps, psec Picosecond

ptc Positive temperature coefficient

ptm Pulse-time modulation

pw Packed weight; pulse width

pw, pW Picowatt

p-wave Pressure wave

pwt. pennyweight

Q

ql Quintal
qt. Quart

R

R Rankine; roentgen
r/a Radioactive
rad. Radian; radius
RAM Random-access memory
rd. Rad
REM Recognition memory
rf Radio frequency
ri Random interval; retrograde inversion
rkva Reactive volt-ampere
rms Root mean square
rmse Root mean square error
Rn Radon
ROM Read-only memory
rps Revolutions per second
r-sq. R-squared
rss Root-sum square
rtn., RTN Routine
rvm Reactive voltmeter

S

s Second
sam. Serial access memory; synchronous

sam., SAM Sequential-access method
s/c Short circuit
scn., SCN Scan
sd Standard deviation
se Spherical equivalent; standard error
s-ft. Second-foot
shf Superhigh frequency
shp Shaft horsepower
sh. tn. Short ton
slf Straight-line frequency
SLIP serial line Internet protocol
s/n Signal to noise (ratio)
so., SO Shift out
sop. Sum of products
sqc Statistical quality control
sq. rt. Square root
st Short ton
sw Shipper's weight
s-w Shortwave
s/w Standard weight

T

t Tonne (metric); troy
T Temperature, tera- (*prefix:* one trillion)
tan. Tangent
t/c Temporary coefficient
TCP/IP Transmission control protocol/Internet protocol
thp Thrust horsepower

tmw Thermal megawatts
TTY Teletypewriter
twx, TWX Teletypewriter exchange

U

u, (u)amu (Unified) Atomic mass unit
uhf, UHF Ultrahigh frequency
ulf, ULF Ultralow frequency
USASCII USA Standard Code for Information Interchange
uv, u-v Ultraviolet

V

v, V Volt
va, v-a, VA Voltampere
VCR video cassette recorder
VDT Video display terminal
vf Video frequency
vga, VGA Visual graphics adaptor
vhf, VHF Very high frequency
vhp, VHP Very high performance
vm Voltmeter
vo Voiceover
vof Variable operating frequency
vox, VOX Voice-operated device

W

w, W Watt
WAIS Wide Area Information Servers (Internet)
WAN Wide area network
w/d Weight displacement (ratio)
wh, Wh Watt hour
wpc Watts per candle

X

x Unknown quantity
xcvr Transceiver
xmt, XMT Transmit

Y

yd. Yard

Z

z Zero
zf Zero frequency
zg Zero gravity
zn. Zenith

Business Organization Abbreviations

A

AAA American Academy of Advertising; American Accounting Association; American Arbitration Association; American Automobile Association

AAAA American Association of Advertising Agencies

AAIE American Association of Industrial Editors; American Association of Industrial Engineers

AAP Association of American Publishers

AASM Association of American Steel Manufacturers

AAUP American Association of University Presses

ABA American Bankers Association; American Bar Association; American Booksellers Association

ABC Audit Bureau of Circulation

ABCA American Business Communications Association

ABT American Board of Trade

ABWA American Business Women's Association

ACM Association for Computing Machinery

ACTSU Association of Computer Time-Sharing Users

ACUG Association of Computing User Groups

ADA Automobile Dealers Association

ADAPSO Association of Data Processing Service Organizations

ADCIS Association for the Development of Computer-Based Instruction Systems

ADMA Association of Direct Marketing Agencies

AEI American Enterprise Institute

AFA Advertising Federation of America

AFBF American Farm Bureau Federation

AFIPS American Federation of Information Processing Societies

AFL-CIO American Federation of Labor and Congress of Industrial Organizations

AFSB American Federation of Small Business

AFTC American Fair Trade Council

AGCA Associated General Contractors of America

AHIA Association of Health Insurance Agents

AIA Aerospace Industries Association; American Institute of Accountants; American Institute of Architects

AIAA Aerospace Industries Association of America

AIB American Institute of Banking

AICPA American Institute of Certified Public Accountants

AIEE American Institute of Electrical Engineers

AIIE American Institute of Industrial Engineers

AIM American Institute of Management

AIME American Institute of Mechanical Engineers

ALDA American Land Development Association

AMA Aircraft Manufacturers Association; American Machinery Association; American Management Association; American Manufacturers Association; American Marketing Association; Automobile Manufacturers Association

AMEME Association of Mining, Electrical, and Mechanical Engineers

AMS Administrative Management Society

ANPA American Newspaper Publishers Association

ANSC American National Standards Committee

AOL America Online

API American Petroleum Institute

APTC Allied Printing Trades Council

ARBA American Road Builders Association

ASA American Standards Association

ASCE American Society of Civil Engineers

ASCHE American Society of Chemical Engineers

ASE American Stock Exchange

ASLA American Savings and Loan Association

ASM American Society for Metals

ASME American Society of Mechanical Engineers

ASQC American Society for Quality Control

ASSE American Society of Safety Engineers

ASSOCHAM Associated Chambers of Commerce

ASTD American Society for Training and Development

ASTE American Society of Tool Engineers

ASTME American Society of Tool and Manufacturing Engineers

ATA Air Transport Association; American Telemarketing Association

ATSU Association of Time-Sharing Users

AUCTU All-Union Council of Trade Unions

B

BBB Better Business Bureau

BEMA Business Equipment Manufacturers Association

BETA Business Equipment Trade Association

BFI Business Forms Institute

BFMA Business Forms Management Association

BIA Building Industry Association

BNF Brand Names Foundation

BPWA Business and Professional Women's Association

C

CBBB Council of Better Business Bureaus

CBEMA Computer and Business Equipment Manufacturers Association

CBOT, CBT Chicago Board of Trade

CCC Commodity Credit Corporation

CCUS Chamber of Commerce of the United States

CFTC Commodity Futures Trading Commission

CIS CompuServe Information Service

CMA Chemical Manufacturers Association

CME Chicago Mercantile Exchange

CPSC Consumer Product Safety Commission

D

DECUS Digital Equipment Computer Users Society

DGTA Dry Goods Trade Association

DMAA Direct Mail Advertising Association

E

EEOC Equal Employment Opportunities Commission
EXIMBANK, Ex-Im Export-Import Bank

F

FASB Financial Accounting Standards Board
FDIC Federal Deposit Insurance Corporation
FEMA Farm Equipment Manufacturers Association
FISC Financial Industries Service Corporation
FMA Financial Management Association
FNMA Federal National Mortgage Association (Fannie Mae)

G

GCA Graphic Communications Association
GNMA Government National Mortgage Association (Ginnie Mae)

I

IBA Independent Bankers Association; Investment Bankers Association
ICBO Interracial Council for Business Opportunities
ICC International Chamber of Commerce; Interstate Commerce Commission
IDA Industrial Development Association

IFC International Finance Corporation

IGA Independent Grocers Alliance

IMA Industrial Marketing Association; International Management Association

IMS Industrial Management Society

ISA International Standards Association

ISO International Organization for Standardization

ITC International Trade Commission

J

JAMA Japan Automobile Manufacturers Association

K

KI Kiwanis International

M

MAPI Machinery and Allied Products Institute

MAUS Metric Association of the United States

MCTA Motor Carriers Traffic Association

MRA Marketing Research Association

MRS Market Research Society

MTA Motor Trade Association

MTBA Machine Tool Builders Association

MVMA Motor Vehicle Manufacturers Association

N

NAA National Association of Accountants

NAB National Alliance of Businessmen; National Association of Businessmen

NADA National Automobile Dealers Association

NADP National Association of Desktop Publishers

NAEA National Advertising Executives Association

NAHB National Association of Home Builders

NAM National Association of Manufacturers

NAPA National Association of Purchasing Agents

NAPM National Association of Purchasing Management

NAR National Association of Realtors

NASA National Appliance Service Association; National Association of Securities Dealers

NATA National Association of Tax Accountants

NBA National Bankers Association; National Bar Association

NBS National Bureau of Standards

NCGA National Computer Graphics Association

NCS Numerical Control Society

NCTA National Cable Television Association

NCUF National Computer Users Forum

NEMA National Electrical Manufacturers Association

NIAA National Industrial Advertisers Association

NIOSH National Institute for Occupational Safety and Health

NIST National Institute of Standards and Technology

NLRB National Labor Relations Board

NMOA National Mail Order Association

NMTBA National Machine Tool Builders Association
NRA National Restaurant Association
NRFA National Retail Furniture Association
NSA National Standards Association
NSRA National Shoe Retailers Association
NTDPMA National Tool, Die, and Precision Machining Association
NTSB National Transportation Safety Board
NYSE New York Stock Exchange

O

OAAA Outdoor Advertising Association of America
OEMA Office Equipment Manufacturers Association
OPIC Overseas Private Investment Corporation
OPMA Office Products Manufacturers Association

P

PIA Plastics Institute of America; Printing Industries of America
PIMA Paper Industry Management Association
PSI Professional Secretaries International

R

RGA Rubber Growers Association
RJA Retail Jewelers of America

S

SAE Society of Automotive Engineers
SBA Small Business Administration
SEC Securities and Exchange Commission
SIE Society of Industrial Engineers

U

USWA United Steel Workers of America

PREFIXES AND SUFFIXES

Prefixes

A

a- On; toward: *aboard*
ab- Away from: *absent*
ad- Toward; near; at: *adjoin*
allo- Other; different: *allonym*
ambi- Both; around: *ambidextrous*
ante- Before: *antedate*
anti- Opposite: *anticompetitive*
apo- Away from; related to: *apothegm*
archi- Chief; primitive: *architect*
audio- Sound; hearing: *audiovisual*
auto- Self; automatic: *autobiography*

B

baro- Weight; pressure: *barometer*
be- Completely; on all sides: *behalf*
bi- Involving two: *biweekly*
bio- Life; living organism: *biotechnology*
by- Out of the way; secondary: *bylaw*

C

cata- Down; reverse: *catalyst*
centi- One hundredth: *centiliter*
chrono- Time: *chronometer*
circum- Around: *circumference*
co- With; together; jointly: *coaction*
com- With; together: *combination*
con- With; together: *concurrent*
contra- Against: *contravene*
counter- Contrary: *counterbalance*
crypto- Hidden; secret: *cryptograph*

D

de- Reverse; remove: *deactivate*
deci- One-tenth: *deciliter*
deka- Ten: *dekameter*
di- Containing two: *diphase*
dia- Across; through; apart: *diametrical*
dis- Negation; reversal; absence of; opposite of: *disable*
duo- Two: *duologue*

E

epi- Over; above; upon: *epicenter*
equi- Equal: *equidistant*
eu- Good; well; true: *euphemism*

PREFIXES AND SUFFIXES

ex- Outside of; former: *ex-president*
extra- Outside; beyond: *extracurricular*
extro- Outward: *extrovert*

F

for- Completely; excessively: *forbid*
fore- Before in time: *forecast*

G

geo- Earth: *geocentric*

H

hecto- One hundred: *hectogram*
hemi- Half; partial: *hemisphere*
homo- Same: *homograph*
hydro- Water; liquid; hydrogen: *hydrodynamics*
hyper- Over; above; beyond: *hyperactive*
hypo- Beneath; under; deficient: *hypocritical*

I

il- Not: *illegible*
im- Not: *imbalance*
in- In; not: *inaccuracy*

infra- Below; within: *infrastructure*
inter- Between; among: *interaction*
intra- Within: *intrastate*
intro- In; inside: *introspection*
ir- In; not: *irrelevant*
iso- Equal: *isometric*

K

kilo- One thousand: *kilobyte*

L

litho- Stone: *lithograph*

M

macro- Large; inclusive: *macroeconomics*
mal- Bad; abnormal: *malfeasance*
meso- Intermediate: *Mesoamerica*
micro- Small: *microanalysis*
mid- Middle: *midcourse*
milli- One-thousandth: *millisecond*
mini- Miniature; small: *minicomputer*
mis- Bad; wrong: *miscalculate*
mono- One; single: *monologue*
morpho- Shape; structure: *morphological*
multi- Many: *multidirectional*

N

neo- New; recent: *neophyte*
non- Not: *nonessential*

O

ob- Inverse; against: *object*
octo- Eight: *octosyllable*
olig- Few: *oligopoly*
out- Exceeding: *outstanding*

P

pan- All: *pandemic*
para- Beside; near: *paradigm*
patho- Disease; suffering: *pathological*
pedi- Foot: *pediform*
per- Through; proportion: *percentage*
peri- Around; about: *periodic*
phono- Sound; speech: *phonotype*
photo- Light: *photocomposition*
physio- Natural: *physiology*
phyto- Plant: *phytochemistry*
poly- Many; much: *polychrome*
post- After: *postgraduate*
pre- Before: *prepublication*
pro- Substituting; supporting: *prodemocracy*

pseudo- False: *pseudonym*
psycho- Mental: *psychodynamics*
pyro- Fire; heat: *pyrotechnic*

Q

quadri- Four: *quadrilateral*

R

radio- Radiation; radiant energy: *radioactive*
re- Back; again: *reaction*
retro- Backward; behind: *retroactive*

S

self- Oneself; automatic: *self-service*
semi- Half: *semiskilled*
sub- Under; inferior: *sublease*
super- Over; superior: *supercharged*
supra- Above; transcending: *supranational*
sym- With; similar: *symbolic*
syn- With; similar: *synchronous*

T

tele- Distance: *telecommunications*

PREFIXES AND SUFFIXES

theo- God; gods: *theological*
topo- Place: *toponym*
trans- Across; transfer: *transmit*

U

ultra- Beyond: *ultramodern*
un- Not; reverse; release: *unconcerned*
under- Below; inferior: *undercapitalized*
up- Up: *upturn*

V

vari- Variety; difference: *variable*
ventro- Ventral: *ventromedial*
vice- Deputy: *vice-chairman*

Z

zero- Dry: *xerography*

Suffixes

A

-ability Ability; inclination: *teachability*
-able Capable of; inclined to: *changeable*
-acity Quality or state of: *tenacity*
-age Collection; result: *breakage*
-agogue Leader; inciter: *demagogue*
-al Relating to: *educational*
-an One belonging to: *librarian*
-ana A collection of items relating to a person or place: *Americana*
-ance State of; action: *continuance*
-ancy Condition; quality; *hesitancy*
-ant Causing; being: *dependant*
-arch Ruler; leadership: *monarch*
-archy Rule; government: *monarchy*
-arium Place; housing: *aquarium*
-art Habitually performing: *braggart*
-ate Characterized by; act on: *demonstrate*

C

-cade Procession: *motorcade*
-centric Having a kind or number of centers: *polycentric*

Prefixes and Suffixes

-chrome Color: *polychrome*
-cide Killer: *pesticide*
-cline Slope: *anticline*
-cracy Government; rule: *democracy*
-cy State; condition: *bankruptcy*

D

-dom Condition: *officialdom*
-drome Field; arena: *airdrome*

E

-ed Having: *wholehearted*
-eer Engaged in: *auctioneer*
-en Consisting of; become or come to have: *lengthen*
-ence State of: *dependence*
-ent State of: *complacent*
-er Performer of action: *worker*
-ery Practice: *bribery*
-escent Becoming: *coalescent*
-ese Relating to: *Japanese*
-et Small: *snippet*

F

-ferous Bearing; containing: *carboniferous*
-fic Causing: *prolific*
-fold Divided into parts: *twofold*

-form Having the form of: *plexiform*
-ful Full of; able to: *useful*
-fy Form; make: *modify*

G

-gen Generator: *halogen*
-genic Suitable for production: *photogenic*
-gon Having angles: *isogon*
-gram Written material: *telegram*
-graph Written material: *monograph*

H

-hood Condition; quality: *falsehood*

I

-ia Things belonging to: *memorabilia*
-ian Of; resembling: *Washingtonian*
-ible Capable of: *reducible*
-ic Characterized by: *academic*
-ician Specialist: *technician*
-ics Pertaining to: *graphics*
-ide Chemical properties: *oxide*
-ile Division: *percentile*
-ine Of; resembling; substance: *glassine*
-ing Action; process: *computing*
-ion Act; process: *completion*

-ish Of; like; preoccupation: *selfish*
-ism System; process: *socialism*
-ist Agent; doer; adherent: *specialist*
-ite Native of; follower: *urbanite*
-ity Condition; degree: *abnormality*
-ive Tending toward: *demonstrative*
-ization Action; process: *centralization*
-ize Cause to be; render: *materialize*

K

-kinesis Motion: *photokinesis*

L

-less Without: *blameless*
-like Resembling: *businesslike*
-ling One characterized by: *underling*
-lith Stone structure: *megalith*
-log(ue) Discourse: *travelog(ue)*
-logy Expression; study of: *methodology*
-ly Like; characterized by: *hourly*
-lyte Substance: *electrolyte*

M

-ment Act; process: *advancement*
-meter Measuring device: *barometer*

-metry Science of measuring: *isometry*
-morphous Having a certain shape or form: *polymorphous*
-most Most; nearest: *innermost*

N

-ness State; quality: *brightness*

O

-oid Resembling: *celluloid*
-ome Mass: *biome*
-on Unit: *photon*
-onym Word; name: *acronym*
-or Performer of action: *accelerator*
-ory Characterized by: *advisory*
-osis Abnormal condition: *symbiosis*
-ous Characterized by: *advantageous*

P

-petal Moving toward: *basipetal*
-phone Sound: *homophone*
-plastic Forming; growing: *metaplastic*

S

-scope Instrument for viewing: *telescope*
-sect Cut; divide: *trisect*

PREFIXES AND SUFFIXES

-ship State; condition; body: *readership*
-some Group or body: *twosome*
-stat Regulating device: *rheostat*

T

-th State; quality: *dearth*
-tude State; quality: *magnitude*
-ty Condition; quality: *realty*

U

-ule Small: *miniscule*
-ure Body; act; process: *erasure*
-urgy Technique or process for working with: *crystallurgy*

W

-ward In a certain direction: *upward*
-ways In a cetain manner; position: *sideways*
-wide Extending throughout: *nationwide*
-wise In a certain direction: *clockwise*
-worthy Suitable or of sufficient worth: *trustworthy*

Y

-y Condition; characterized by: *thrifty*

APPENDIX

Fraction and Decimal Equivalents

Fraction	Decimal	Fraction	Decimal
1/2	0.500	4/5	.800
1/3	.333	4/6	.667
1/4	.250	4/7	.571
1/5	.200	4/8	.500
1/6	.167	4/9	.444
1/7	.143	4/10	.400
1/8	.125		
1/9	.111	5/6	.833
1/10	.100	5/7	.714
		5/8	.625
2/3	.667	5/9	.556
2/4	.500	5/10	.500
2/5	.400		
2/6	.333	6/7	.857
2/7	.286	6/8	.750
2/8	.250	6/9	.667
2/9	.222	6/10	.600
2/10	.200		
		7/8	.875
3/4	.750	7/9	.778
3/5	.600	7/10	.700
3/6	.500		
3/7	.429	8/9	.889
3/8	.375	8/10	.800
3/9	.333	9/10	0.900
3/10	.300		

Large Numbers
(American System)

Name	Value in Powers of 10	No. Zeros
billion	10^9	9
trillion	10^{12}	12
quadrillion	10^{15}	15
quintillion	10^{18}	18
sextillion	10^{21}	21
septillion	10^{24}	24
octillion	10^{27}	27
nonillion	10^{30}	30
decillion	10^{33}	33
undecillion	10^{36}	36
duodecillion	10^{39}	39
tredecillion	10^{42}	42
quattuordecillion	10^{45}	45
quindecillion	10^{48}	48
sexdecillion	10^{51}	51
septendecillion	10^{54}	54
octodecillion	10^{57}	57
novemdecillion	10^{60}	60
vigintillion	10^{63}	63
centillion	10^{303}	303

Note: The British system of writing large numbers is different. In it, for example, an *octillion* has 48 zeros, whereas in the American system it has 27 zeros.

Roman Numerals

I (i)	1	XX (xx)	20
II (ii)	2	XXX (xxx)	30
III (iii)	3	XL (xl)	40
IV (iv)	4	L (l)	50
V (v)	5	LX (lx)	60
VI (vi)	6	LXX (lxx)	70
VII (vii)	7	LXXX (lxxx)	80
VIII (viii)	8	XC (xc)	90
IX (iv)	9	C (c)	100
X (x)	10	CC (cc)	200
XI (xi)	11	CCC (ccc)	300
XII (xii)	12	CD (cd)	400
XIII (xiii)	13	D (d)	500
XIV (xiv)	14	DC (dc)	600
XV (xv)	15	DCC (dcc)	700
XVI (xvi)	16	DCCC (dccc)	800
XVII (xvii)	17	CM (cm)	900
XVIII (xviii)	18	M (m)	1,000
XIX (xix)	19	MM (mm)	2,000

Notes: (1) Repeating a letter will repeat its value: *I = 1 and II = 2.* (2) Placing a letter *after* another letter of greater value adds to it. Thus if *X = 10* and *I = 1, XI = 11.* But placing a letter *before* another letter of greater value subtracts from it. Thus *IX = 9.* (3) Placing a dash over a numeral multiplies the value by 1,000. Thus if *X = 10, $\bar{X}$ = 10,000.*

Cardinal and Ordinal Numbers in Five Languages

FRENCH

Cardinal Numbers

one: un
two: deux
three: trois
four: quatre
five: cinq
six: six
seven: sept
eight: huit
nine: neuf
ten: dix
eleven: onze
twelve: douze
thirteen: treize
fourteen: quatorze
fifteen: quinze
sixteen: seize
seventeen: dix-sept
eighteen: dix-huit
nineteen: dix-neuf
twenty: vingt
thirty: trente
forty: quarante
fifty: cinquante
sixty: soixante
seventy: soixante-dix
eighty: quatre-vingts
ninety: quatre-vingt-dix
hundred: cent
thousand: mil
million: million

Ordinal Numbers

first: premier
second: second
third: troisième
fourth: quatrième
fifth: cinquième
sixth: sixième
seventh: septième
eighth: huitième
ninth: neuvième
tenth: dixième
hundredth: centième
thousandth: millième

GERMAN

Cardinal Numbers

one: eins
two: zwei
three: drei
four: vier
five: fünf
six: sechs
seven: sieben
eight: acht
nine: neun
ten: zehn
eleven: elf
twelve: zwölf
thirteen: dreizehn
fourteen: vierzehn
fifteen: fünfzehn
sixteen: sechzehn
seventeen: siebzehn
eighteen: achtzehn
nineteen: neunzehn
twenty: zwanzig
thirty: dreissig
forty: vierzig
fifty: fünfzig
sixty: sechzig
seventy: siebzig
eighty: achtzig
ninety: neunzig
hundred: hundert
thousand: tausend
million: Million

Ordinal Numbers

first: erste
second: zweite
third: dritte
fourth: vierte
fifth: fünfte
sixth: sechste
seventh: siebente
eighth: achte
ninth: neunte
tenth: zehnte
hundredth: hundertste
thousandth: tausendste

ITALIAN

Cardinal Numbers

one: uno
two: due
three: tre
four: quattro
five: cinque
six: sei
seven: sette
eight: otto
nine: nove
ten: dieci
eleven: undici
twelve: dodici
thirteen: tredici
fourteen: quattordici
fifteen: quindici

sixteen: sedici
seventeen: diciassette
eighteen: diciotto
nineteen: diciannove
twenty: venti
thirty: trenta
forty: quaranta
fifty: cinquanta
sixty: sessanta
seventy: settanta
eighty: ottanta
ninety: novanta
hundred: cento
thousand: mille
million: milione

Ordinal Numbers

first: primo
second: secondo
third: terzo
fourth: quarto
fifth: quinto
sixth: sesto

seventh: settimo
eighth: ottavo
ninth: nono
tenth: decimo
hundredth: centesimo
thousandth: millesimo

LATIN

Cardinal Numbers

one: unus
two: duo
three: tres
four: quattuor
five: quinque
six: sex
seven: septem
eight: octo
nine: novem
ten: decem
eleven: undecim
twelve: duodecim
thirteen: tredecim
fourteen: quattuordecim
fifteen: quindecim
sixteen: sedecim
seventeen: septendecim
eighteen: duodeviginti
nineteen: undeviginti
twenty: viginti
thirty: triginta
forty: quadraginta
fifty: quinquaginta
sixty: sexaginta
seventy: septuaginta
eighty: octoginta
ninety: nonaginta
hundred: centum
thousand: mille
million: decies centena mil(l)ia

Ordinal Numbers

first: primus
second: secundus
third: tertius
fourth: quartus
fifth: quintus
sixth: sextus
seventh: septimus
eighth: octavus
ninth: nonus
tenth: decimus
hundredth: centesimus
thousandth: millesimus

SPANISH

Cardinal Numbers

one: uno
two: dos
three: tres
four: cuatro
five: cinco
six: seis
seven: siete
eight: ocho
nine: nueve
ten: diez
eleven: once
twelve: doce
thirteen: trece
fourteen: catorce
fifteen: quince
sixteen: dieciseis
seventeen: diecisiete
eighteen: dieciocho
nineteen: diecinueve
twenty: veinte
thirty: treinta
forty: cuarenta
fifty: cincuenta
sixty: sesenta
seventy: setenta
eighty: ochenta
ninety: noventa
hundred: ciento
thousand: mil
million: millón

Ordinal Numbers

first: prim(er)o
second: segundo
third: tercero
fourth: cuarto
fifth: quinto
sixth: sexto
seventh: sé(p)timo
eighth: octavo
ninth: noveno
tenth: décimo
hundredth: centésimo
thousandth: milésimo

Mathematical Signs and Symbols

Sign	Meaning
+	Plus
−	Minus
×	Multiplied by
÷	Divided by
=	Equal to
±	Plus or minus
∓	Minus or plus
⩲	Plus or equal to
++	Double plus
≜	Difference between
−∶	Difference excess
≡	Identical with, congruent
≢	Not identical with
≠	Not equal to
≈	Nearly equal to
≅	Equals approximately
≊	Equals approximately
≧	Equal to or greater than
≦	Equal to or less than
<	Less than
⊏	Less than
>	Greater than
⊐	Greater than
≷	Greater than or less than
≮	Not less than

431

Appendix

Sign	Meaning
≯	Not greater than
≤	Less than or equal to
≦	Less than or equal to
≼	Less than or equal to
⪯	Less than or equal to
≶	Less than or greater than
≥	Greater than or equal to
≧	Greater than or equal to
≽	Greater than or equal to
⪰	Greater than or equal to
≎	Equivalent to
≢	Not equivalent to
≢	Not equivalent to
⊂	Included in
⊃	Excluded from
∼	Difference
∽	Difference
⋕	Equal and parallel
≐	Approaches a limit
≘	Is measured by
⊥	Perpendicular to
⊥s	Perpendiculars
∥	Parallel
∥s	Parallels
∦	Not parallel
∠	Angle
⌐	Angle
⊄	Angle
⌐s	Angles
∟	Right angle
⩬	Equal angles
△	Triangle
△s	Triangles
/	Rising diagonal
\	Falling diagonal
∥	Parallel rising diagonal

APPENDIX

Sign	Meaning
∥	Parallel falling diagonal
∥∥	Rising parallels
∥∥	Falling parallels
∥∥	Triple vertical
≡	Quadruple parallels
∩	Arc
∪	Arc
⌔	Sector
∅	Diameter
∴	Hence, therefore
∵	Because
·	Multiplied by
:	Ratio
::	Proportion
∺	Geometrical proportion
√	Square root
∛	Cube root
∜	Fourth root
ⁿ√	nth root
⎯	Horizontal radical
Σ	Summation
Π	Product sign
π	Pi
∪	Union sign
∩	Intersection sign
!	Factorial sign
∅	Empty set; null set
∈	Is an element of
∉	Is not an element of
Δ	Delta
∝	Variation
∞	Infinity
⊢	Assertion sign
∂	Partial differential
∂	Partial differential
∫	Integral

APPENDIX

Sign	Meaning
∮	Contour integral
⨍	Horizontal integral
╱	Single bond
╲	Single bond
╲	Single bond
│	Single bond
│	Single bond
│	Single bond (punched to right)
╲╲	Double bond
‖	Double bond
⫽	Double bond
‖	Double bond
⫶	Triple bond
↔	Reaction goes both right and left
↕	Reaction goes both up and down
⇋	Equilibrium reaction beginning at right
⇌	Equilibrium reaction beginning at left
⇌	Reversible reaction beginning at left
⇋	Reaction begins at right and is completed to left
⇋	Reaction begins at right and is completed to right
⇌	Reaction begins at left and is completed to right
⇌	Reaction begins at left and is completed to left
⇌	Reversible reaction beginning at right
⇕	Reversible
⇑	Elimination
⇓	Absorption
⇅	Exchange
⤢	Reversible reaction
⤡	Reversible reaction

Greek Letter Symbols

Name	Uppercase Letter	Lowercase Letter
alpha	A	α
beta	B	β
gamma	Γ	γ
delta	Δ	δ
epsilon	E	ϵ
zeta	Z	ζ
eta	H	η
theta	Θ	θ
iota	I	ι
kappa	K	κ
lambda	Λ	λ
mu	M	μ
nu	N	ν
xi	Ξ	ξ
omicron	O	o
pi	Π	π
rho	P	ρ
sigma	Σ	σ, ς
tau	T	τ
upsilon	Υ	υ
phi	Φ	ϕ
chi	X	χ
psi	Ψ	ψ
omega	Ω	ω

Foreign Currency

Note: Some countries, especially recently formed countries, may change their currencies from time to time. Contact banks for current information, or check the latest issue of a financial guide, such as the *MRI Bankers' Guide to Foreign Currency* (Monetary Research International).

A

Afghanistan: afghani (Af) = 100 puls
Albania: lek (L) = 100 quintars
Algeria: Algerian dinar (DA) = 100 centimes
Andorra: French franc (F) = 100 centimes; Spanish peseta (Pta) = 100 céntimos
Angola: kwanza (Kz) = 100 kwei
Antigua and Barbuda: East Caribbean dollar (EC$) = 100 cents
Argentina: peso (ARP) = 100 centavos
Armenia: ruble (R) = 100 kopeks
Australia: Australian dollar ($A) = 100 cents
Austria: Austrian schilling (S) = 100 groschen
Azerbaijan: manat (N.A.) = 10 rubles

B

Bahamas, The: Bahamian dollar (B$) = 100 cents
Bahrain: Bahraini dinar (BD) = 1,000 fils
Bangladesh: taka (Tk) = 100 paise

Barbados: Barbadian dollar (Bds$) = 100 cents
Belarus: rubel (N.A.) = 10 Russian rubles
Belgium: Belgian franc (BF) = 100 centimes
Belize: Belizean dollar (Bz$) = 100 cents
Benin: CFA franc (CFAF) = 100 centimes
Bhutan: ngultrum (Nu) = 100 chetrum
Bolivia: boliviano ($B) = 100 centavos
Bosnia and Herzegovina: dinar (D) = 100 paras
Botswana: pula (P) = 100 thebe
Brazil: cruzeiro (Cr$) = 100 centavos
Brunei: Bruneian dollar (B$) = 100 cents
Bulgaria: lev (Lv) = 100 stotinki
Burkina Faso: CFA franc (CFAF) = 100 centimes
Burma: See *Myanma*.
Burundi: Burundi franc (FBu) = 100 centimes

C

Cambodia: riel (CR) = 100 sen
Cameroon: CFA franc (CFAF) = 100 centimes
Canada: Canadian dollar (Can$) = 100 cents
Cape Verde: Cape Verdean escudo (CVEsc) = 100 centavos
Central African Republic: CFA franc (CFAF) = 100 centimes
Chad: CFA franc (CFAF) = 100 centimes
Chile: Chilean peso (Ch$) = 100 centavos
China: yuan (¥) = 10 jiao
Colombia: Colombian peso (Col$) = 100 centavos
Comoros: Comoran franc (CF) = 100 centimes
Congo: CFA franc (CFAF) = 100 centimes

Costa Rica: Costa Rican colón (C) = 100 centimos
Croatia: Croatian dinar (CD) = 100 paras
Cuba: Cuban peso (Cu$) = 100 centavos
Cyprus: Cypriot pound (£C) = 100 cents
Czech Republic: koruna (Kc) = 100 haleru

D

Denmark: Danish krone (DKr) = 100 re
Djibouti: Djiboutian franc (DF) = 100 centimes
Dominica: East Caribbean dollar (EC$) = 100 cents
Dominican Republic: Dominica peso (RD$) = 100 centavos

E

Ecuador: sucre (S/) = 100 centavos
Egypt: Egyptian pound (£E) = 100 piasters
El Salvador: Salvadoran colón (C) = 100 centavos
Equatorial Guinea: CFA franc (CFAF) = 100 centimes
Eritrea: N.A.
Estonia: Estonian kroon (EEK) = 100 (N.A.)
Ethiopia: birr (Br) = 100 cents

F

Fiji: Fijian dollar (F$) = 100 cents
Finland: markkaa (FMk) = 100 pennia
France: franc (F) = 100 centimes

APPENDIX 439

G

Gabon: CFA franc (CFAF) = 100 centimes
Gambia, The: dalasi (D) = 100 bututs
Georgia: Russian ruble (R) = 100 kopeks (lari to be introduced)
Germany: deutsche mark (DM) = 100 pfennige
Ghana: cedi (C) = 100 pesewas
Greece: drachma (Dr) = 100 lepta
Grenada: East Caribbean dollar (EC$) = 100 cents
Guatemala: quetzal (Q) = 100 centavos
Guinea: Guinean franc (FG) = 100 centimes
Guinea-Bissau: Guinea-Bissauan peso (PG) = 100 centavos
Guyana: Guyanese dollar (G$) = 100 cents

H

Haiti: gourde (G) = 100 centimes
Honduras: lempira (L) = 100 centavos
Hungary: forint (Ft) = 100 fillér

I

Iceland: Icelandic krona (IKr) = 100 aurar
India: Indian rupee (Re) = 100 paise
Indonesia: Indonesian rupiah (Rp) = 100 sen (sen discontinued)
Iran: Iranian rial (IR) = 10 tomans
Iraq: Iraqi dinar (ID) = 1,000 fils
Ireland: Irish pound (£IR) = 100 pence

Israel: new Israeli shekel (NIS) = 100 new agorot (sing. agora)
Italy: Italian lira (Lit) = 100 centesimi
Ivory Coast: CFA franc (CFAF) = 100 centimes

J

Jamaica: Jamaican dollar (J$) = 100 cents
Japan: yen (¥) = 100 sen
Jordan: Jordanian dinar (JD) = 1,000 fils

K

Kazakhstan: Russian ruble (R) = 100 kopeks
Kenya: Kenyan shilling (KSh) = 100 cents
Kiribati: Australian dollar ($A) = 100 cents
Korea, North: North Korean won (Wn) = 100 chon
Korea, South: South Korean won (W) = 10 chon (theoretical)
Kuwait: Kuwaiti dinar (KD) = 1,000 fils
Kyrgyzstan (Kirghizia): som (new currency)

L

Laos: new kip (KK) = 100 at
Latvia: lat = 100 N.A.
Lebanon: Lebanese pound (£L) = 100 piasters
Lesotho: loti (L) = 100 lisente
Liberia: Liberian dollar (L$) = 100 cents
Libya: Libyan dinar (LD) = 1,000 dirhams
Liechtenstein: Swiss franc (SwF) = 100 centimes

APPENDIX 441

Lithuania: talonas, to be replaced with litas
Luxembourg: Luxembourg franc (LuxF) = 100 centimes

M

Macedonia: denar (N.A.) = 100 N.A.
Madagascar: Malagasy franc (FMG) = 100 centimes
Malawi: Malawian kwacha (MK) = 100 tambala
Malaysia: ringgit (M$) = 100 sen
Maldives: rufiyaa (Rf) = 100 laaris
Mali: CFA franc (CFAF) = 100 centimes
Malta: Maltese lira (LM) = 100 cents
Marshall Islands: U.S. dollar (US$) = 100 cents
Mauritania: ouguiya (UM) = 5 khoums
Mauritius: Mauritian rupee (MauR) = 100 cents
Mexico: New Mexican peso (Mex$) = 100 centavos
Micronesia: U.S. dollar (US$) = 100 cents
Moldova: Russian ruble (R) = 100 kopeks (lei to be introduced)
Monaco: French franc (F) = 100 centimes
Mongolia: tughrik (Tug) = 100 mongos
Morocco: Moroccan dirham (DH) = 100 centimes
Mozambique: metical (Mt) = 100 centavos
Myanma (Burma): kyak (K) = 100 pyas

N

Namibia: South African rand (R) = 100 cents
Nauru: Australian dollar ($A) = 100 cents

Nepal: Nepalese rupee (NR) = 100 paisa
Netherlands, the: guilder, gulden, or florin (f.) = 100 cents
New Zealand: New Zealand dollar (NZ$) = 100 cents
Nicaragua: córdoba (C$) = 100 centavos
Niger: CFA franc (CFAF) = 100 centimes
Nigeria: naira (N) = 100 kobo
Norway: Norwegian krone (NKr) = 100 re

O

Oman: Omani rial (RO) = 1,000 baiza

P

Pakistan: Pakistan rupee (PRe) = 100 paisa
Panama: balboa (B) = 100 centesimos
Papua New Guinea: kina (K) = 100 toea
Paraguay: guaraní (G) = 100 centimos
Peru: nuevo sol (S/.) = 100 centavos
Philippines: Philippine peso (P) = 100 centavos
Poland: zloty (Zl) = 100 groszy
Portugal: Portuguese escudo (Esc) = 100 centavos

Q

Qatar: Qatari riyal (QR) = 100 dirhams

R

Romania: leu (L) = 100 bani
Russia: ruble (R) = 100 kopeks
Rwanda: Rwandan franc (RF) = 100 centimes

S

Saint Kitts and Nevis: East Caribbean dollar (EC$) = 100 cents
Saint Lucia: East Caribbean dollar (EC$) = 100 cents
Saint Vincent and the Grenadines: East Caribbean dollar (EC$) = 100 cents
San Marino: Italian lira (L) = 100 centesimi; also national coins
São Tomé and Príncipe: dobra (Db) = 100 centimos
Saudi Arabia: Saudi rial (SR) = 100 halalas
Senegal: CFA franc (CFAF) = 100 centimes
Serbia and Montenegro: Yugoslav new dinar (YD) = 100 paras
Seychelles: Seychelles rupee (SRe) = 100 cents
Sierra Leone: leone (Le) = 100 cents
Singapore: Singapore dollar (S$) = 100 cents
Slovakia: koruna (Kc) = 100 haleru
Slovenia: tolar (SIT) = 100 N.A.
Solomon Islands: Solomon Islands dollar (SI$) = 100 cents
Somalia: Somali shilling (So.Sh.) = 100 centesimi
South Africa: rand (R) = 100 cents
Spain: peseta (Pta) = 100 centimos
Sri Lanka: Sri Lankan rupee (SLRe) = 100 cents
Sudan: Sudanese pound (£Sd) = 100 piasters
Suriname: Surinamese guilder, gulden, or florin (Sf.) = 100 cents

Swaziland: lilangeni (E) = 100 cents
Sweden: Swedish krona (SKr) = 100 öre
Switzerland: Swiss franc (SwF) = 100 centimes
Syria: Syrian pound (£S) = 100 piasters

T

Taiwan: New Taiwan dollar (NT$) = 100 cents
Tajikistan: Russian ruble (R) = 100 kopeks
Tanzania: Tanzanian shilling (TSh) = 100 cents
Thailand: baht (B) = 100 satang
Togo: CFA franc (CFAF) = 100 centimes
Tonga: pa'anga (T$) = 100 seniti
Trinidad and Tobago: Trinidad and Tobago dollar (TT$) = 100 cents
Tunisia: Tunisian dinar (TD) = 1,000 millimes
Turkey: Turkish lira (TL) = 100 kurus
Turkmenistan: Russian ruble (R) = 100 kopeks (manat to be introduced)
Tuvalu: Tuvaluan dollar ($T) = 100 cents or Australian dollar ($A) = 100 cents

U

Uganda: Uganda shilling (USh) = 100 cents
Ukraine: karbovanet (hryvnya to be introduced)
United Arab Emirates: Emirian dirham (Dh) = 100 fils
United Kingdom: British pound (£) = 100 pence
Uruguay: new Uruguayan peso (N$Ur) = 100 centésimos
Uzbekistan: Russian ruble (R) = 100 kopeks

V

Vanuatu: vatu (VT) = 100 centimes
Venezuela: bolívar (Bs) = 100 centimos
Vietnam: new dong (D) = 100 xu

W

Western Samoa: tala (WS$) = 100 sene

Y

Yemen: Yemeni rial (new currency to replace North Yemeni rial and South Yemeni dinar); North Yemeni rial (YR) = 100 fils; South Yemeni dinar (YD) = 1,000 fils

Z

Zaïre: zaïre (Z) = 100 makuta
Zambia: Zambian kwacha (ZK) = 100 ngwee
Zimbabwe: Zimbabwe dollar (Z$) = 100 cents

Principal National Holidays of Other Countries

Note: All countries observe an independence day or other principal national holiday, such as the Fourth of July in the United States, as well as many other general or religious holidays. Recently independent or emerging nations may establish a new holiday; in addition, dates in some countries may vary from year to year.

A

Afghanistan: Islamic Revolution Day, April 27
Albania: Liberation Day, November 29
Algeria: Anniversary of the Revolution, November 1
Andorra: Mare de Deu de Meritxell, September 8.
Angola: Independence Day, November 11
Antigua and Barbuda: Independence Day, November 1
Argentina: Independence Day, May 25
Armenia: Independence Day, September 21
Australia: Australia Day, January 26
Austria: National Holiday, October 26
Azerbaijan: Independence Day, May 28

APPENDIX

B

Bahamas, The: National Day, July 10
Bahrain: National Day, December 16
Bangladesh: National Day, March 26
Barbados: Independence Day, November 30
Belarus: Day of Independence, June 27
Belgium: National Day, July 21
Belize: Independence Day, September 21
Benin: National Day, August 1
Bhutan: National Day, December 17
Bolivia: Independence Day, August 6
Bosnia and Herzegovina: N.A.
Botswana: Botswana Day, September 30
Brazil: Independence Day, September 7
Brunei: National Day, February 23
Bulgaria: National Liberation Day, March 3
Burkina Faso: Anniversary of the Revolution, August 4
Burma: See *Myanma.*
Burundi: Independence Day, July 1

C

Cambodia: N.A.
Cameroon: National Day, May 20
Canada: Canada Day, July 1
Cape Verde: Independence Day, July 5
Central African Republic: National Day, December 1
Chad: Independence Day, August 11

Chile: Independence Day, September 18
China: National Day, October 1
Colombia: Independence Day, July 20
Comoros: Independence Day, July 6
Congo: Congolese National Day, August 15
Costa Rica: Independence Day, September 15
Croatia: Statehood Day, May 30
Cuba: Rebellion Day, July 26
Cyprus: Independence Day, October 1
Czech Republic: Independence Day, October 28

D

Denmark: Birthday of the Queen, April 16
Djibouti: Independence Day, June 27
Dominica: Independence Day, November 3
Dominican Republic: Independence Day, February 27

E

Ecuador: Independence Day, August 10
Egypt: Anniversary of the Revolution, July 23
El Salvador: Independence Day, September 15
Equatorial Guinea: Independence Day, October 12
Eritrea: Independence Day, May 24
Estonia: Independence Day, February 24
Ethiopia: National Day, May 28

F

Fiji: Independence Day, October 10
Finland: Independence Day, December 6
France: National Day, July 14

G

Gabon: Renovation Day, March 12
Gambia, The: Independence Day, February 18
Georgia: Independence Day, April 9
Germany: German Unity Day, October 3
Ghana: Independence Day, March 6
Greece: Independence Day, March 25
Grenada: Independence Day, February 7
Guatemala: Independence Day, September 15
Guinea: Anniversary of the Second Republic, April 3
Guinea-Bissau: Independence Day, September 10
Guyana: Republic Day, February 23

H

Haiti: Independence Day, January 1
Honduras: Independence Day, September 15
Hungary: Day of the Proclamation of the Republic, August 20

I

Iceland: Anniversary of the Establishment of the Republic, June 17

India: Anniversary of the Proclamation of the Republic, January 26

Indonesia: Independence Day, August 17

Iran: Islamic Republic Day, April 1

Iraq: Anniversary of the Revolution, July 17

Ireland: St. Patrick's Day, March 17

Israel: Independence Day, May 14 (varies April-May on lunar calendar)

Italy: Anniversary of the Republic, June 2

Ivory Coast: National Day, December 7

J

Jamaica: Independence Day, first Monday in August

Japan: Birthday of the Emperor, December 23

Jordan: Independence Day, May 25

K

Kazakhstan: Independence Day, December 16

Kenya: Independence Day, December 12

Kiribati: Independence Day, July 12

Korea, North: DPRK Foundation Day, September 9

Korea, South: Independence Day, August 15

Kuwait: National Day, February 25

Kyrgyzstan (Kirghizia): National Day, December 2

APPENDIX 451

L

Laos: National Day, December 2
Latvia: Independence Day, November 18
Lebanon: Independence Day, November 22
Lesotho: Independence Day, October 4
Liberia: Independence Day, July 26
Libya: Revolution Day, September 1
Liechtenstein: Assumption Day, August 15
Lithuania: Independence Day, February 16
Luxembourg: National Day, June 23

M

Macedonia: N.A.
Madagascar: Independence Day, June 26
Malawi: Republic Day, July 6
Malaysia: Independence Day, August 31
Maldives: Independence Day, July 26
Mali: Anniversary of the Proclamation of the Republic, September 22
Malta: Independence Day, September 21
Marshall Islands: Proclamation of the Republic, May 1
Mauritania: Independence Day, November 28
Mauritius: Independence Day, March 12
Mexico: Independence Day, September 16
Micronesia: Proclamation of the Federated States of Micronesia, May 10
Moldova: Independence Day, August 27

Monaco: National Day, November 19
Mongolia: National Day, July 11
Morocco: National Day, November 18
Mozambique: Independence Day, June 25
Myanma (Burma): Independence Day, January 4

N

Namibia: Independence Day, March 21
Nauru: Independence Day, January 31
Nepal: Birthday of His Majesty the King, December 28
Netherlands, the: Queen's Day, April 30
New Zealand: Waitangi Day, February 6
Nicaragua: Independence Day, September 15
Niger: Republic Day, December 18
Nigeria: Independence Day, October 1
Norway: Constitution Day, May 17

O

Oman: National Day, November 18

P

Pakistan: Pakistan Day, March 23
Panama: Independence Day, November 3
Papua New Guinea: Independence Day, September 16
Paraguay: Independence Days, May 14–15

APPENDIX

Peru: Independence Day, July 28
Philippines: Independence Day, June 12
Poland: Constitution Day, May 3
Portugal: Day of Portugal, June 10

Q

Qatar: Independence Day, September 3

R

Romania: National Day of Romania, December 1
Russia: Independence Day, June 12
Rwanda: Independence Day, July 1

S

Saint Kitts and Nevis: Independence Day, September 19
Saint Lucia: Independence Day, February 22
Saint Vincent and the Grenadines: Independence Day, October 27
San Marino: Anniversary of the Foundation of the Republic, September 3
São Tomé and Príncipe: Independence Day, July 12
Saudi Arabia: Unification of the Kingdom, September 23
Senegal: Independence Day, April 4
Serbia and Montenegro: N.A.
Seychelles: Liberation Day, June 5

Sierra Leone: Republic Day, April 27
Singapore: National Day, August 9
Slovakia: Slovak National Uprising, August 29
Slovenia: Statehood Day, June 25
Solomon Islands: Independence Day, July 7
Somalia: N.A.
South Africa: Republic Day, May 31
Spain: National Day, October 12
Sri Lanka: Independence and National Day, February 4
Sudan: Independence Day, January 1
Suriname: Independence Day, November 25
Swaziland: Somhlolo (Independence) Day, September 6
Sweden: Day of the Swedish Flag, June 6
Switzerland: Anniversary of the Founding of the Swiss Conferation, August 1
Syria: National Day, April 17

T

Taiwan: National Day, October 10
Tajikistan: Independence Day, September 9
Tanzania: Union Day, April 26
Thailand: Birthday of His Majesty the King, December 5
Togo: Independence Day, April 27
Tonga: Emancipation Day, June 4
Trinidad and Tobago: Independence Day, August 31
Tunisia: National Day, March 20
Turkey: Anniversary of the Declaration of the Republic, October 29

APPENDIX

Turkmenistan: Independence Day, October 27
Tuvalu: Independence Day, October 1

U

Uganda: Independence Day, October 9
Ukraine: Independence Day, August 24
United Arab Emirates: National Day, December 2
United Kingdom: Birthday of the Queen, second Saturday in June
Uruguay: Independence Day, August 25
Uzbekistan: Independence Day, September 1

V

Vanuatu: Independence Day, July 30
Venezuela: Independence Day, July 5
Vietnam: Independence Day, September 2

W

Western Samoa: National Day, June 1

Y

Yemen: Proclamation of the Republic, May 22

Z

Zaïre: Anniversary of the Regime, November 24
Zambia: Independence Day, October 24
Zimbabwe: Independence Day, April 18

Area Codes: United States and Canada

Area Code	Location
201	New Jersey
202	District of Columbia
203	Connecticut
204	Manitoba (Canada)
205	Alabama
206	Washington
207	Maine
208	Idaho
209	California
210	Texas
212	New York
213	California
214	Texas
215	Pennsylvania
216	Ohio
217	Illinois
218	Minnesota
219	Indiana
281	Texas
301	Maryland
302	Delaware
303	Colorado
304	West Virginia
305	Florida
306	Saskatchewan (Canada)
307	Wyoming
308	Nebraska
309	Illinois
310	California
312	Illinois
313	Michigan
314	Missouri
315	New York
316	Kansas
317	Indiana
318	Louisiana
319	Iowa
320	Minnesota
330	Ohio
334	Alabama
352	Florida
360	Washington
401	Rhode Island
402	Nebraska
403	Alberta, Yukon Territory, Northwest Territories (Canada)
404	Georgia
405	Oklahoma
406	Montana
407	Florida

Appendix

Area Code	Location
408	California
409	Texas
410	Maryland
412	Pennsylvania
413	Massachusetts
414	Wisconsin
415	California
416	Ontario (Canada)
417	Missouri
418	Quebec (Canada)
419	Ohio
423	Tennessee
501	Arkansas
502	Kentucky
503	Oregon
504	Louisiana
505	New Mexico
506	New Brunswick (Canada)
507	Minnesota
508	Massachusetts
509	Washington
510	California
512	Texas
513	Ohio
514	Quebec (Canada)
515	Iowa
516	New York
517	Michigan
518	New York
519	Ontario (Canada)
520	Arizona
540	Virginia
562	California
573	Missouri
601	Mississippi
602	Arizona
603	New Hampshire
604	British Columbia (Canada)
605	South Dakota
606	Kentucky
607	New York
608	Wisconsin
609	New Jersey
610	Pennsylvania
612	Minnesota
613	Ontario (Canada)
614	Ohio
615	Tennessee
616	Michigan
617	Massachusetts
618	Illinois
619	California
630	Illinois
701	North Dakota
702	Nevada
703	Virginia
704	North Carolina
705	Ontario (Canada)
706	Georgia
707	California
708	Illinois
709	Newfoundland, Labrador (Canada)
712	Iowa
713	Texas
714	California
715	Wisconsin
716	New York

Appendix

Area Code	Location
717	Pennsylvania
718	New York
719	Colorado
770	Georgia
801	Utah
802	Vermont
803	South Carolina
804	Virginia
805	California
806	Texas
807	Ontario (Canada)
808	Hawaii
809	Caribbean Islands
810	Michigan
812	Indiana
813	Florida
814	Pennsylvania
815	Illinois
816	Missouri
817	Texas
818	California
819	Quebec (Canada)
847	Illinois
860	Connecticut
864	South Carolina
901	Tennessee
902	Prince Edward Island, Nova Scotia (Canada)
903	Texas
904	Florida
905	Ontario (Canada)
906	Michigan
907	Alaska
908	New Jersey
909	California
910	North Carolina
912	Georgia
913	Kansas
914	New York
915	Texas
916	California
917	New York
918	Oklahoma
919	North Carolina
941	Florida
970	Colorado
972	Texas

Time-Period Designations

Designation	Time Period
annual	yearly
biannual	twice a year
bicentennial	200 years
biennial	2 years
bimonthly	every 2 months; twice a month
biweekly	every 2 weeks; twice a week
centennial	100 years
decennial	10 years
diurnal	daily; in a day
duodecennial	12 years
millennial	1,000 years
novennial	9 days, years, etc.
octennial	8 years
perennial	year after year
quadrennial	4 years
quadricentennial	400 years
quincentennial	500 years
quindecennial	15 years
quinquennial	5 years
semiannual	twice a year
semicentennial	50 years
semidiurnal	twice a day
semiweekly	twice a week
septennial	7 years
sesquicentennial	150 years

Designation	Time Period
sexennial	6 years
tricennial	30 years
triennial	3 years
trimonthly	every 3 months
triweekly	every 3 weeks; 3 times a week
undecennial	11 years
vicennial	20 years

Dates and Times in Five Languages

FRENCH

Days
Sunday: dimanche
Monday: lundi
Tuesday: mardi
Wednesday: mercredi
Thursday: jeudi
Friday: vendredi
Saturday: samedi

Months
January: janvier
February: février
March: mars
April: avril
May: mai
June: juin
July: juillet
August: août
September: septembre
October: octobre
November: novembre
December: décembre

Seasons
spring: printemps
summer: été
autumn: automne
winter: hiver

Time
second: seconde
minute: minute
hour: heure
day: jour
week: semaine
month: mois
year: année

GERMAN

Days
Sunday: Sonntag
Monday: Montag
Tuesday: Dienstag
Wednesday: Mittwoch
Thursday: Donnerstag
Friday: Freitag
Saturday: Sonnabend, Samstag

Months
January: Januar
February: Februar
March: März
April: April
May: Mai
June: Juni
July: Juli
August: August
September: September
October: Oktober
November: November
December: Dezember

Seasons
spring: Frühling
summer: Sommer
autumn: Herbst
winter: Winter

Time
second: Sekunde
minute: Minute
hour: Stunde
day: Tag
week: Woche
month: Monat
year: Jahr

ITALIAN

Days
Sunday: domenica
Monday: lunedì
Tuesday: martedì
Wednesday: mercoledì
Thursday: giovedì
Friday: venerdì
Saturday: sabato

Months
January: gennaio
February: febbraio
March: marzo
April: aprile
May: maggio
June: giugno
July: luglio
August: agosto
September: settembre
October: ottobre
November: novembre
December: dicembre

Seasons
spring: primavera
summer: estate
autumn: autunno
winter: inverno

Time
second: secondo
minute: minuto
hour: ora
day: giorno
week: settimana
month: mese
year: anno

LATIN

Days
Sunday: dies solis, dies dominica
Monday: dies lunae
Tuesday: dies Martis
Wednesday: dies Mercurii
Thursday: dies Iovis
Friday: dies Veneris
Saturday: dies Saturni

Months
January: Januarius
February: Februarius
March: Martius
April: Aprilis
May: Maius
June: Junius
July: Julius
August: Augustus
September: September
October: October
November: November
December: December

Seasons
spring: ver
summer: aestas
autumn: autumnus
winter: hiems

Time
second: momentum (temporis)
minute: momentum
hour: hora
day: dies
week: hebdomas
month: mensis
year: annus

SPANISH

Days
Sunday: domingo
Monday: lunes
Tuesday: martes
Wednesday: miércoles
Thursday: jueves
Friday: viernes
Saturday: sábado

Months
January: enero
February: febrero
March: marzo
April: abril
May: mayo
June: junio
July: julio
August: agosto
September: se(p)tiembre
October: octubre
November: noviembre
December: diciembre

Seasons
spring: primavera
summer: verano
autumn: otoño
winter: invierno

Time
second: segundo
minute: minuto
hour: hora
day: día
week: semana
month: mes
year: año

Easily Misspelled Words

abdicate
aberration
abhorrence
absence
absurd
accede
accept
acceptance
access
accessible
accessory
accidentally
accommodate
accompanied
accompanying
accordance
accrued
accumulate
accuracy
accustom
achieve
achievement
acknowledgment *or*
  acknowledgement
acquaintance
acquainted
acquiesce
acquire
acquitted
across
adapt
address

adequate
adjustment
admirable
advantageous
advertisement
advertising
advisable
advise
adviser *or* advisor
advisory
aerogram *or*
  aerogramme
aesthetic
affect (*vb.: influence*)
affects
affidavit
affluent
aggravate
agreeable
aisle
allotment
allotted
allowable
allowance
all right
almost
already
altar (*n.: structure*)
alter (*vb.: change*)
altogether
aluminum

alumnus
amateur
ambassador
amendment
among
amortize
analogous
analyses (*pl.*)
analysis (*s.*)
analyze
angel
angle
announce
announcement
annoyance
annual
antecedent
anticipate
anxiety
anxious
apocalypse
apologize
apparatus
apparel
apparent
appearance
appliance
applicable
applicant
appointment
appraisal
appreciable

appropriate
approximate
archaeology
archetype
archipelago
architect
archive
arctic
argument
arrangement
article
ascend
ascertain
assessment
assignment
assistance
assistant
associate
assured
attendance
attention
attorneys
auditor
authorize
auxiliary
available
awkward
baccalaureate
bachelor
balloon
bankruptcy
barbarous
bargain
baroque
barren
basis
beggar
beginning
believe

believing
beneficial
beneficiary
benefited
binary
bloc (*n.: political unit*)
bookkeeper
boundary
boutonniere
brilliant
brochure
bruised
budget
bulletin
buoy
buoyant
bureau
business
businessperson
busy
cafeteria
calendar
campaign
canceled *or* cancelled
cancellation
candidate
cannot
capital (*n.: money; town*)
capitol (*n.: building*)
career
carriage
casualty
catalog *or* catalogue
catechism
category
Caucasian

cede
cellar
cemetery
chancellor
changeable
changing
characteristic
chauffeur
chlorophyll
choice
choose
cigarette
cinnamon
circuit
circumstances
client
clientele
clique
coalesce
coarse
codicil
collar
collateral
colloquial
colonel
column
coming
commission
commitment
committed
committee
commodity
comparable
comparative
comparatively
comparison
compel
compelled
competent

Appendix

competitor
complement (*n.: that which completes; vb.: complete*)
compliment (*n.: flattery; vb.: flatter*)
compromise
concede
conceivable
conceive
concern
concession
concurred
conference
confident
confidential
configuration
congratulate
connoisseur
conscience
conscientious
conscious
consensus
consequence
consignment
consistent
consonant
consul (*n.: diplomatic official*)
consulate (*n.: consul's residence*)
contemptible
continuous
controlling
controversy
convenience

convenient
cordially
correspondent (*n.: law*)
corporation
correspondence
correspondent (*n.: writer*)
corroborate
council
councilor *or* councillor (*n.: council member*)
counsel (*n: lawyer*)
counselor *or* counsellor (*n.: lawyer*)
courteous
courtesy
coverage
credibility
creditor
crescendo
criticism
criticize
cruelty
cryptic
curiosity
current
curriculum
cursor
customer
database *or* data base
dealt
debater
debtor
deceitful
deceive

decide
decision
deducible
deductible
defendant
defense
deference
deferred
deficient
deficit
definite
definitely
definitive
delegate
delicatessen
demagogue
dependent
depositor
depreciation
derivative
descendant
describe
description
desirable
desktop publishing
desperate
destructible
deteriorate
develop
development
device (*n.: object*)
devise (*vb.: arrange*)
diagnostic
dialogue *or* dialog
diaphragm
dictionary
dietitian *or* dietician
difference
different

dilemma
dilettante
director
disappear
disappoint
disastrous
discipline
discourse
discrepancy
discriminate
disk
disparate
dissatisfaction
dissatisfied
dissipate
drought
drudgery
dying (*pres. part.* of die: *to be near death*)
dyeing (*pres. part* of dye: *to color*)
eagerly
ecclesiastical
economical
ecstasy
edible
edition
effect (*n.: result; vb.: to bring about*)
effects (*n.: personal or real property*)
efficiency
efficient
effluent
eighth
eligible
eliminate
eloquent

embarrass
embarrassment
emergency
eminent
emphasis
emphasize
employee
enclose
encumbrance
encyclopedia
endeavor
endorse
endorsement
enemy
enterprise
enthusiasm
envelop (*vb.*)
envelope (*n.*)
environment
equaled *or* equalled
equipment
equipped
equivalent
especially
essence
essential
etiquette
euphoria
exaggerate
exceed
excel
excellence
excellent
except
excessive
exercise
exhaust
exhibit
exhilarate

exhilaration
existence
expedite
expenditure
expense
experience
explanation
extension
extraordinary
extremely
facilitate
facilities
familiar
familiarize
fantasy
fascinate
favorable
favorite
feasible
February
fiery
finally
financial
financially
financier
flaunt
flowchart *or* flow chart
forbade
forcible
foreign
foremost
forfeit
formally
formerly
fortuitous
forty
forward
fourth

Appendix

frantically	hesitate	independence
fraudulent	heterogeneous *or*	independent
freight	heterogenous	indict
friend	hindrance	indigestible
fulfill *or* fulfil	holiday	indispensable
fulfillment	homogeneous *or*	individual
fungus	homogenous	induce
furthermore	hoping	inducement
gaily	horrible	industrious
gallant	humorous	inevitable
gasoline	hundredths	infinite
gauge *or* gage	hurriedly	influential
generally	hygienic	inimitable
genius	hyperbole	initial
genuine	hypocrisy	innocence
glamour *or* glamor	identical	inoculate
good-bye *or* good-by	idiosyncrasy	inquiry
gourmet	ignorant	insignia
government	illegible	insistent
governor	imaginary	installment
grammar	imitation	instance
grandeur	imitative	integral
grateful	immediately	intellectual
grief	immigration	intelligence
grievance	imminent	intelligible
grievous	imperative	intention
guarantee	imperiled *or*	intentionally
guerrilla *or* guerilla	imperilled	intercede
guidance	impossible	interest
handkerchief	impromptu	interface
handled	inasmuch (as)	interrupted
harangue	inaugurate	intervene
harass	incarcerate	inventory
hardware	incidentally	investor
hazardous	inconvenience	irrelevant
height	incredible	irresistible
heinous	incredulous	irritable
hesitancy	incurred	itemized
hesitant	indebtedness	itinerary

itself
jeopardize
jeopardy
judge
judgment *or*
   judgement
juggle
justifiable
knowledge
knowledgeable
kosher
laboratory
landlord
legible
legitimate
leisure
lenient
length
letterhead
liable
liaison
library
license
lightning
likable
likelihood
likely
liquefy
literature
livelihood
loneliness
loose (*adj.:*
   unfastened)
lose (*vb.: mislay*)
magazine
maintain
maintenance
management
manual

manufacturer
manuscript
marital
marriage
Massachusetts
material (*n.:*
   substance)
materiel (*n.:*
   equipment)
mathematics
maximum
meager
medical
medicinal
medicine
medieval
megabyte
memorandum
menus
merchandise
messenger
microprocessor
mileage
miniature
minimum
miscellaneous
mischievous
misspell
Mississippi
modernize
momentous
monochrome
monolog *or*
   monologue
morale
mortgage
murmur
muscle
necessary

negligible
negotiate
neighborhood
neither
nestle
nevertheless
newsstand
niche
nickel
nil
ninetieth
ninety
ninth
nobody
no one
noticeable
notoriety
nowadays
nuclear
nucleus
oblige
oblivious
obstacle
occasion
occasionally
occupant
occur
occurred
occurrence
occurring
offense
offering
official
omission
omit
omitted
operate
opinion
opportunity

APPENDIX

optimistic
ordinary
organization
organize
original
oscillate
outrageous
overdue
overrun
pageant
paid
pamphlet
pantomime
paradigm
parallel
paralyze
parliament
partial
participant
particularly
pastime
patronage
peculiar
perceive
percent
peremptory
periphery
permanent
permissible
permitted
perseverance
persistent
personal (*adj.:
 private*)
personnel (*n.:
 employees*)
persuade
phase
physician

physically
piece
planning
pleasant
pleasure
plebeian
plebiscite
plow
politician
portentous
possess
possession
possibly
practical
practically
practice
precede
precedence
precedent
precision
predictable
preferable
preference
preferred
prejudice
preliminary
premium
preparation
presence
prevalent
previous
price list
primitive
principal (*n.:
 person; money;
 adj.: chief*)
principle (*n.: rule*)
privilege
probably

procedure
proceed
prodigy
professor
programmer
prominent
promissory
pronunciation
propeller *or*
 propellor
prophecy *or*
 prophesy (*n.:
 prediction*)
prophesy (*vb.:
 predict*)
prosecute
protocol
pseudonym
psyche
psychiatrist
psychology
purchase
pursue
quantity
quay
questionnaire
queue
quiet
quite
quixotic
quiz
quizzes
realize
really
rearrange
reasonable
recede
receipt
receive

recently
recipe
recognize
recognized
recommend
reconnaissance
recurrence
refer
referee
reference
referred
referring
region
registrar
regrettable
reign
reimburse
relieve
religious
remember
reminisce
remittance
renewal
repeat
repetition
representative
respectively
requirement
reservoir
residual
resistance
respectfully
response
responsible
responsibility
restaurant
reticence
retractable
retrieve

rhetoric
rheumatism
rhythm
rhythmical
ridiculous
route
saccharin
sacrifice
sacrilegious
safety
salable *or* saleable
salary
sarcasm
satisfactory
scarcely
scenery
scepter
schedule
schism
science
scythe
secede
secession
secretary
securities
seize
semantic
sensible
sentinel
separate
sequence
sequential
sergeant
several
severely
serviceable
sheriff
shipment
shipping

shone
shown
siege
significant
similar
simile
simultaneous
sincerity
smolder
solemn
soliloquy
someone
somewhat
sophomore
specimen
speech
specialize
spell-checker *or*
 spell checker
stationary (*adj.:*
 immobile)
stationery (*n.: paper*)
statistics
strenuous
strictly
studying
suave
submitted
subpoena
subscriber
substantial
succeed
successful
suddenness
sufficient
suffrage
summarize
superintendent
supersede

supervisor
suppress
surprise
survey
sustainable
syllable
syllabus
symmetrical
symmetry
synchronize
tariff
telecommunications
temperament
temperature
temporary
tendency
terrestrial
theater
their
there
thesaurus
thorough
thousandth
throughout
tied
time-sharing *or* time sharing
tournament
toward *or* towards
tragedy
tranquillity *or* tranquility
transfer
transferred
trauma
treacherous
treasurer
tremendous
tried

trivial
truly
twelfth
tying
typeface
typical
typing
tyranny
ultimately
unanimous
underrate
undoubtedly
unfortunately
universally
unnecessary
until
unusual
urgent
usable
usage
usually
vacancy
vaccination
vacillate
vacuum
valuable
various
vector
vehicle
vendor
vengeance
vicinity
vicious
victory
vigilance
villain
visible
vitiate
vivacious

volatile
volume
voluntary
volunteer
warehouse
warrant
weather
Wednesday
weird
whether
wholesale
wholly
withhold
worthwhile
wreck
wrestle
writing
written
yacht
yaw
yea
yearn
yield
zebra
zephyr
zero
zigzag
zinc

Index

A-1, 319
abandon, 3
abandonment, 3–4
abbreviations, 4, 94
   business organization, 395–403
   general business, 333–363
   technical business, 364–394
abecedarian, 301
abjure, 301
a bon marché, 285
abort, 3, 267
ab ovo usque ad mala, 285
abozzo, 301
abrogate, 5
absentee owner, 5
abstract, 5, 225
abstract of record, 5
abstract of title, 5
academe, 301
acalculia, 301
acceleration clause, 5, 83
acceptilation, 301. *See also* acknowledgment
access, 267. *See also* computers
accessorize, 267
accomodation endorsement. *See* endorsement
account, 6, 84
   capital stock, 55
   cash, 55
   chart of accounts, 59
   for earnest money, 92
   See also credit
accounting, 6–8
   amortization, 15
   audit, 31
   balance sheet, 37
   cash flow, 55
   closing in, 62
   credit in, 77
   See also journal; ledger; spreadsheet
accoutrement, 301
accrual accounting. *See* accounting
accrued dividend. *See* dividends
accumulated dividend. *See* dividends
ace in the hole, 319
acid test, 319
acknowledgment, 8–9, 13
à compte, 285. *See also* credit
acronym. *See* abbreviations
across the board, 267
actions speak louder than words, 319
actual cash value, 10
actuary, 10
acuity, 301
acumen, 301
acuminate, 301
addendum, 10
add-on, 267
address, 10

INDEX

adduce, 301
ad hoc, 285
ad infinitum, 285
adjourned meeting, 10
adjustable-rate mortgage (ARM). *See* mortgage
adjustment bond. *See* bonds
adminicle, 301
ad referendum, 285
adumbrate, 301
ad valorem, 285
advance, 11
adventitious, 301
adversaria, 302
affidavit, 8, 11–13, 190
aficionado, 285
a fortiori, 285
aftermarket, 267
Age Discrimination Act of 1967, 87
agency, 13, 37. *See also* fiduciary
agent. *See* agency
agiotage, 302. *See also* stock; stock exchange
agreements, 5, 14, 43
  and bonds, 46
  breach of warranty, 50
  and calls, 53
  leases, 140–141
  performance bond, 49
  See also contracts; covenants
a la carte, 285
a la mode, 285
aleatory, 302
Algol (algorithmic language). *See* languages
algorism, 302
algorithm, 14, 106, 120
algorithmic language (Algol). *See* languages
alien corporation. *See* corporations
aliquot, 302
A-list, 267
all in a day's work, 319
allograph, 302
allonym, 302
all in the same boat, 319
all wet, 319
alphanumeric, 14, 20, 104
alpha and omega, 267. *See also* Greek alphabet
alpha storage, 267. *See also* capital
alternative dispute resolution. *See* arbitration
amalgamation, 14

ambagious, 302
ambidextrous, 302
amendments, 14–15, 52, 198
Americans with Disabilities Act of 1990, 87
American Standard Code for Information Interchange (ASCII), 21–26, 58
American Stock Exchange (AMEX). *See* stock exchange
American Stock Exchange (AMEX) Market Value Index. *See* stock index
America Online, 131
AMEX (American Stock Exchange). *See* stock exchange
amicus curiae, 285
amortization, 15–16, 41, 114–115
amotion, 302
amphigaean, 302
ana, 302
analects, 302
analog, 16, 86
anastatic, 302. *See also* printing
angel, 267
animadversion, 302
anno Domini, 285
annual reports, 10, 16, 31
annuity, 16–17
annuity premiums, 10
anopisthographic, 303. *See also* printing
answer, 17
antitrust laws, 18, 179, 206
APL (programming language). *See* languages
apophasis, 303
apothegm, 303
appendix. *See* back matter
applications software. *See* software
appreciation, 18
a priori, 285
apropos of, 285
arb (arbitrageur), 267, 303. *See also* stock
arbitrageur, 267, 303
arbitration, 18–19
archetype, 303. *See also* prototype
area codes in United States and Canada, 457–459
arithmetic mean. *See* mean
ARM (adjustable-rate mortgage). *See* mortgage
armed to the teeth, 319
arm's length, 319
array, 19

arrearage. *See* arrears
arrears, 20
arriviste, 303
arrogate, 303
articles of incorporation, 20, 70. *See also* corporations
artifice, 303
artificial intelligence, 20–21, 78
artificial language. *See* languages
ascesis, 303
ASCII (American Standard Code for Information Interchange), 21–26, 58
asked price. *See* quotation
assembler, 26–27
assembly language. *See* assembler; languages
assets, 27–28
   in accounting, 6
   amortization of, 15
   appreciation of, 18
   and auditing, 31
   on balance sheet, 37
   in bankruptcy, 40
   and basis, 41
   and book value, 49
   and capital, 54
   cash flow, 55
   depreciation of, 85
   and goodwill, 114
asseverate, 303
assigned-risk plan, 28
assignment, 29
assumable mortgage. *See* mortgage
atelier, 285
athenaeum, 303
at liberty, 267
at one's fingertips, 319
attaché, 285
attachment, 10, 28, 29
attestation, 29–30
attestation clause. *See* attestation
attitude, 267
au contraire, 285
audioconference. *See* teleconferences
audit, 16, 30–31
au fait, 285
aussitôt dit, aussitôt fait, 285
autobahn, 285
autodidact, 303
autognosis, 303
automation, 31
Automation Alley, 267
auxiliary storage, 81
avant-propos, 286. *See also* front matter

avec plaisir, 286
average, 31–32
avoid like the plague, 319
axe to grind, 319
axis, 32

baby bond. *See* bonds, 33
backhanded compliment, 319
backlog, 33
back matter, 33–36
back to back, 268
back to the drawing board, 319
back to square one, 319
back to the wall, 319
backup, 36, 88
bag of tricks, 319
bailment, 37, 69
bait and switch pricing, 268
balance sheet, 6, 16, 37–38, 39, 55
balloon mortgage. *See* mortgage
balloon payment, 38
ballpark figure, 268
bank draft, 38, 42. *See also* bill of exchange
bankruptcy, 29, 38, 40. *See also* insolvency; liquidation
barcode, 40
bargain and sale deed. *See* deed
bark up the wrong tree, 319
barter, 40–41
baseland, 268. *See also* computers; LANs
BASIC (Beginners All-Purpose Symbolic Instruction Code). *See* languages
basis, 18, 41
batch processing, 41, 175
baud, 41
bean counter, 268
bear, 268
bear the brunt, 320
bearer bond. *See* bonds
beat around the bush, 320
bed of roses, 320
Beginners All-Purpose Symbolic Instruction Code (BASIC). *See* language
beg the question, 320
being all things to all people, 320
belles lettres, 286
bells and whistles, 268
beneficiary, 17, 42, 83
beside the point, 320
bête noire, 286

better late than never, 320
bibliography. *See* back matter
bid and asked price. *See* quotation
bide time, 320
bid price. *See* quotation
Big Blue, 268
Big Board. *See* stock exchange
bilateral contract. *See* contracts
bill of exchange, 42
bill of lading, 42
bill of sale, 42
binary, 21, 27, 41–43, 86. *See also* languages
binder, 43
bird's eye view, 320
bissextile, 303
bite the bullet, 320
bite off more than you can chew, 320
bits, 21, 41, 43, 52
blank endorsement. *See* endorsement
blanket insurance, 43–44
blanket mortgage. *See* mortgage
blaze a trail, 320
blessing in disguise, 320
blind trust. *See* trust
block, 44
blow hot and cold, 320
blow off steam, 320
blue chip, 268. *See also* stock
blueprint, 44
blue-sky laws, 45
board of directors, 16, 45, 51
boilerplate, 268. *See also* covenants
bolshoi, 286
bona fide, 286
bon appétit, 286
bond discount. *See* bonds
bond dividend. *See* dividends
bonding, 49
bond premium. *See* bonds
bond redemption. *See* bonds
bonds, 46–48
  block of, 44
  and calls, 53
  point, 203–204
bone of contention, 320
book value, 49, 114
both feet on the ground, 320
bottom line. *See also* net income
Bowash, 268
bravura, 286
breach of contract, 49–50, 79, 157. *See also* contracts
breach of warranty, 50. *See also* warranty

breakeven point, 50
breviate, 303
broadcast, 50
bucket shop, 268
budgeting. *See* zero-base budgeting
buffer, 50
bug, 269. *See also* computers; software
bull, 269
bulletin board system, 51
bumping, 269
burden of proof, 320
burden rate. *See* overhead
burn a candle at both ends, 320
burn the midnight oil, 320
burnout, 269
bury the hatchet, 320
bus. *See* central processing unit (CPU)
business abbreviations, 333–403
business as usual, 320
bus topology. *See* local area networks (LANs)
by the book, 320
bylaws, 45, 51–52, 166, 198
by leaps and bounds, 321
by the same token, 320
byte, 52, 58
by word of mouth, 320

cache, 286
cachet, 304
cacoepy, 304
cacography, 304
cacology, 304
CAD (computer-aided design). *See* graphics
cafeteria plan, 269
call, 47, 53
callable bond. *See* bonds
callable preferred stock. *See* stock
call a halt, 321
call into question, 321
call option. *See* call
call price. *See* call
camaraderie, 286
camarilla, 304
cambistry, 304
cameralistics, 304
camera-ready copy, 53–54, 207
Canadian area codes, 457–459
candy-store problem, 269
cap, 269
capital, 17, 31, 37, 54. *See also* corporations
capital asset. *See* assets

480 INDEX

capital goods, 54
capitalization, 20, 54
capital stock, 55, 74. *See also* stock
capital structure. *See* capitalization
captain of industry, 321
CAR (computer-assisted retrieval). *See* micrographics
cardinal numbers in five languages, 427–430
carpe diem, 286
carrier. *See* common carrier
carte blanche, 286
cartography, 304
cash disbursements journal. *See* journal
cash dividend. *See* dividends
cash flow, 55
cashier's check, 55
cash receipts journal. *See* journal
catachresis, 304
catbird seat, 321
catechetical, 304
cathode ray tube (CRT), 56, 66, 119
catholicon, 304
causa sine qua non, 286
causative factor, 269
cause célèbre, 286
causerie, 304
caveat, 286
caveat emptor, 286
caveat lector, 286
cavil, 304
CD-ROM. *See* disk
cell. *See* cellular technology; spreadsheet
cellular technology, 56–57
central bank, 57, 206
centralization, 57, 81
central processing unit (CPU), 57, 66, 119. *See also* chip; microprocessor
Centrex. *See* telephone system
centrifugal, 304
centripetal, 304
certificate of incorporation. *See* articles of incorporation
certified check, 58
certified public accountants (CPAs), 8, 58
certiorari, 286
chacun à son goût, 286
chaffer, 304
change agent, 269
change of heart, 321
channel, 269. *See also* Internet
Chapter 7, 11, 13 bankruptcy. *See* bankruptcy

character, 58
charitable corporation. *See* corporations
chart of accounts, 6, 59, 60
charter. *See* articles of incorporation
chattel mortgage. *See* chattel; mortgage
checkered career, 321
chef de cuisine, 286
chef d'oeuvre, 286
chew out, 321
Chicago Manual of Style, The, 34, 72
chicano, 287
chip, 59
chrematistics, 304
circumforaneous, 304
civil law, 59
Civil Rights Act of 1964, 87, 96. *See also* discrimination; equal opportunity
class action, 59–60
clavis, 304
Clayton Act. *See* antitrust laws
clean as a whistle, 321
clear the air, 321
clearinghouse, 61
cliches, 317–331
clip art, 61
cloisonné, 287
close corporation. *See* corporations
closed-circuit television, 61. *See also* teleconferences
closed corporation. *See* corporations
closed end, 51–52
closed-end fund. *See* mutual fund
closely held corporation. *See* corporations
close shop, 321
closing, 62
closing the books. *See* closing
closing entries. *See* closing
closing statements. *See* closing
cloud on the title. *See* encumbrance; title
coacervate, 304
coadjuvancy, 304
COBOL (Common Business Oriented Language). *See* languages
codicil, 62
coeval, 304
cogito ergo sum, 287
coinsurance, 62–63
collateral, 29
collocate, 305
collusion, 63
colophon, 305
color coding, 63

INDEX

comaker, 64
comity, 305
command-driven program. *See* commands
commands, 64, 65
commercial paper, 64, 178
commodities, 64
  clearinghouse in, 61
  and exchange rate, 99
  futures contracts, 112–113
  PPI (producer price index), 209
  and price fixing, 205
  See also stock; stock exchange; stock index
commodities exchange. *See* commodities
commodities futures. *See* commodities
Commodities Futures Trading Commission. *See* commodities
Common Business Oriented Language (COBOL). *See* languages
common carrier, 65
common law, 65, 70, 72, 235
common logarithm. *See* logarithm
common stock. *See* stock
communications protocol. *See* protocol
communiqué, 287. *See also* reports
compact disk. *See* disk
comparative negligence. *See* contributory negligence
compatibility, 65
compendious, 305
compiler. *See* languages
complaint, 17, 65
compound interest. *See* interest
CompuServe, 131
computer-aided design (CAD). *See* graphics
computer-assisted retrieval (CAR). *See* micrographics
computer conference. *See* teleconferences
computer document conference. *See* teleconferences
computer graphics. *See* graphics
computer printing. *See* printing
computers, 66
  address in, 10
  artificial intelligence, 20–21, 78
  ASCII (American Standard Code for Information Interchange), 21–26, 58
  assembler, 26–27
  auxiliary storage, 81
  and backup, 36, 88
  and batch processing, 41, 175
  binary system, 21, 27, 41–43, 86
  broadcasting, 50
  buffers in, 50
  bulletin board system, 51
  characters in, 58
  commands for, 64, 65
  configuration in, 68
  CPU (central processing unit), 57, 66
  database, 79, 80
  data processing, 44, 80
  default settings in, 83–84
  desktop publishing, 61, 72, 85, 164, 207
  diagnostic routine, 86
  digital, 16, 86
  documentation for, 90
  and E-mail, 50, 93–94, 161, 243
  ENIAC (Electronic Numerical Integrator and Calculator), 66
  and fiber optics, 103
  fields in, 103–104
  files in, 104–105
  hard copy, 90, 94, 118
  integrated circuits, 59, 103, 118, 126–127
  languages for, 138–140
  linear programming, 156–157
  menu, 167–168
  operating system, 68, 193
  peripherals, 65, 118, 202, 312
  protocol for, 215–216, 278
  See also Internet; memory; modem; programming
computer-telephone integration. *See* telephone system
concatenation, 305
conditional endorsement. *See* endorsement
conditional sale, 67
conference proceedings. *See* conferences
conferences, 67–68. *See also* meetings; teleconferences
confidential mailbox. *See* mailbox
configuration, 68
configuration file. *See* configuration
congeries, 305
conglomerate. *See* corporations
connoisseur, 287
consideration. *See* contracts; mortgage
consignment, 37, 69
constructive receipt, 69
consuetude, 305
consumer price index (CPI), 69, 125

continuous inventory. *See* inventory
contra, 287
contracts, 71–72
  acceleration clause, 5, 83
  bailment for hire, 37
  and bill of lading, 42
  binders in, 43
  breach of, 49–50, 157
  and calls, 53
  and chattel, 54
  escalation clause in, 97–98
  and escrow, 98
  execution of, 99
  futures, 112–113
  leases, 140–141
  recission of, 226
contributory negligence, 71
control account. *See* account; ledger
conventional mortgage. *See* mortgage
conventional wisdom, 321
conventions. *See* conferences
convertible bond. *See* bonds
convertible preferred stock. *See* stock
cool and whizzy, 269. *See also* computers; hardware; software
copula, 305
copy, 71–72
copyedit, 53, 71, 72
copying. *See* xerography
copyright, 72–73, 216–217. *See also* patent; trademark
copyright infringement. *See* copyright
corporate bond. *See* bonds
corporate raider, 269
corporations, 16, 19, 73–76
  articles of incorporation, 20
  and blue-sky laws, 45
  and bonds, 46
  and capital, 54
  and capital stock, 55
  commercial paper, 64
  and contracts, 70
  and dividends, 89–90
  equity in, 96
  and Eurocurrency, 99
  incorporators' meeting, 122, 124
  See also limited liability company
corpus, 287
corpus juris civilis, 287. *See also* civil law
correlation, 76
correlation coefficient. *See* correlation
correspondence format. *See* format
cortege, 287

costa, 287
cost accounting. *See* accounting
cost-plus contract. *See* contracts
coterie, 287
coup d'état, 287
coupon bond. *See* bonds
coupon yield. *See* yield
covenants, 76–77, 82, 163
CPAs (certified public accountants), 8, 58
CPR (consumer price index), 69, 125
CPU (central processing unit), 57, 66. *See also* chip; microprocessor
cream of the crop, 321
credit, 47, 77
  and central bank, 57
  commercial paper, 64
  and Eurocurrency, 99
credit line. *See* credit
critique, 287
cross a bridge when one comes to it, 321
crossover, 269
crosstalk, 269
CRT (cathode ray tube), 56, 66, 119
cumbrous, 305
cumulative preferred stock. *See* stock
cumulative trauma disorders. *See* ergonomics
cunctation, 305
Curb, the. *See* stock exchange
currency, foreign, 436–445
current asset. *See* assets
current yield. *See* yield
curriculum vitae, 287
Cu See-Me conference. *See* teleconferences
cut and dried, 321
cybernetics, 77–78
cyberspace, 270. *See also* computers

damage control, 270
damages, 50, 65, 71, 79
data, 10, 14, 66, 79
  American Standard Code for Information Interchange (ASCII), 21–26
  array, 19
  and backup, 36
  and bauds, 41
  CPU (central processing unit), 57
  on disks, 87–88
databank. *See* database
database management system, 80
data-bases, 31, 79, 80

data processing, 44, 80
dates and times in five languages, 462–466
dead end, 270
dead letter, 322
dead to rights, 322
debacle, 287
debenture. *See* bonds
debit and credit, 6, 80–81. *See also* credit
debonair, 287
debug, 270. *See also* computers
decadic, 305
decentralization, 57, 81
decibel, 81
decimal and fraction equivalents, 423
decree. *See* judgment
deductible, 63, 81–82
deed, 76, 82–83, 92, 163
deed of trust. *See* bonds; deed; mortgage; trust
deep-six, 322
de facto, 287
de facto corporation. *See* corporations
defalcation, 305
defamation. *See* libel; slander
default, 5, 63, 83–84
 and calls, 53
 in computers, 68–69
 grace period, 115
 and guarantees, 117
default settings. *See* default
defeasance clause. *See* mortgage
deficit, 84
deflation, 84, 125
de gustibus non est disputandum, 288
de jure, 288
de jure corporation. *See* corporations
demand deposit, 84
démarche, 288
dementi, 305
demit, 305
demography, 305
demotic, 305
denouement, 288
Deo gratias, 288
Deo volente, 288
depositary. *See* depository
deposition, 87, 190
deposition on written interrogatories. *See* deposition
depository, 84–85
depreciation, 85
 in actual cash value, 10
 and amortization, 15
 and basis, 41
 and book value, 49
 and fixed assets, 27
desideratum, 306
desinence, 306
desktop publishing (DTP), 61, 72, 85, 164, 207
de trop, 288
Dewey Decimal system, 145–148
diagnostic routine, 86
dialog box. *See* menu
diatribe, 306
Die gratia, 288
die is cast, the, 322
differential cost. *See* marginal cost
digerati, 270
digital, 16, 86
diglot, 306
ding hao, 288
di rigueur, 288
disclaimer, 86
discrimination, 86–87. *See also* equal opportunity
dishonor, 87
disinflation. *See* deflation
disk, 3, 36, 66, 87–88
disk drive, 88–89, 118
diskette. *See* disk
display screen. *See* cathode ray tube (CRT)
disposable income, 89
diurnal, 306
divestiture, 89
dividends, 10, 89–90
documentation, 90
document conference. *See* teleconferences
dog, 270
domestic corporation. *See* corporations
Domestic Mail Manual, 194
Dominus vobiscum, 288
dossier, 288
dot the i's and cross the t's, 322
dot matrix printer. *See* printing
double-entendre, 288
double-entry bookkeeping. *See* debit and credit
Dow Jones Industrial Average. *See* stock index
download, 270. *See also* computers; modem
downsize, 270
downtick, 270

dragoman, 306
dragoon, 306
draw the line at, 322
DRIP, 270. *See also* dividend; stock; stockholder
drop ship, 90–91
dry as dust, 306
dubiety, 306
dumb terminal. *See* workstation
dumping, 270–271. *See also* stock
duplexing. *See* duplex system
duplex system, 91
Dvorak keyboard, 66, 91, 119
dye-sublimation printer. *See* printing
dye-thermal printer. *See* printing
dynamic scoring, 271

earnest money, 43, 92
easement, 92–93
easily mispelled words, 467–480
ecce homo, 288
economy of scale, 93. *See also* marginal cost
ectype, 306
effective interest rate. *See* yield
effendi, 288
élan, 288
elasticity of demand, 93
electronic mailbox. *See* electronic mail (E-mail); mailbox
electronic-mail (E-mail), 50, 93–94, 161, 243
Electronic Numerical Integrator and Calculator (ENIAC), 66
eleemosynary, 306
elenchus, 206
eleventh hour, 322
E-mail (electronic-mail), 50, 93–94, 161, 243
eminent domain, 94
emolument, 306
emoticon, 271. *See also* E-mail; network
enchiridion, 306
encumberances, 82, 94–95, 155, 163
endnotes. *See* back matter
endorsement, 29, 95–96
end user, 271
en famille, 288
enfilade, 306
English creep, 271
ENIAC (Electronic Numerical Integrator and Calculator), 66
ennui, 288
en plein jour, 288

en poste, 288
en rapport, 288
entertain high hopes, 322
entourage, 288
entre nous, 288
entrepôt, 289
e plurbis unum, 289
Equal Employment Opportunity Act of 1972, 87
Equal Employment Opportunity Commission, 96
equal opportunity, 96. *See also* discrimination
equitable lien. *See* liens
equity, 6, 27, 63, 96
equity of redemption. *See* foreclosure
erasable optical disk. *See* disk
ergo, 289
ergonomics, 96–97. *See also* workers' compensation laws
eristic, 306
erratum/errata, 289
ersatz, 289
escalation clause, 97–98
escalator clause. *See* escalation clause
escheat, 306
escrow, 92, 98. *See also* earnest money
esoteric, 306
estrade, 306
et alli, 289
ethics, 98
et uxor, 289
et vir, 289
Eurobank. *See* Eurocurrency
Eurocurrency, 99, 178
Eurodollar. *See* Eurocurrency
every man has his price, 322
ex cathedra, 289
exchange. *See* stock exchange
exchange rate, 99
execution, 99, 135
execution time, 99–100
exegesis, 307
ex gratia, 289
exiguous, 307
exit, 271. *See also* computers
ex more, 289
ex officio, 289
exordium, 307
exoteric, 307
ex parte, 289
explore every avenue, 322
exponent, 100
ex post facto, 289

INDEX

ex relatione, 289

facadism, 271
face the music, 322
face value, 48, 101
facient, 307
facsimile (fax), 50, 101–102, 161, 243
fair shake, 322
fait accompli, 289
fallout, 271
false alarm, 322
Fannie Mae mortgage. *See* mortgage
far cry, 322
FASB (Financial Accounting Standards Board), 7
fast track, 271
fat cat, 322
faux pas, 289
fax (facsimile), 50, 101–102, 161, 243
Federal Deposit Insurance Corporation, 178
Federal Home Loan Mortgage Corporation (FHLMC), 181
Federal Housing Administration (FHA), 181
Federal National Mortgage Association (FNMA), 181
Federal Reserve System, 57. *See also* central bank
Federal Savings and Loan Insurance Corporation, 178–179
feedback, 102
feel the pinch, 322
fee simple. *See* deed
felicitous, 307
feracious, 307
few and far between, 322
FHA (Federal Housing Administration), 181
FHA mortgage. *See* mortgage
FHLMC (Federal Home Loan Mortgage Corporation), 181
fiat, 289
fiber optics, 102–103
fidelity bond. *See* bonding
fiduciary, 46, 49, 103
fields, 103–104
fifth-generation computer, 271–272. *See also* computers; programming
fight tooth and nail, 323
file, 3, 14, 36, 104–105
filename, 105
file-transfer protocol. *See* protocol
filing system. *See* file

fill the bill, 323
final injunction. *See* injunction
finance charge, 106
Financial Accounting Standards Board (FASB), 7
finis, 289
finishing touch, 323
firmware. *See* software
first generation, 272
first magnitude, of the, 323
fiscal period, 16, 55, 106, 187
fiscal year. *See* period
fixed annuity. *See* annuity
fixed assets. *See* assets
fixed capital. *See* capital goods
fixed-rate mortgage (FRM). *See* mortgage
flanker, 272
flexible mortgage. *See* mortgage
flexible-payment mortgage. *See* mortgage
flipflop, 272
floor trader. *See* stock exchange
floppy disk. *See* disk
flowchart, 106–107
fly-by-night, 323
fly in the face of, 323
fly in the ointment, 323
FNMA (Federal National Mortgage Association), 181
focus group, 272
food for thought, 323
footnotes. *See* back matter
force majeure, 289
force to be reckoned with, 323
foreclosure, 108
foregone conclusion, 323
foreign corporation. *See* corporations
foreign currency, 436–445
foreign expressions, 283–298
format, 65, 110, 164
Formula Translation (FORTRAN). *See* languages
for-profit corporation. *See* corporations
Forth. *See* languages
FORTRAN (Formula Translation). *See* languages
Fortune 500, 272
forward P/E. *See* price-earnings ratio
fourth estate, 323
fourth-generation language (4GL). *See* languages
fraction and decimal equivalents, 423
frame of reference, 272

franchise, 15, 27, 75, 110
fraud, 63, 111
Freddie Mac mortgage. *See* mortgage
free ride, 272
freeze, 272
French dates and times, 462
French numbers, 426
fringe benefit, 111
FRM (fixed-rate mortgage). *See* mortgage
from A to Z, 323
from the word go, 323
front matter, 5, 72, 111–112
frozen asset. *See* assets
fugacious, 307
full-duplex system. *See* duplex system
full lot. *See* odd lot
full steam ahead, 323
fungible, 307
futures, 64, 112–113
futures contracts. *See* commodities; futures

game plan, 272
gamer, 272
garnishment, 114
gate, 272
gateway. *See* Internet; local area networks (LANs)
gauche, 290
general journal. *See* journal
general obligation bond. *See* bonds
general partnership. *See* partnerships
gentrification, 272
geodesic, 307
German dates and times, 463
German numbers, 427
get down to brass tacks, 323
get a handle on, 323
get it down pat, 323
get sacked, 324
get to the bottom of, 324
gingerbread, 272
Ginnie Mae mortgage. *See* mortgage
give the benefit of the doubt, 324
give short shrift to, 324
give a wide berth to, 324
glass ceiling, 272
glossary. *See* back matter
glotogonic, 307
GNMA (Government National Mortgage Association), 181
gnome, 307
GNP (gross national product), 116

go against the grain, 324
go for broke, 324
going in circles, 324
going-concern will. *See* goodwill
golden handcuffs, 273. *See also* contracts
golden parachute, 273
gomei kaisha, 290
good old boy, 324
goodwill, 27, 114–115
Gothic type. *See* typeface, 115
gourmet, 290
Government National Mortgage Association (GNMA), 181
grace period, 115
graded lease. *See* lease
graduated-payment mortgage. *See* mortgage
grandfather clause, 115
graphics, 58, 61, 67, 85, 115–116
gratis, 290
gravamen, 307
graveyard shift, 273
Greek letter symbols, 435
green, 273
greenmail, 273. *See also* stock
grimthorpe, 307
grist for the mill, 324
gross income, 6, 116
gross margin. *See* gross profit
gross national product (GNP), 116
gross profit, 6, 54, 116
groupware, 273. *See also* software
guarantee, 117
guaranty. *See* guarantee
gym rat, 273

habitué, 290
hacker, 273
haircut, 273
half the battle, 324
half-duplex system. *See* duplex system
halftone, 118
handwriting on the wall, 324
hang in the balance, 324
hardball, 273
hard copy, 90, 94, 118
hard disk. *See* disk
hard and fast, 324
hardware, 66, 68, 86, 118–119
Harvard Law Review Association, *Uniform System of Citation,* 72
haute couture, 290
have a bone to pick, 324
heavy industry, 119

INDEX

hebdomadal, 308
hedge, 119
hedging. *See* hedge
hegemony, 308
hesperian, 308
heteronym, 308
heuristic, 14, 120
hidden asset. *See* assets
high-level language. *See* languages
high tech, 273
hit, 273. *See also* database
hit the nail on the head, 324
hive of industry, 324
hoc anno, 290
hoi polloi, 325
hold forth, 325
holding the bag, 325
holding company. *See* corporations
holidays (national) of other countries, 446–456
holograph, 308
home page, 274
homme d'affaires, 290
homonym, 308
homophone, 308
honorarium, 120
horatatory, 308
horizontal market, 274
host, 274. *See also* computers; database; peripherals; workstations
hostile takeover. *See* leveraged buyout
housekeeping routine, 274. *See also* computers
humanum est errare, 290
hybrid telephone system. *See* telephone system
hype, 274
hyperbole, 308
hypertext, 274. *See also* computers; graphics
hypobulia, 308
hypothesis, 120–121

ideogram, 308
ideograph, 309
id est, 290
illation, 309
imbroglio, 290
immiscible, 309
impasse, 290
implied contract. *See* contracts
implied easement. *See* easement
imprest fund. *See* petty cash
imprimatur, 309

income bond. *See* bonds
income statement, 6, 16, 37, 55, 122, 123
incomunicado, 290
incorporators' meeting, 122, 124. *See also* articles of incorporation
incremental cost. *See* marginal cost
indefectible, 309
indemnify, 124
indenture. *See* bonds
independent contractor, 124
index. *See* back matter; stock index
indirect costs and expenses. *See* overhead
individual retirement account (IRA). *See* retirement plan
inexpugnable, 309
inflation, 69, 84, 119, 124
infobahn, 274
information processing. *See* data processing
information superhighway, 274. *See also* computers; Internet
infra, 290
infrastructure, 274
in-house, 274
inineratry, 132
initialisms. *See* abbreviations
injuction, 125–126
ink-jet printer. *See* printing
in loco parentis, 290
in the long run, 325
in medias res, 290
in a nutshell, 325
in perpetuum, 290
in propria persona, 291
input, 275. *See also* computers
in rerum natura, 291
insider trading, 275. *See also* stock
in situ, 291
insolvency, 38, 126. *See also* bankruptcy; liquidation
ins and outs, 325
installment sale, 126
in statu quo, 291
intangible asset. *See* assets
intangible property, 3
integer, 126
integrated circuits, 59, 103, 118, 126–127
integrated system, 127
intelligent workstation. *See* workstations
interactive processing. *See* batch processing
inter alia, 291

488 INDEX

intercalate, 309
interchangeable bond. *See* bonds
interest, 16, 46, 57, 128–131, 178
interface, 275. *See also* computers
interlocutory injunction. *See* injuction
internal storage. *See* memory
Internet, 80, 93, 131–132, 161–162. *See also* wide area network
interpreter. *See* languages
interstate commerce, 18, 132, 206
intervivos trust. *See* trust
in toto, 291
intrastate commerce, 132
inventory, 27, 91, 132
involuntary bankruptcy. *See* bankruptcy
in a word, 325
ipso facto, 291
ipso jure, 291
IRA (individual retirement account). *See* retirement plan
irrevocable power of attorney. *See* power of attorney
isochronous, 309
isogenesis, 309
Italian dates and times, 464
Italian numbers, 428

jargon, 265–282
jaundiced eye, 325
jaweb, 309
jejune, 309
job order. *See* job lot
job queue. *See* queue
John Hancock, 325
joint bond. *See* bonds
joint tenancy, 133
joint venture, 133
jot lot, 133
journal, 133–135. *See also* accounting; ledger
judgment, 134–135
judgment lien. *See* liens
judicial precedent. *See* common law
junk bond, 275. *See also* bonds; yield
jural, 309
jurat, 291. *See also* affidavit
jure divno, 291
jus, 291
jus canonicum, 291
jus civile, 291. *See also* civil law
jus commune, 291. *See also* common law
jus gentium, 291
jus proprietatis, 291
justification, 136

just-in-time, 275. *See also* inventory
justitia omnibus, 291

keep the ball rolling, 325
keep one's head above water, 325
Keogh plan. *See* retirement plan
keyboard. *See* Dvorak keyboard; input; qwerty keyboard
kickback, 275
killer technology, 275
kill two birds with one stone, 325
know the ropes, 325
KSU-less telephone system. *See* telephone system

labile, 309
laches, 309
laissez-faire, 291
landlord's lien. *See* liens
languages, 138–140
  dates and times, 462–466
  machine, 26
  numbers in, 427–430
LANs (local-area networks), 93, 101, 103, 158–159, 173
large numbers, 424
laser printer. *See* printing
last will and testament. *See* will
Latin dates and times, 465
Latin numbers, 429
layaway, 140
lay one's cards on the table, 326
LCDs (liquid crystal displays), 156, 157
leading. *See* point
lease, 3, 10, 97–98, 140–141
lease with an option to buy. *See* lease
leaseback. *See* lease
leasehold, 27. *See also* lease
leave no stone unturned, 326
leave out in the cold, 326
ledger, 6, 7, 59, 142, 143
LED (light-emitting diode), 156
LED printer. *See* printing
legist, 309
lemma, 310
le style, c'est l'homme, 292
let the chips fall where they may, 326
le tout ensemble, 292
letter of credit. *See* credit
letter format. *See* format
letter-perfect, 326
leveraged buyout, 142–143
liabilities, 143–144
  in accounting, 6

and auditing, 31
on balance sheet, 37
liaison, 292
libel, 144. *See also* slander
library classification system, 144–155
Library of Congress system, 148–155
licentiate, 310
liens, 82, 155–156, 163
light-emitting diode (LED), 156, 209
light industry, 156
limited liability. *See* corporations; limited liability company
limited liability company, 156, 200
limited partnerships. *See* partnerships
linear programming, 156–157
line of credit. *See* credit
line drawing. *See* halftone
liquid asset. *See* assets
liquidated damages, 157. *See also* breach of contract; damages; default
liquidation, 157. *See also* bankruptcy; insolvency
liquid crystal displays (LCDs), 156, 157
liquid ink-jet printer. *See* printing
liquidity. *See* capital
lis pendens, 292
list price, 158
litigious, 310
litotes, 310
live and learn, 326
living trust. *See* trust
living will. *See* will
load, 158
load fund. *See* load; mutual fund
local-area networks (LANs), 93, 101, 103, 158–159, 173
lock, stock, and barrel, 326
locus in quo, 292
locus sigilii, 292
logarithm, 159
log in. *See* log on
logo, 159
logogram, 310
log on, 276. *See also* computers
logotype. *See* logo
longiloquence, 310
long sale. *See* short sale
long shot, 326
lost cause, 326
lot. *See* job lot
low-level language. *See* languages

machine language. *See* languages
macroscopic, 310

magisterial, 310
magnetic disk. *See* disk
mailbox, 94, 161
mainframe computer. *See* computers
main memory. *See* memory
maintain the status quo, 326
majority stockholder. *See* stockholders
make or break, 326
mala praxis, 292
malversation, 310
management information system (MIS), 162
mandatory injunction. *See* injunction
man-hours, 276
MAN (metropolitan area network), 172
manuduction, 310
manuscript. *See* copy
marcreconomics, 161
margin, 162–163
marginal cost, 163. *See also* economy of scale
markdowns, 158, 163
marketable title, 163. *See also* title
market research, 164
market share, 164
market value. *See* face value
markup, 164
mathematical signs and symbols, 431–434
maturity
  and bonds, 47, 164–165
  and calls, 53
  commercial paper, 64
maturity date. *See* maturity, 165
maturity value. *See* face value
matutinal, 310
MCI, 131
mea culpa, 292
mean, 32, 165
mechanic's lien. *See* liens
mediation. *See* arbitration, 165
meetings, 10, 15, 51, 122, 124, 165–166. *See also* conferences
mélange, 292
melee, 292
meliorate, 310
memory, 166–167
  abandon, 3
  address in, 10
  auxiliary storage, 81
  and bytes, 52
  characters in, 58
  and chips, 59
  and configuration, 68
  CPU (central processing unit), 57

menu, 167–168
menu bar. *See* menu
menu-driven program. *See* commands
merit rating, 168
metage, 310
métier, 292
metric system, 168–172
metropolitan area network (MAN), 172
mi casa es su casa, 292
Mickey Mouse, 276
microchip. *See* chip; integrated circuits
microcomputer. *See* computers
microeconomics, 172
microfiche. *See* micrographics
microfilm. *See* micrographics
microform. *See* micrographics
microform reader. *See* micrographics
micrographics, 173–174
micromanagement, 276. *See also* centralization
microprocessor, 59, 174. *See also* chip; integrated circuits
Microsoft, 131
Midas touch, 326
mikado, 293
milieu, 293
millennium, 293, 310
Miller-Tydings Act. *See* antitrust laws
minicomputer. *See* computers
minimum wage, 174
minority stockholder. *See* stockholders
minutes, 174–175, 176
mise en scène, 292
MIS (management information system), 162
misocainea, 311
misspelled words, 467–480
mobile telephone. *See* cellular technology
mode, 175, 177
modem, 41, 51, 177
 and faxes, 101–102
 and the Internet, 131
 See also E-mail
modular, 177–178
modular accounting. *See* modular
modular/demodulator. *See* modem
modular programming. *See* modular
module. *See* modular
modus operandi, 292
moment of truth, 326
mommy track, 276
mon ami, 292
monde, 292

money, foreign, 436–445
money market, 178–179
monitor. *See* cathode ray tube (CRT)
monolithic, 311
monopoly, 179
month of Sundays, 326
month-to-month lease, 179
moratorium, 179
more than one bargained for, 326
morphing, 276
mortgage, 3, 15, 179–183
 and chattel, 59
 closed end, 62
 and deeds, 82
mortgage bond. *See* bonds
mortmain, 311
motion. *See* parliamentary procedure
mouse, 66, 167, 183
mouse milking, 276
movers and shakers, 326
MRI Bankers' Guide to Foreign Currency, 436
muddy the water, 326
mulct, 311
multiple. *See* price-earnings ratio
multiple listing, 183–184
municipal bond. *See* bonds
muniment, 311
mutatis mutandis, 292
mutual fund, 62, 178, 184–185

NASDAQ Composite Index. *See* stock index
NASDAQ (National Association of Securities Dealers Automated Quotations). *See* over-the-counter
national holidays of other countries, 446–456
natural language. *See* languages
nee, 292
negative proof. *See* proof
negligence. *See* contributory negligence
negotiable instrument, 87, 186
nemine contradicente, 293
nemine dissentiente, 293
neologism, 311
neoteric, 311
nescience, 311
net income, 6, 54
netiquette, 276. *See also* Internet
net loss, 84, 187
net-net, 276
net profit. *See* net income
net result, 327

network, 56, 187. *See also* Internet; LAN; MAN; WAN
networking, 277. *See also* network
net working capital. *See* capital
net worth, 96, 187–188
news release, 188, 189
New York Stock Exchange Composite Index. *See* stock index
New York Stock Exchange (NYSE). *See* stock exchange
New York Times Manual of Style and Usage, The, 72
nexus, 311
niche market, 277
Nikkei Stock Average. *See* stock index
nimiety, 311
node. *See* local area networks (LANs)
nodus, 311
noesis, 311
no-fault insurance, 188–189
nolens volens, 293
nolle prosequi, 293
no-load fund. *See* load; mutual fund
nolo contendere, 293
nom de gueere, 293
nom de plume, 293
nominal yield. *See* yield
noncompete agreement, 189–190
noncumulative preferred stock. *See* stock
noncurrent assets. *See* assets
nonnegotiable instrument, 190
nonparticipating preferred stock. *See* stock
nonprofit corporation. *See* corporations
non prosequitur, 293
non sequitur, 293
nonvolatile memory. *See* memory
no-par stock. *See* stock
nose to the grindstone, 327
notary public, 8, 11, 190
notebook computer. *See* computers
notes, 29, 64, 178, 190. *See also* back matter
not-for-profit corporation. *See* corporations
nous, 311
nouveau riche, 293
no-win situation, 327
nuance, 293
nul tort, 293
numbers
   decimal and fraction equivalents, 423
   in French, 426
   in German, 427
   in Italian, 428
   large numbers, 424
   in Latin, 429
   Roman numerals, 424
   in Spanish, 430
numerical control, 191
NYSE (New York Stock Exchange). *See* stock exchange

obiit, 293
obiter dictum, 293
objet d'art, 293
objurgate, 311
obrogate, 311
obsignation, 312
occidental, 312
OCR (optical chart recognition), 194
odd lot, 192
oeuvre, 293
off the beaten track, 327
off line, 277. *See also* on line
offset press. *See* printing
of and running, 327
okimono, 293
old-boy network, 327
oligopoly, 312
ombudsperson, 192
on the fence, 327
on line, 277. *See also* central processing unit (CPU)
open and aboveboard, 327
open account. *See* credit
open book, 327
open end, 193
open-end fund. *See* mutual fund
open-end mortgage. *See* mortgage
open question, 327
operating ratio, 193. *See also* balance sheet; income statement
operating system, 68, 193
operations research, 193
operative, 277
opere citato, 293
OPM financing, 277
optical chart recognition (OCR), 194
optical disk. *See* disk
optimize, 277
optimum, 277
option, 277
optional dividend. *See* dividends
options trading. *See* futures
opus, 293
oral contract. *See* contracts
oral deposition. *See* deposition

ordinal numbers in five languages, 427–430
organization abbreviations, 395–403
orismology, 312
orthoepy, 312
orthography, 312
out on a limb, 327
out-of-state corporation. *See* corporations
output, 277
output contract. *See* contracts
outside director. *See* board of directors
outsourcing, 277
over a barrel, 327
overhead, 194
over-the-counter (OTC) market, 195
overtime, 195
owner's equity. *See* equity
oxymoron, 312

package mortgage. *See* mortgage
packets, 278. *See also* data; network
pack it in, 327
page layout. *See* desktop publishing; word processing
page proof, 44. *See also* proof
panache, 294
pandemic, 312
panoptic, 312
paper over, 327
paper tiger, 327
paradigm, 278
parameter, 68, 196
par avion, 294
parent corporation. *See* corporations
par excellence, 294
pari passu, 294
parliamentary law. *See* parliamentary procedure
parliamentary procedure, 11, 15, 51, 166, 174–175, 196–199
paroemia, 312
participating preferred stock. *See* stock
partnerships, 75, 133, 156, 199–200
par value. *See* face value
par-value stock. *See* stock
Pascal. *See* languages
pasha, 294
patent, 3, 27, 200–201, 216–217. *See also* copyright; trademark
payroll, 201
pay through the nose, 327
PBX (private branch exchange) telephone system. *See* telephone system

peculate, 312
pecuniary damage. *See* damages
peer-to-peer, 278. *See also* computers; network
peewee tech, 278
peice de resistance, 294
penchant, 294
pension, 111, 201. *See also* retirement plan
per annum, 294
P/E ratio. *See* price-earnings ratio
per diem, 294
performance bond. *See* bonding
periodic tenancy. *See* lease
peripherals, 65, 118, 202, 312
permanent injunction. *See* injunction
perpetual inventory. *See* inventory
per se, 294
persona grata, 294
personal computer. *See* computers
personal property, 37, 59, 155, 202
personalty. *See* personal property
persona non grata, 294
perspicuous, 312
petty cash, 202
phon, 312
phoneme, 312
phonogram, 313
photocopier. *See* printing
photocopying. *See* xerography
pica. *See* point
pick someone's brain, 328
pièce de résistance, 294
pied-à-terre, 294
piggybacking. *See* telephone system
pis aller, 294
plain as day, 328
plat, 203
plate, 203
play fast and loose, 328
play one's cards right, 328
pledge, 47, 63, 83, 203
pleno jure, 294
pleonasm, 313
plethoric, 313
plus ça change, plus c'est la même chose, 294
point, 85, 164, 203–204. *See also* typeface
point of no return, 328
poison pill, 278
polling, 204
portable mortgage, 204
portfolio, 204

post mortem, 294
postprandial, 313
potpourri, 294
power of attorney, 205
PPI (producer price index), 125, 209. *See also* consumer price index
praxis, 313
précis, 294
preferred stock. *See* stock
prefixes, 407–413
preliminary injunction. *See* injunction
premiums, 82, 205
Prentice Hall Style Manual, The, 34, 72, 108
preowned, 278
preprandial, 313
prescriptive, 313
press proof. *See* proof
press release. *See* news release
preternatural, 313
price-earnings ratio, 205–206
price fixing, 70, 206
prime interest rate. *See* prime rate
prime rate, 206. *See also* central bank
primus inter pares, 294
principal, 16, 206–207
 and bonds, 47
 and calls, 53
 and deductible, 81
 and interest, 128–131
 See also amortization; installment sale
principals, 29
printing, 44, 119, 207–209
 buffers in, 50
 camera-ready copy, 53–54
 from computers, 66, 83
 defaults in, 83
 markup, 164
 point, 204
 in publishing, 72
prioritize, 278
pristine, 313
private branch exchange (PBX). *See* telephone system
private ledger. *See* ledger
privately held corporation. *See* corporations
private-purpose bond. *See* bonds
pro, 294
pro bono, 294
procurement, 209
producer price index (PPI), 125, 209. *See also* consumer price index
product line, 209

proem, 313
professional corporation. *See* corporations
profit. *See* gross profit; net income
profit and loss statement. *See* income statement
profit sharing, 210
pro forma, 294
program. *See* software
program flowchart. *See* flowchart
programming, 86, 210
programming language, 26. *See also* language
prohibitory injunction. *See* injunction
prolepsis, 313
promethean, 313
promissory note. *See* notes
promo, 278
proof, 210–211
proof of pages, 44
proofreading, 44–45, 53, 71–72, 211–213
property, abandonment of, 3–4. *See also* real property
property dividend. *See* dividends
proposal, 214–215
proprietary lease. *See* lease
proprietorship, 96, 215
pro rata, 294
prosumer, 278
protégé, 295
pro tempore, 295
protocol, 215–216, 278
prototype, 216
protreptic, 313
proximate, 313
proxy, 216
public corporation. *See* corporations
public domain, 73, 216–217
public easement. *See* easement
publicly held corporation. *See* corporations
public-purpose bond. *See* bonds
public service corporation. *See* corporations
public utility corporation. *See* corporations
pull it off, 328
punitive damages. *See* damages
purchase-money mortgage. *See* mortgage
put all one's eggs in one basket, 328
put a good face on it, 328
put it on the back burner, 328
put one's best foot forward, 328

put one's money on the line, 328
puts, 53, 217
putting the cart before the horse, 328
pyramiding, 217–218

qualified endorsement. *See* endorsement
quality control, 219
quasi, 295
quasi contract. *See* contracts
queue, 219
queue time. *See* queue
quick study, 328
quiddity, 313
quid pro quo, 295
quit-claim deed. *See* deed
quod erat demonstrandum, 295
quod vide, 295
quo jure?, 295
quotation, 219–220
quotidian, 313
quo warranto, 295
quroum. *See* meetings
qwerty keyboard, 66, 91, 119, 220

raconteur, 295
radix, 314
raider, 278. *See also* stock
raison d'être, 295
RAM (random-access memory). *See* memory
random-access memory (RAM). *See* memory
random sample, 221. *See also* sample; universe
rank and file, 328
rate class. *See* premiums
ratio, 221
ratiocinate, 314
raw data, 221
read between the lines, 329
read-only memory (ROM). *See* memory
read-out, 221
read something into it, 329
real estate closing. *See* closing
real property, 27, 43, 202, 222
  and bonds, 47
  closing in, 62
  and deeds, 82
  and earnest money, 92
  and escrow, 98
  leases, 140–141
  liens on, 155
real time, 222
recherche, 295

recission, 226
record. *See* fields
records management, 104–105, 222
recto, 314
recycling, 222–223
redeemable bond. *See* bonds
redeemable preferred stock. *See* stock
redemption, 223
redemption price. *See* call; redemption
red herring, 329
red ink, 278
red-letter day, 329
reference list. *See* back matter
registered agent. *See* resident agent
registered bond. *See* bearer bond
registered office, 224
registered trademark. *See* trademark
reich, 295
reify, 314
rendezvous, 295
rep, 278
repetitive-strain injury. *See* ergonomics
répondez s'il vous plaît, 295
reports, 5, 72, 224–226
  back matter in, 33
  front matter in, 111–112
reprographics, 226
research, 226–227
resident agent, 227
resolution. *See* minutes
restraining order. *See* injunction
restrictive covenant. *See* covenants
restrictive endorsement. *See* endorsement
retail, 90, 227
retirement plan, 227–228. *See also* pension
revenue bond. *See* bonds
reverse-annuity mortgage. *See* mortgage
reverse mortgage. *See* mortgage
revolving account, 228
ricochet, 295
rider. *See* endorsement
ring topology. *See* local area networks (LANs)
risk, 28, 62, 119, 228. *See also* underwriting
risk capital. *See* capital
risk classification. *See* risk
risqué, 295
Robert's Rules of Order, 166. *See also* parliamentary procedure
Robinson-Patman Act. *See* antitrust laws
rococo, 295
rollback, 279

rollover, 279
rollover mortgage. *See* mortgage
roll with the punches, 329
Roman numerals, 424
ROM (read-only memory). *See* memory
round lot. *See* lot
routine. *See* diagnostic routine
rubber check, 329
rubric, 314
rug ranking, 279
rules of order. *See* bylaws
rule of thumb, 329
run its course, 329
run of the mill, 329

S&P (Standard & Poor's) 500 Index. *See* stock index
sacred cow, 279
sale and leaseback. *See* lease
salon, 296
sample, 230. *See also* random sample; universe
sans doute, 296
sans gêne, 296
sans pareil, 296
sans peine, 296
sans serif type. *See* typeface
sans souci, 296
satellite office. *See* telecommunications
save face, 329
savings bond. *See* bonds
savoir-faire, 296
scenario, 279
scholium, 314
scilicet, 296
scorched earth, 279
S corporations, 156. *See also* corporations
screamer, 279
second mortgage. *See* mortgage
second to none, 329
SEC (Securities and Exchange Commission), 7, 16
secundum, 296
secured loan, 230
Securities and Exchange Commission (SEC), 7, 16. *See also* stock exchange
sedulous, 314
see eye to eye, 329
seize the bull by the horns, 329
seller-financed mortgage. *See* mortgage
semeiology, 314
seminar. *See* conferences

semper fidelis, 296
semper idem, 296
semper paratus, 296
separate the men from the boys, 329
serial bond. *See* bonds
seriatim, 314
series bond. *See* bonds
serif type. *See* typeface
service mark. *See* trademark
service of process. *See* summons
service provider, 231
session. *See* adjourned meeting
sexual harassment. *See* discrimination
share. *See* stock
shareholder. *See* stockholders
shark repellent, 279
sheriff's deed. *See* deed
Sherman Act. *See* antitrust laws
ship of state, 329
short end of the stick, at the, 329
short list, 279
short sale, 231
shot in the dark, 329
sight draft. *See* bank draft
sight unseen, 329
sigillum, 296
silent partner. *See* partnerships
silicon chip. *See* chip; integrated circuits
s'il vous plaît, 296
simple interest. *See* interest
simulacrum, 314
sine die, 296
sine qua non, 296
sinking-fund bond. *See* bonds
SI (Système International). *See* metric system
sit tight, 329
sixth sense, 330
slammer, 279
slander, 232. *See also* libel
sleaze factor, 279
smart card, 279. *See also* microprocessor
smart money, 279
snake-check, 279
sodality, 314
soft copy. *See* read-out
soft soap, 330
software, 21, 51, 65, 66, 232–233
    configuration of, 68
    database, 79
    desktop publishing, 85
    diagnostic routine, 86
    menues on, 167–168
sole proprietorship. *See* proprietorship

solid ink-jet printer. *See* printing
solidus, 314
sound bite, 279
sound as a dollar, 330
sour grapes, 330
Spanish dates and times, 466
Spanish numbers, 430
special endorsement. *See* endorsement
spin control, 279
split, 233
split hairs, 330
split up. *See* split
spot market. *See* commodities
spread. *See* quotation
spreadsheet, 65, 234, 235. *See also* accounting
square deal, 330
Standard & Poor's 500 (S&P 500) Index. *See* stock index
standing rules. *See* bylaws
star topology. *See* local area networks (LANs), 234
statement of revenue and expenditures. *See* income statement
statistical inference. *See* parameter; sample
statute of frauds, 70, 92, 234–235
statute of limitations, 235
statutory deed. *See* deed
statutory law, 18, 45, 65, 235
 and copyrights, 72
 and deeds, 82
stem the tide, 330
step-up lease. *See* lease
sticker for the rules, 330
stochastic, 314
stock, 29, 47, 235–237
 block of, 44
 and calls, 53
 capital, 55
 odd lot, 192
 point, 203
 puts, 217
 See also commodities; corporations; stock exchange; stock index
stock average. *See* stock index
stock certificate. *See* stock
stock dividend. *See* dividends
stock exchange, 237–239
 clearinghouse in, 61
 and over-the-counter (OTC) market, 195
 See also commodities; stock; stock index

stockholders, 16, 29, 45, 51, 239. *See also* corporations
stockholders' equity. *See* equity
stock index, 32, 239–241. *See also* commodities; stock; stock exchange
stonewall, 279
straight loan, 241
string along, 330
style guide. *See* back matter; copyedit
Style Manual of the American Institute of Physics, 34
subchapter S corporation. *See* corporations
sublease. *See* lease
sub nom, 296
subpoena, 241
subprogram. *See* subroutine
subroutine, 241–242
subsidiary. *See* corporations
subsidiary journal. *See* journal
subsidiary ledger. *See* ledger
subvention, 314
sub verbo, 296
suffixes, 414–419
summons, 242
summum bonum, 296
sumptuary, 314
suo jure, 296
suo loco, 296
supra, 296
suretyship. *See* guarantee
surfing, 279. *See also* Internet
suum cuique, 296
syllogism, 314
syndicate, 242
synergism, 315
systematic sampling. *See* sample
systematize, 279
Système International (SI). *See* metric system
systems analysis, 242
systems flowchart. *See* flowchart
systems software. *See* software

table d'hôte, 297
take with a grain of salt, 330
talk it up, 330
tangible property. *See* abandonment; real property
Tao, 297
taxonomy, 315
tectonics, 315
teflon, 280

INDEX

telecommunications, 10, 41, 50, 243. *See also* computers; Internet; modem; network
telecommuting, 243
teleconferences, 243–245. *See also* conferences
teleginic, 315
telephone system, 245–246
tempora mutantur, 297
temporary injunction. *See* injunction
tempus fugit, 297
tenancy at will. *See* lease
tenancy by the entirety, 246
tenancy in common, 133, 246–247
tendentious, 315
tergiversate, 315
terminal. *See* workstations
term insurance, 247
terraqueous, 315
testamentary trust. *See* trust
tête-à-tête, 297
thermal ink-jet printer. *See* printing
thermal wax-transfer printer. *See* printing
thorn in one's side, 330
throughput, 280. *See also* computers; data processing
throw light on, 330
tighten one's belt, 330
time deposit, 247–248
time draft. *See* bank draft
time frame, 280
time-period designations, 460–461
time-sharing, 248
tip of the iceberg, 330
title, 3, 5, 13, 248–249
 and bill of exchange, 42
 breach of warranty, 50
 in conditional sale, 67
 and deeds, 82
 See also marketable title
Tokyo Stock Price Index (TOPIX). *See* stock index
tong, 297
TOPIX (Tokyo Stock Price Index). *See* stock index
top of the line, 280
topology. *See* local area networks (LANs)
toponym, 315
tort, 79, 144, 249
tour de dorce, 297
tout de suite, 297
track record, 330

trademark, 27, 159, 249–250. *See also* copyright; patent
traduce, 315
trailing P/E. *See* price-earnings ratio
translator. *See* assembler; languages
trojan horse, 280
trompe-l'oeil, 297
trope, 315
trust, 37, 42, 49, 250–251
 deed of, 83
 and escrow, 98
 See also will
trust account. *See* trust
trust deed. *See* deed
trust estate. *See* trust
trust fund. *See* trust
trust mortgage. *See* mortgage
turnaround time, 280
turnover, 280
turn the tables, 330
turn the tide, 330
twenty/twenty hindsight, 330
two-line telephone system. *See* telephone system
typeface, 85, 164, 251. *See also* point

UCC (Uniform Commercial Code), 70, 186, 252–253
ULSI (ultralarge-scale integration). *See* integrated circuits
ultrafiche. *See* micrographics
ultralarge-scale integration (ULSI). *See* integrated circuits
ultra vires, 297
underwriting, 228, 252. *See also* risk
unemployment compensation. *See* unemployment insurance
unemployment insurance, 252
Uniform Commercial Code (UCC), 70, 186, 252–253
Uniform System of Citation, Harvard Law Review Association, 72
unilateral contract. *See* contracts
United States area codes, 457–459
United States Government Printing Office Style Manual, 72
U.S. Patent and Trademark Office, 250
U.S. Postal Service, 194
universe, 253. *See also* random sample; sample
unsecured loan, 253
untoward, 315
unusual words, 298–316
upgrade, 280

upload, 280. *See also* computers; network
uptick, 280
uptime, 280
up to snuff, 331
user friendly, 280
usufruct, 315
ut infra, 297
ut supra, 197

Value Line Composite Index. *See* stock index
VA mortgage. *See* mortgage
variable annuity. *See* annuity
VA (Veterans Administration), 181
v-chip, 281
veni, vidi, vici, 297
venture capital. *See* capital
verbatim, 297
verbatim et literatim, 197
verso, 316
versus, 297
vertex, 316
vertical market, 281
Veterans Administration (VA), 181
viable, 281
videlicet, 297
videoconference. *See* teleconferences
video display. *See* cathode ray tube (CRT)
virus, 51, 281. *See also* computers; data
vis-à-vis, 297
voice-data system, 254. *See also* E-mail; facsimile; computers; voice messaging
voice messaging, 254–255. *See also* E-mail; voice-data system
voilà, 298
volatile memory. *See* memory
voluntary bankruptcy. *See* bankruptcy
voucher, 255
voucher system. *See* voucher
vox populi, 298

waiver, 256
wannabee, 281
warranty, 82, 117, 256
warranty deed. *See* deed
waste disposal. *See* recycling
wasting asset, 281. *See also* assets
wave of the future, 331

Web (World Wide Web), 131, 281. *See also* Internet
weltanschauung, 298
wen, 298
whistleblower, 281
white knight, 281. *See also* corporations
whole ball of wax, 331
whole life insurance. *See* term insurance
whole new ball game, 331
wholesale, 257
wholesale price index. *See* producer price index (PPI)
whys and wherefores, 331
wide area network (WAN), 257. *See also* Internet; LAN; MAN
widget, 316
will, 42, 62, 257–258. *See also* trust
Wilshire 5000 Equity Index. *See* stock index
window, 281
wise, 281
Wissenschaft, 298
with flying colors, 331
word processing, 61, 65, 72, 258
 desktop publishing, 85
 printing, 208
workers' compensation insurance. *See* workers' compensation laws
workers' compensation laws, 259–259
working capital. *See* capital
workshop. *See* conferences
workstations, 158, 259
workup, 282. *See also* diagnostic routine
World Wide Web (Web), 131, 281. *See also* Internet
wraparound mortgage. *See* mortgage
WWW (World Wide Web), 131, 281. *See also* Internet

xenophile, 316
xenophobe, 316
xerography, 261. *See also* printing
x-height, 261. *See also* point; typeface
XMODEM, 282. *See also* protocol

yield, 262

zero-base budgeting, 263
ZMODEM, 282. *See also* Internet; protocol
zoning, 263